Globalization and Regional Dynamics

East Asia and the European Union from the Japanese and the German Perspective

Springer
Berlin
Heidelberg
New York
Barcelona
Hong Kong
London
Milan
Paris
Tokyo

Wolfgang Klenner
Hisashi Watanabe
Editors

Globalization and Regional Dynamics

East Asia and the European Union from the Japanese and the German Perspective

With 13 Figures
and 51 Tables

Springer

Prof. Dr. Wolfgang Klenner
Ruhr-Universität Bochum
Sektion Wirtschaft Ostasiens
Universitätsstraße 150
44780 Bochum
Germany

Prof. Dr. Hisashi Watanabe
Tokyo Keizai University
Faculty of Economics
Minamicho 1-7-34, Kokubunji-shi
Tokyo 185-8502
Japan

Symposium sponsored by Fritz Thyssen Stiftung
Printing sponsored by Förderverein für japanisch-deutsche Kulturbeziehungen e. V. Köln

ISBN 3-540-42599-3 Springer-Verlag Berlin Heidelberg New York

Library of Congress Cataloging-in-Publication Data applied for
Die Deutsche Bibliothek – CIP-Einheitsaufnahme
Globalization and Regional Dynamics: East Asia and European Union from the Japanese and the German Perspective / Wolfgang Klenner; Hisashi Watanabe ed. – Berlin; Heidelberg; New York; Barcelona; Hong Kong; London; Milan; Paris; Tokyo: Springer, 2002
ISBN 3-540-42599-3

Springer-Verlag Berlin Heidelberg New York
a member of BertelsmannSpringer Science+Business Media GmbH

http://www.springer.de

Hardcover-Design: Erich Kirchner, Heidelberg

SPIN 10852205 42/2202-5 4 3 2 1 0 – Printed on acid-free paper

Foreword

The writings by Japanese and German economists presented here originated against the backdrop of ongoing globalization processes and notable fluctuations in regional economic dynamics observable at the same time, primarily in the East and South East Asian area. They provided the occasion for these writers to come to terms with globalization processes, and in particular with the stabilizing and destabilizing elements at work in them. This is the basis for their investigation of the options provided by economics and economic policy for stabilizing an ever more tightly interwoven world economy. The regional focal points of the contributions are the East Asian realm and the European Union, and the points of view are in every case both from the Japanese and the German side.

Questions of international competition and mechanisms of the spread of the crisis in the wake of globalization processes lie at the centre of the analyses by Hisashi Watanabe and Willy Kraus. Hisashi Watanabe focusses on the relationship, an especially important one from the Japanese perspective, between Japan and South Korea and takes up the problem of South Korea's demand that Japan should energetically promote its own transition to a service-sector-oriented society and withdraw from certain areas of manufacturing. This, it is argued, will grant Japan's Asian neighbours better chances for development and make a positive contribution to the economic stabilization of the region. Willy Kraus deals with the sequence of phases exerting the pressures of economic dynamics, but also with the mechanisms at work in the spread of the crisis, and presents various stabilizing options for the Asian region.

Monetary effects of globalization processes and the manifestations of the crisis are treated by Michiteru Nagamine, Rainer Beckmann, Jürgen Born and Wim Kösters. Michiteru Nagamine concentrates especially upon financial measures of the Japanese government towards stabilization of the East Asian region and their consequences for the regional importance of the yen. Rainer Beckmann, Jürgen Born and Wim Kösters take a starting point more strongly orientated to the world economy and examine the chances of the euro and the yen to establish themselves as important international currencies and to diminish the role of the U.S. dollar in the world economy and in the East Asian realm.

Changes in the competitive and cooperative relationships in Asia are examined by Sachio Imakubo and Wolfgang Klenner. Sachio Imakubo chooses a sectoral approach and focusses on the changing competitive and cooperative relationships mainly in the sector of the electronics industry. Wolfgang Klenner examines changes in the regional balances of the two most important Asian partners and competitors, Japan and China. Their future positioning in the world economy will depend in part upon the extent to which they open themselves to globalizing processes through, among other factors, the opening of the conditions of their regulatory policies. Because international mergers and acquisitions contribute in a very special way to the adaptation to regulatory and organizational structures, their development in Japan and China is also studied.

Globalizing processes and the manifestations of crisis demand adaptations in regional and sectoral structures of employment. These are dealt with by Shuichi Yatsubayashi and Christian Watrin. Both writers suggest that globalizing processes lead to a new form of the division of labour and analyze the necessary preconditions for it and the changes it may be expected to bring. Shuichi Yatsubayashi takes the point of view that Japan's concepts of production and employment show sufficient flexibility. In order to satisfy the requirements imposed by globalizing processes, fundamental systemic changes are not, in his opinion, necessary. Christian Watrin, on the contrary, notes in his analysis, which concentrates on Germany, a great need for adaptation. The benefits of social welfare, he argues, have never simply dropped into the laps of the concerned parties; they are, rather, the outcome of a competitive regimen, which can, under certain circumstances, make very painful cutbacks necessary.

Both impulses to development and crisis-triggering effects proceed from the international flows of capital. Their development and effects upon stability are examined by Johzen Takeuchi, Günter Heiduk and Nicole Pohl. On the basis of an analysis of the procurement and client relationships of firms in the automobile parts industry in the Asian area, Johzen Takeuchi draws the conclusion that tightly woven networks among entrepreneurs can work against potentially destabilizing effects of international capital movements, primarily financial investments. Günter Heiduk and Nicole Pohl turn their attention to connections between non-monetary developmental processes and the need for regulatory frameworks, and stress the necessity of synchronizing them.

Takafusa Nakamura and Herbert Hax concentrate upon the contradictions resulting from the fact that a financial system is basically defined in national terms, but movements of capital know no national borders. Takafusa Nakamura focusses on developments in Japan at the end of the 1990s and presents the argument that the functional capacity of Japan's financial system was diminished by weak monitoring bodies and an unstable political environment. Herbert Hax, in an analysis which concentrates more upon fundamental principles, confirms this argument and sets forth certain requirements for a national financial system aimed at reducing to an absolute minimum problems of moral hazard and the dangers emanating from the presence of a lender of last resort.

The Arisawa Lecture held by Takafusa Nakamura occupies a special position. It is intended to honour the memory of Hiromi Arisawa, a highly esteemed economist and formulator of economic policy. Hiromi Arisawa, whose intellectual inspiration came primarily from Germany, played an outstanding role in Japanese economic policy and as an academic teacher during the 1950s. Takafusa Nakamura is a student of this economist, whose fame extends far beyond the borders of Japan. The Arisawa Lecture is equally important as an indicator of the scholarly contacts, going back many years and now firmly established, between Japanese and German economists. These connections first led to a convention with participation from both sides in 1966. Among the Japanese initiators were Hiromi Arisawa, Kazuo Okochi, and Tomoo Matsuda and among the Germans Karl Hax and Willy Kraus. At these shared conventions current economic and social problems in both countries are presented both from Japanese and German perspectives. The present collection is based upon lectures given at the twelfth of these symposia.

The editors wish to thank the *Fritz Thyssen Stiftung* for its generous support of the symposium and the *Förderverein japanisch-deutscher Kulturbeziehungen e. V. Köln* for its financial support of the printing of this publication. They also thank William Walker for his translation of the texts into English, as well as Sabine Pfaar, Mathias Klasberg and the other coworkers in the Department of East Asian Economics for the work they took on during the symposium and the printing of this book.

Wolfgang Klenner

Table of Contents

International Competition, Globalization and Mechanisms of the Expanding Crisis. Is the Simultaneity of the Crises in Japan and Korea a Coincidence?

Hisashi Watanabe

Kyoto University

1 Introduction

In April 1997, the Japanese economy, which had suffered from a depression that had dragged on since since March 1991, was struck by a new crisis. At the end of 1997 Korea too was hit by a currency and financial crisis. This simultaneity is the primary phenomenon in the bilateral economic relationship between Japan and Korea since the end of the Second World War, i.e., since the founding of the Republic of Korea in 1948. When we consider this remarkable circumstance, the question immediately arises as to whether the simultaneity should be seen as a coincidence or a determined event.

As regards Japan, there are of course extensive public discussions about the diagnosis and therapy of the great depression in that country during the last decade of the 20th century. Even so, very few people have been made aware of the simultaneity in the economic setbacks of the two countries, which could after all have reciprocal effects. To be sure, there is a general perception that the more globalization progresses, the more tightly inderdependent the national economies become. Hence it is probably no wonder if the simultaneity in this case is not considered especially remarkable here in Japan. But if it is interpreted as only one aspect of the general globalization process, the meaning of the peculiar tension between these two national economies can hardly be gasped; the tension can only be explained through the historical structure of the Japanese-Korean relationship.

Therefore I intend to deal here with what has perhaps been *consciously* disregarded both in Japan and in Korea. This is the fact that we need to consider the excessive competition in capital investment, carried on as an *idée fixe*, as one of the primary causes of the simultaneity of the suffering on both sides.

2 Japan's Great Depression

In October 1993, Japan's business cycle hit its nadir after the bursting of the bubble boom in March 1991, and then began a slow recovery. But before an upswing could properly begin, there was another downturn in April 1997. Accordingly, in 1997 and 1998 the Japanese economy showed negative growth rates in its GDP twice in a row, the first since the first oil crisis in 1974. Finally, in 1999, the first stages of improvement were noticeable and a positive growth rate in the GDP was again achieved. But this was a mere 0.5% for the fiscal year, and this pitiful figure was only made possible by reckless expenditures from the national budget, leading to a catastrophic level of state debt. To be sure, an early indication of reconstruction was unmistakably present. But the initial steps towards autonomous and reciprocal effects between private consumption and capital investment are still not yet strong enough.

The most vivid illustration of Japan's great depression of the 1990s is the unbroken increase in the unemployment rate. As late as 1991, it was still only 2.1%, and in fact it had been below 3% ever since the 1950s. But then it began to rise, reached 3% in 1995, exceeded 4% in 1998, and topped out at 4,9% in July 1999. For fiscal 1999 it was 4.7%, a figure almost inconceivable five years earlier. Of course it seems relatively mild, compared with the rates in the OECD member nations. But since low unemployment rates had been taken as a symbol of the inexhaustible growth potential of the Japanese economy since its reconstruction after the Second World War, the new situation on the job market indicates that the economy has been hit by a crisis unique in the past half century. Indeed, a positive view of the prospects for revitalization of private consumption is hardly possible. Although it is hard to imagine such a revitalization without an improvement of the job situation, restructuring of the firms usually leads to a radical downsizing of personnel, which obviously increases unemployment or at least hinders its reduction. Private consumption has also been dampened by pessimistic expectations of the future overload of taxation, since the enormous state expenditures to overcome the slump inevitably cause a progressive accumulation of deficits in the state finances.

If we now direct our attention to Korea, we see that the Korean economy as well posted negative growth rates in its GDP in 1998. But the reconstructive power of Korea's young national economy outstrips that of Japan, and the country was able to climb up from its nadir the following year. The growth rate of its GDP was a striking 10.7% in 1999. The unemployment rate, which hit its highest mark in February 1999 of 8.6%, dropped half a year later to 5.9%. In May 2000 it declined further to 3.9%, after a low of 3.0% in December 1997. Despite all this it remains an open question as to whether these striking achievements of the Korean economy should be seen as a complete recovery from the crisis or only an apparent rehabilitation. Indeed, the system of chaebols (groups of concerns based on familial operations), which has been accepted as the backbone of the Korean national economy, has been subjected to a crisis over its very existence. Of the five biggest chaebols (Samsung, Hyundai, Daewoo, LG and SK), Daewoo collapsed in 1999. The two leaders, Samsung and Hyundai, are now equally under pressure to conduct a drastic reconstruction of their systems.

There are of course differences between the symptoms of crisis in the two countries. But both national economies have in common an emphasis in their industrial structures upon the *primacy of industry, and above all of the manufacturing industries.* But is this merely the result of a periodic surplus of investment capital, or is it the result of a falsely programmed and monocultural overindustrialization?

3 Diagnoses of the Great Depression

As regards the perceptions of the crisis among the Japanese public, the main theme is the evaluation of Japan's traditional industralism. There are those who argue that the industrial structure of the Japanese economy in its traditional form should be preserved, since the comparative advantage will surely continue to be in this sector. Even if radical industrialism has led to Japanese firms being satisfied with only a moderate fixation on profits, a position now seen as something of a weakness, given presentday global competitive pressures, especially compared with Anglo-American firms and their clear orientation towards maximizing profits, one can still take for granted that there is a conviction of Japan's technological superiority in the manufacturing sectors.

On the other hand, there are those who argue for a transfer of the main emphasis of the industrial structure to the service sector, and for two reasons: First, Japan's credit institutions failed, because of their low productivity, to invest the accumulated financial wealth of the population effectively. Second, since the long-term tendency for a reduction of the workforce in the manufacturing sectors due to ageing is unavoidable, Japan will be forced in any event to transfer manufacturing operations to national economies with younger age structures, such as Korea. This argument is often connected with a pessimistic outlook on Japan's technological superiority in the manufacturing industries.

The two sides, then, have in common that they are both naive adherents of the Petty-Clark Principle. By chance, I met one adherent of this classic law in Korea. At a Japanese-Korean symposium at Seoul National University in December 1994 I was severely criticized by a colleague from the SNU. He commented somewhat reproachfully on my explanation of Japanese structural industrialism that since Japan, in its present stage of economic development, was still the unchallenged pacesetter in its relationship to Korea, it should shift the emphasis of its industrial structure to the service sector, on the Anglo-American model, and leave the manufacturing businesses to Korea. Japan's resistance to this, he claimed, had led to excessive competition between the two countries. I am sure I can take his opinion as not only personal but as representative of public opinion in Korea.

Accordingly, we are dealing here more with a dichotomous way of thinking (industry *or* service), a strong trait in both nations, rather than with orientation towards industry in itself. It is precisely from this either-or thinking that the gap formed by mutual negative perceptions arises, according to which Korea regards Japan as a hard-hearted pacesetter, always blocking Korea's attempts at industrialization, and Japan regards Korea as a chauvinistic neighbour with a tendency to near-misses.

4 Comparison of Japan, Korea, the United States, OECD-Europe and Germany

Now I wish to deal with the matter of determining the transformation of the position of the manufacturing industries in the industrial structures of each of the two countries. In so doing, I shall make use primarily of data from publications of the OECD.

At the end of 1996, Korea entered the OECD as the second Asian member after Japan, resulting in the availability of informative statistical data for the relativizing of comparisons between Japan and Korea, Japan and the USA, and Japan and Europe. First I wish to confirm the change in the relative positions among the member states of Japan and Korea. In 1997 the total populations of Japan and Korea were 126m and 46m, respectively, i.e., Japan's population is 2.7 times that of Korea's. Japan's population is the second-largest of the member nations (after the USA), Korea's ninth-largest (after Italy). Korea's GDP in 1970 was one 25th of Japan's and in 20th place among the 26 member states, followed by Poland, the Czechoslovakia and Hungary. But in 1997, Korea's GDP had moved up to an 8th of Japan's and had taken 9th place among 29 member states. The per capita GDP of Korea in 1970 was one 8th of Japan's and the lowest of the 26 member states. But in 1997 it was a third of Japan's and in 22nd place among the 29 member states. The GDP per capita index in terms of purchasing power parity in 1970 was 86 for Japan and 19 for Korea (OECD=100). In 1997 it was 114 for Japan and 67 for Korea. These data demonstrate the dramatic catching up process of the Korean economy, powered mainly by accelerated industrialization.

In order to determine the transformation of comparative positions of the manufacturing industries, I shall now compare five regions: Japan, Korea, the USA, OECD-Europe, and Germany, using long-term dynamics of national economic criteria. Since the publications of the OECD for Korea only present the data since 1970 or 1974, the temporal span is limited to the dynamics since 1974.

4.1 Employment Structure (see Table 1)

(1) Employment in the Agricultural Sector

The pace of reduction was greatest in Korea, meaning that the process of de-agriculturalization in the five regions for the period in question was most drastic in Korea and that its process of urbanization caused a dramatic gap, mainly between city and countryside. Such a dynamic also conceals the fact that there has long been an increased contrast between the fishing industries in Japan and Korea.

(2) Employment in the Industrial Sector

In 1974 Japan hit its peak, followed by Korea in 1991, followed by a slow falling off. In consequence, both countries were at the same level in the 1990s. The USA has lagged behind Korea since the 1980s. OECD-Europe has trailed Japan since the 1990s, and since the 1990s has also been behind Korea. Germany, by way of exception, surpassed both Japan and Korea in 1995.

(3) Employment in the Manufacturing Industries

In Japan, the USA, OECD-Europe and Germany, the proportions trended down, while only Korea's increased until 1989. Accordingly, Korea surpassed Japan in 1986, but Germany surpassed both countries in 1995.

(4) Employment in the Service Sector

In addition to the USA, the leading nation, four other regions followed its upward trend. In the 1990s, Japan and OECD-Europe were on the same level. The gap between Japan and Korea tended to close. German has trailed Japan since the 1970s, with this gap also tending to close.

(5) Rate of Unemployment

The unemployment rate in Japan slowly increased, whereas in Korea it tended to decrease, resulting in the same level for both countries in the first half of the 1990s. In the USA it fell during the 1990s, while increasingly strongly in Germany and OECD-Europe.

4.2 Industrial Structure (see Table 2)

(6) Share in Value Creation of the Agricultural Sector

Japan and Korea followed the trend in the leading USA and OECD-Europe, but at a much faster pace. It is striking that Japan has been behind OECD-Europe ever since the 1970s.

(7) Share in Value Creation of the Industrial Sector

Japan and Korea topped out in 1974 and 1991, respectively, followed by a decrease in both countries. In the mid-1980s, Korea surpassed Japan and the gap increased. It is notable that both Japan and Korea, as regards value creation, in contrast to employment, surpassed Germany as early as the mid-1980s, and that the gap then increased.

(8) Share of Value Creation of the Manufacturing Industries

Japan's share has tended downwards since the beginning of the 1990s, after increasing up to 1988. Korea surpassed Japan in 1986, and even Germany in 19888, whereas Japan surpassed Germany in 1993. It can now be seen that the comparative advantage of the industrial sector, i.e., of the producing industries, initially lay more with Japan than Germany, and subsequently more with Korea than Japan.

(9) Share of Value Creation of the Service Sector

Both in the USA and Japan, the share of value creation was overall less than employment, whereas in Korea the former exceeded the latter until the 1980s. In OECD-Europe, the former exceeded the latter from the beginning on.

4.3 Structure of Expenditures (see Table 3)

(10) Share of Private Consumption

By way of exception, only Korea's share showed a declining tendency, whereas in all the other regions, it rose. Thus Korea showed the lowest share in the 1990s, although it had had the highest in the 1970s. It is also notable that Japan has surpassed Germany in this criterion ever since the 1970s.

(11) Share of State Consumption

In all the regions the share was practically at the same level. It is notable that the share in Japan and Korea in contrast with the USA and OECD-Europe was essentially lower. The share in Germany was the highest.

(12) Share of Gross Investment in Fixed Assets

From 1974 to 1995 this decreased in Japan, the USA and OECD-Europe, whereas in Korea it tended to increase and remained on almost the same level in Germany. Thus Korea surpassed Japan in this respect in the 1980s. In any case, Japan and Germany were far ahead of the USA and OECD-Europe, including Germany.

(13) Share of the Construction Industry (not including Housing)

The share stayed at the same level in Japan, but increased strongly in Korea. As a result, Korea surpassed Japan in the first half of the 1990s. In any event, both countries far outstripped the USA and OECD-Europe, including Germany, by this standard.

(14) Share of the Investment in Equipment

This share only increasedd in Germany, while remaining unchanged in Japan, Korea, the USA and OECD-Europe. Even so, Japan and Korea were ahead of the USA and OECD-Europe, including Germany, in this respect.

(15) Exports of Goods and Services in Terms of GDP

In Japan percentages fell from 12% to 9%, while staying at ca. 30% in Korea. Thus a gap was created. In the USA the percentage rose in the meantime from 8% to 10% and surpassed Japan in the first half of the 1990s. In OECD-Europe there was only a slight rise, from 25% to 27%. In consequence, Japan remained the country with the weakest orientation towards exports of all the member states. Be that as it might, Japan and the USA formed one side of the picture, with Korea and OECD-Europe on the other.

(16) Imports of Goods and Services in Terms of GDP

Percentages trended down in Japan, but remained at over 30% in Korea. In the USA there was an increase from 8% to 10%, and in OECD-Europe they hovered around 26%. In terms of its import dependency as well, Japan remained the weakest of these countries in 1995. In any event, in this respect, too, Japan and the USA were on one side, and Korea and OECD-Europe on the other.

(17) Balance of Foreign Trade in Terms of GDP

Japan consisted produced surpluses, except for 1974, when only Germany could show a positive balance. Korea's drastic deficit in the 1970s decreased substantially in the meantime. Korea's foreign trade balance, however, still remained basically negative. The USA showed a structurally negative balance. OECD-Europe achieved a positive balance in the 1980s, and its surplus increased.

(18) Net Savings in Terms of GDP

In Korea the percentage tended to increase, whereas in all the other regions it decreased. Hence Korea surpassed Japan in the 1980s. In 1995, Korea had the highest percentage, with a huge lead even on Japan, which was in second place.

Our final result is that in terms of ten criteria out of 18 (2, 3, 5, 7, 8, 11, 12, 13, 14, 18), Japan and Korea were close to each other during the period in question. In terms of six criteria (7, 8, 12, 13, 14, 18), Korea surpassed not only Japan but also other regions during the 1990s. This state of affairs shows not only the comparative benefit of the industrial sector in both countries (leaving Germany out of consideration for the moment), but also the vigorous industrialization of Korea. The latter is beyond any doubt the cause of the former. The question now is, what was the decisive motive force behind such a rapid industrialization of Korea?

5 Industrialization and Export Orientation of the Korean Economy

For a long time now there has apparently been no disagreement that Germany and Japan are leading industrial nations. Thus, for example, the share of the industrial sectors in investments for research and development between 1975 and 1996 increased in Japan from 94.3% to 96.2%, and in Germany from 91.4% to 94.4%. By contrast, this share decreased in the USA from 97.0% to 80.3%, and in the EU from 90.8% to 87.1%. These opposing dynamics could be taken as a convincing argument for the *primacy of industry* in Japan and Germany. Now Korea is about to catch up with these two pacesetters as the industrially oriented state in third place. Therefore, one needs to examine the meaning of the phrase *primacy of industry* in each country, and to keep two points in mind when doing so.

First, it is now established that Germany may still have surpassed Japan and Korea in its shares of the industrial sector and of producing operations providing employment in the mid-1990s, but that in terms of shares of value creation, it was surpassed by both Japan and Korea as early as the 1980s, and that the gap became ever greater. At the same time, the facts show that in Germany since the mid-1970s, the labour productivity of the service sector has exceeded that of the industrial sector. Hence, Germany can hardly still be termed an industrial nation in the narrow sense.

Second, these three industrial nations display striking differences in their export orientation. Japan is low down on the scale, Germany in the middle, and Korea at the top. What explains this contrast between Japan and Korea? We have to take into account the fact that from the earliest phase of its industrialization, Japan's export dependency has always been relatively low (hardly over 20% in terms of GDP). Can we really resolve this question with economic arguments alone?

In Japan, intensive capital investment is regarded as the foundation of the ever-expanding domestic demand, whereas in Korea, capital investment is seen more as an approach to export orientation, to a degree found elsewhere only in small European states such as Switzerland and the Benelux countries. Both for Japan and Korea, export is really seen as a means of acquiring foreign currencies indispensable for imports, whereas Germany regards export as a source of profits. Germany imports in order to export, but Japan and Korea export in order to import. For Korea, however, the importance of exports is even greater.

Export, for Korea, is the true criterion for the optimal measurement of progress in the competitiveness of the Korean economy against the Japanese economy. In this respect, Korea proceeds not from a purely economic concern, but from one outside the economic realm: Korea believes it is the highest priority in securing its national interest to catch up with Japan in as many economy areas as possible, and as early as possible. The government, the business community, and the population at large are in complete agreement on this point. Every measure affecting economic policy or business strategy has to be tested and approved in terms of this *raison d'état*. What is the origin of this peculiar national motivating force?

The cornerstone of the present economic system in South Korea was laid by the Park Jeong-Hee regime. The preceding period, including the First Republic (1948-1960 under President Lee) and the Second Republic (1960-1961 under Prime Minister Chang), was that of the formation of the South Korean complex of ideologies, namely, of anticommunism (i.e., of the legitimacy of the South Korean system) and of anti-Japanese thinking (i.e., of Korean nationalism), in other words, the period of the *primitive accumulation* of Korean ideology. When Park, at the beginning of 1962, after his successful coup in May 1961 established the first five-year plan for economic development, he proceeded from this double ideology, but also from a clear and objective perception of the status quo. For him, the pertinent question was no longer reunification of the two Koreas, but competition between the two systems. This led inevitably to a dilemma.

On the one hand, the anti-Japanese attitude of the South Korean people was all the more reinforced by their awareness of the political reality of the division of the nation, since the national identity could only be affirmed by this means, given the hard facts. But on the other hand, South Korea was compelled to attach itself once again to Japan economically, since South Korea could only overcome the military and industrial superiority of North Korea at the time through a rapid industrialization of its own, a process without which the economic and technological help both of the USA and Japan was indispensable. The importation of Japanese developmental technology was of decisive importance for this process, which now aggressively undertook this industrialization with precisely the same basic system inherited from the colonial domination of Japan. And so, to prevail against the North Korean system, South Korea aimed at a reconstruction of its close relationship with the Japanese economy. But was this nothing more than a return to the subordination of Korea to the dominance of Japan?

In order to escape this dilemma, the Park regime set itself a new goal, that of catching up with Japan on the same track as that of Japan's own industrialization process. This ambitious strategy of industrialization proved successful beyond all expectation, since it mobilized the accumulation of national emotion of the South Korean people in a purposeful way and since Japan largely accommodated itself to it, in due recognition of the fact that the achievement of South Korean economic independence from Japan in stages by no means signified a real loss of its influence upon the South Korean economy. In any event, it was surely to the substantial disadvantage of North Korea, which had not been given South Korea's room for manoeuver and accordingly could draw only upon the developmental assistance of China, the USSR, and the East European states, a form of aid which did not accord at all with the industrial heritage of Japanese dominance.

The smaller the gap became between Japan and Korea on the track of the industrialization process, the stronger South Korea's economic position became in comparison to North Korea's. But by the time the Fourth Republic ended in 1979 with the assassination of President Park, at which point South Korea had caught up with North Korea, it had become an end in itself to catch up with and pass the Japanese economy. This aim has functioned as a reason of state ever since.

But how can we determine the stepwise realization of Korean economic independence from Japan? In realizing this goal, Korea has hardly been satisfied with a mere increase in the speed of the growth rate leading to a diminution of the gap in per capita GDP between itself and Japan. Korea itself has regarded its achievements in foreign trade as the adequate yardstick for confirming to itself its progress in competitiveness against Japan. Now it has been the general strategy of state capitalism to challenge Japan on the overseas market and deprive it of its market share. In so doing, Korea has usually proceeded from the notion that its own domestic market is too small. It has also calculated that export and foreign investment can be appropriate ways of approving Korea's technical standards. Therefore, Korea's tendency to think in terms of a small domestic market is probably better seen as self-manipulation designed to justify its aggressive export operations and premature foreign investments. But as a consequence of such excessive orientation towards exports and foreign investments, Korea has neglected to look after its own domestic market effectively. The development of the trade network as an infrastructure for the opening up and expansion of the domestic market has hardly advanced hand in hand with the analogous development in industrial production.

It is surely the final goal of Korea's aggressive export strategy to enter the Japanese market, first with standard then with high-quality goods from the range of capital- and technology-intensive products, such as, e.g., the new type of television with significantly higher quality offered to the Japanese market by LG Electronics in the autumn of 1999. The tendency has unavoidably evolved that the export goods structure of the two countries increasingly resemble each other, which has also necessarily led to increasing similarity in their industrial structures. Today the industrial structures of both countries have a high degree of similarity. For instance, they have about the same competitive advantage in the building industry on the world market, whereas both are equally weak in the chemical and pharmaceutical industries.

The organization of firms has followed the market strategy. In contrast to Taiwan, where another market strategy, and therefore other company organizational forms, have been preferred, Korea's organization is based on the familial concern, or *chaebol*. Up until quite recently, *chaebols* were able to function as the optimal complex of firms for the financing of economies of scale, through which the competitive pricing of Korean finished goods against Japanese equivalents on the overseas market could be effectively intensified. Beyond any doubt the *chaebol*-system supplied the motive force for the entire process of Korea's aggressive industrialization down to the mid-1990s.

But there was always a dark side to the process, namely, deformities both in small and medium-sized firms and among parts suppliers, and, furthermore, the patriarchal organizational principle of the *chaebol*, along with an irrational linkage of politics and economics. It is still an open question whether the current boom in foundings of venture outfits in the area of the so-called IT-intensive *New Economy* can really lead to a breakthrough in the bottleneck of the *chaebol* system.

6 Conflicting Results of Korea's Industrialization

Korea has succeeded in proving itself as the third industrially oriented nation after Germany and Japan. Its export orientation exceeds even that of Germany. But in contrast to Germany and Japan, Korea is compelled to be highly dependent upon imports of capital goods and of half- and partially finished products in order to improve the competitive pricing of its export goods. Consequently, Korea's foreign trade structure has been drawn into such a vicious circle that its extreme export orientation inevitably leads to a negative foreign trade balance, which in turn reinforces its export orientation.

Furthermore, Korea is compelled to rely primarily upon Japan for its indispensable capital goods and its half- and partially finished products, to the extent that it wants to produce goods "made in Japan" itself. This is the main cause of the structural deficits in Korea's foreign trade balance with Japan. According to Japanese statistics, the deficits in Korea's foreign trade balance with Japan before the 1970s were always over 200% and from 1974 to 1995 on average 69% of Korea's exports to Japan. In 1998, the percentage fell to its lowest level due to Korea's economic crisis, but it was still 27,1%. Here the imports of capital goods and of half- and partially finished products played a decisive role. According to the foreign trade statistics of the OECD, Korea's deficits with Japan were especially striking in the following categories in the SITC: power-generating machinery and equipment, special machinery, metal-working machinery, other industrial machinery and parts, office machines and automatic data processing machines, road vehicles, and other transport equipment. Examples of ratios between imports from and exports to Japan from 1994 to 1997 are: iron and steel, 1.4:1; power-generating machinery and equipment, 7.3:1; specialized machinery, 24:1; metal working machinery, 26.5:1; other industrial machinery and parts, 11.9:1. This shows that overall Korea is compelled to rely mainly upon Japanese suppliers for its capital goods and its half- and partially finished products. The challenge posed by goods made in Korea to the dominant goods made in Japan on the overseas market has on the one hand caused an accumulation of deficits in

Korea's foreign trade balance with Japan, and on the other hand led to an overcapacity in the manufacturing sector.

The countereffect of the competitive pressure from Korea has been to force the Japanese firms to oppose every Korean challenge with more active investments in equipment and with rationalization measures. In so doing, they tried on the one hand to create differences in their products by developing higher levels of quality, which only stimulated Korea to set itself ever new goals in order to close the quality gap, as in the case of the shipbuilding industry. On the other hand, since the mid-1980s, Japanese firms have relocated their production sites for mass-produced goods to the ASEAN countries and to China, so that they can effectively counter the competitive prices of Korean goods. Then, the Korean firms followed the example of the Japanese pacesetters. The competition accelerated the race for investments in plant and equipment on both sides. When the earning power of employed capital finally dropped off the chart, the surpluses of investment capital were revealed as a structural problem for both sides simultaneously.

Therefore, one still should not regard the latent danger of oversupply as eliminated, in so far as Korea wants to maintain its tenacious orientation towards exports. Even in the process of regulating overcapacity, vigorous competition has already arisen between the two countries. On the Korean side, the government is trying through the so-called *Big-Deal*, i.e., the exchange of business sectors among the *chaebol*, essentially to eliminate the potential of the exaggerated domestic competition. One must expect that in the near future, the Korean firms, with increased capital productivity due to rationalization, but mainly due to IT-intensive investments, will prove more powerful challengers than their Japanese rivals. On the Japanese side, *the law on special measures for the revitalization of industry* that took effect in 1999 and will apply until March 2003, has as its main goal the drastic restructuring of the firms. Therefore, the pressure of oversupply could be further increased in the East Asian region, even if any intention on China's part of advancing to the fore as a new competitor seems for the present to be excluded.

7 Overview

There is no denying, then, that the reciprocal competitive pressure between Japan and Korea, with its burden of historical backgrounds, must be seen as one component of the interactive complex of causes which led both countries to a structural surplus of investment capital. Viewed short-term, the outlook hardly seems to offer grounds for optimism. But in the long term, complete pessimism seems equally unfounded. What sort of option exists that allows an escape from this hectic competition?

It is surely not a realistic alternative to guide the industrial structures of the two countries by means of structural policy to a new, bilateral division of labour, with Japan transferring its main industrial structure from manufacturing to service sectors while Korea takes over manufacturing, as a sort of Big Deal between the countries handed down from on high. It is likely more realistic to examine this imaginary dichotomy between *industrial society* and *service society* in both countries , in order to transfer the accumulated technology and know-how in manufacturing in both countries as far as possible to other sectors, including the weakened agricultural sector. Competition for the extent and the rapidity of a technology transfer in this sense could be a step towards the creation of new prospects for the horizontal interdependence of the two neighbouring national economies.

In fact, Korea's government under Kim Dae Jung has already taken the first bold step. In November 1998 it decided to embark on negotiations for a free trade agreement with Japan, and immediately thereafter it was decided to open preliminary negotiations for a bilateral agreement on investments at the Japanese-Korean Conference of Ministers. At the end of 1998, Korea partly abolished the now ineffectual dispersion system of the producing countries, which had resulted in a de facto exclusion of Japanese products from the Korean market. At the end of June 1999, its abolition was completed.

In the meantime, negotiations for a bilateral agreement on investments have progressed, although those for the free trade agreement have not proceeded as well as initially expected, since Korea is now no longer interested so much in a bilateral, but in a trilateral free trade agreement which will include China. On the other hand, Korea has decided to take up preliminary negotiations for a free trade agreement with Chile and Thailand. Thus it can hardly be doubted that in the long term the Korean market will increasingly open to the outside world.

This process will certainly compel Korean firms to change course in their previous marketing strategy and concentrate upon the domestic market, since the domestic market will no longer be sustainable through protective policies from above, but only through efforts at self-help from its own firms. In this respect one should note that the Korean market, with its 46 million members, now is considered to have the most dynamic growth of all the OECD nations. True, Korea's GDP is less than Canada's, but it is already greater than Spain's. If we consider the inexhaustible growth potential of the Korean economy, then even the prospects of the domestic market should be of strategic importance for Korean firms.

Changing course in marketing strategy will necessarily involve a certain shift in the competitive interest of the Korean firms over against their Japanese rivals, which can surely be a step in the transition from an emotional and in marketing terms inadequate competition to one which is objective and more adequate. This in no way means that there will be less competitive pressure from Korea.

Therefore, both the business strategy and the economic policy of Japan will also be forced to change course. And so it will also be an important part of this transition to make the industrial orientation of both countries, which has certainly contributed decisively to their striking economic growth, work in a mutually stimulating rather than a mutually opposing way. In this sense we should now speak of the elimination of the *fourth* surplus, namely that of historical emotion. And in this case, Japan, as the former colonial master of Korea, has the responsibility for taking the initiative.

Table 1 Employment

		1974	74-79	80-89	90-95	1995
In agriculture as a percentage of civilian employment	J	12.9	12.1	8.9	6.3	5.7
	K	48.0	42.3	26.8	15.2	12.5
	US	4.2	3.9	3.2	2.9	2.9
	OE[1]	16.0	15.2	12.8	10.2	10.2
	G[2]	7.0	6.2	4.6	3.6	3.3
In industry as a percentage of civilian employment	J	37.0	35.7	34.7	34.2	33.6
	K	21.2	25.6	29.9	34.3	33.2
	US	32.5	31.2	28.2	24.7	24.0
	OE	38.4	37.1	33.3	30.5	29.1
	G	46.7	45.0	41.3	39.0	37.5
In manufacturing as a percentage of civilian employment	J	27.2	25.4	24.6	23.7	22.5
	K	17.3	20.6	23.9	25.1	23.4
	US	24.2	23.0	19.8	16.9	16.4
	OE	28.1	27.0	23.9	20.8	18.0
	G	35.8	34.5	32.4	29.2	27.0
In services as a percentage of civilian employment	J	50.1	52.3	56.4	59.5	60.7
	K	30.8	32.1	43.3	50.5[3]	54.3
	US	63.4	64.9	68.6	72.4	73.1
	OE	45.5	47.7	54.0	59.2	60.6
	G	46.3	48.8	54.1	57.4	59.1
Unemployment as a percentage of total labour force	J	1.4	1.9	2.5	2.5	3.2
	K	4.0	3.8	3.8	2.4	2.0
	US	5.5	6.7	7.2	6.4	5.5
	OE	3.2	4.9	8.8	9.4	10.2
	G	2.1	3.4	6.8	7.1	8.1

Notes: 1 OE=Total OECD-Europe. Czech Republic, Hungary and Poland are not included in OE.
2 G=Germany. Since 1991 data refer ot Germany. Prior to 1991 they refer to Western Germany.
3 Original misprint is corrected
Source: OECD (1997), *Historical Statistics 1960-1995*, Paris.

Table 2 Industrial Structure of GDP

		1974	74-79	80-89	90-95	1995
Value added in agriculture as a percentage of GDP	J	5.6	5.1	3.2	2.2	1.9
	K	24.8	22.5	12.4	7.4	6.5
	US	3.7	3.2	2.2	1.8[3]	..
	OE[1]	6.2	5.8	4.3	3.2	2.9
	G[2]	2.7	2.6	1.9	1.3	1.0
Value added in industry as a percentage of GDP	J	44.7	42.4	41.1	39.7	38.0
	K	32.6	35.3	41.3	43.7	43.3
	US	33.4	33.4	31.3	26.7[3]	..
	OE[1]	39.3	37.9	34.7	30.9	29.9
	G[2]	46.2	44.3	40.6	35.6	33.1
Value added in manufacturing as a percentage of GDP	J	33.6	30.5	28.9	26.3	24.7
	K	25.7	26.7	29.8	27.7	26.8
	US	23.3	23.2	20.4	18.1[3]	..
	OE[1]	28.8	27.3	24.2	21.3	20.6
	G[2]	36.0	34.5	31.5	26.7	24.1
Value added in services as a percentage of GDP	J	49.7	52.6	55.8	58.1	60.0
	K	42.6	42.2	46.3	48.9	50.1
	US	62.9	63.4	66.6	71.4[3]	..
	OE[1]	54.5	56.2	61.0	65.3	67.1
	G[2]	51.2	53.1	57.5	63.2	65.8

Notes: 1 & 2 as Table 1.
3 Average of 1990-1994
Source: As Table 1.

Table 3 Structure of Final Demand

		1974	74-79	80-89	90-95	1995
Private final consumption expenditure as a percentage of GDP	J	54.3	57.2	58.9	58.6	60.2
	K	70.4	65.2	58.2	53.6	53.0
	US	62.7	63.1	65.0	67.7	68.0
	OE[1]	59.1	59.6	60.2	60.6	60.5
	G[2]	53.6	55.6	56.3	57.0	57.1
Government final consumption expenditure as a percentage of GDP	J	9.1	9.7	9.6	9.3	9.8
	K	9.7	10.5	10.5	10.5	10.3
	US	17.6	17.3	17.6	16.9	15.8
	OE	16.5	17.4	18.4	18.6	18.3
	G	19.8	20.3	20.5	19.7	19.5
Gross fixed capital formation as a percentage of GDP	J	34.8	31.8	29.1	30.0	28.3
	K	27.0	28.9	29.4	36.7	36.6
	US	18.9	19.4	18.9	16.3	17.2
	OE	23.9	22.4	20.5	20.0	19.0
	G	21.3	20.5	20.2	22.2	21.7
Non-residential construction as a percentage of GDP	J	14.2	13.4	12.6	13.5	13.0
	K	8.8	9.6	11.3	15.1	15.6
	US	6.7	6.3	6.3	4.8	4.8
	OE	8.0	7.3	6.4	6.3	5.8
	G	7.7	6.8	6.1	6.5	6.6
Machinery & equipment as a percentage of GDP	J	12.7	10.8	10.8	11.0	10.1
	K	11.6	13.5	13.3	13.5	13.1
	US	7.7	8.0	8.1	7.5	8.3
	OE	9.4	9.0	8.8	8.5	8.0
	G	7.4	7.9	8.4	9.0	7.6
Exports of goods and services as a percentage of GDP	J	13.6	12.6	12.9	9.8	9.4
	K	27.8	29.3	35.9	29.9	33.1
	US	8.6	8.5	8.6	10.5	11.3
	OE	25.6	25.0	27.7	27.1	29.3
	G	24.7	23.7	27.9	24.3	23.6
Imports of goods and services as a percentage of GDP	J	14.3	12.2	10.9	8.1	7.9
	K	38.8	34.6	34.8	30.8	34.1
	US	8.7	9.0	10.6	11.6	12.8
	OE	27.2	25.4	27.4	26.4	27.7
	G	20.6	21.4	25.2	23.4	22.8
External balance of goods and services as a percentage of GDP	J	-0.7	0.4	1.9	1.7	1.5
	K	-11.0	-5.3	1.0	-0.9	-1.1
	US	-0.2	-0.5	-2.0	-1.2	-1.5
	OE	-1.6	-0.4	0.3	0.7	1.6
	G	4.1	2.3	2.7	0.9	0.8
Net savings as a percentage of GDP	J	23.1	20.2	18.0	17.4	14.8
	K	12.4	17.1	20.4	25.4	25.8
	US	10.1	9.1	6.1	4.1	5.1
	OE	13.2	11.4	8.7	7.7	8.2
	G	12.5	10.2	8.9	8.9	8.2

Notes: 1 & 2 as Table 1.
Source: As Table 1.

List of References

Asahi Shimbun

Fukugawa, Yukiko: *Kankoku-Senshinkoku Keizairon: Seijukukateino Mikurobunseki (On the Economy of Korea as a Developed Country: Microanalysis of its Process to Maturity)*, Tokyo: Nihonkeizaishimbunsha, 1997

Hori, Kazuo: *Chousenkougyoukano Shitekibunseki: Nihonshihonshugito Shokuminchikeizai (Historical Analysis of Korean Industrialization: Japanese Capitalism and Colonial Economy)*, Tokyo: Yuhikaku, 1995

Kaneko, Itsurou, Momose, Shigeo and Okamoto, Yoshihiro: *Kankokukeizai: Kigyouno Hattento Genjou (Economy of Korea: Development and Present State of its Enterprises)*, Tokyo: Keisoshobo, 1999

Kimura, Mitsuhiko: *Kitachosenno Keizai: Kigen, Keisei, Houkai (North Korean Economy from Emergence to Collapse)*, Tokyo: Sobunsha, 1999

Moriyama, Shigenori: *Kankoku Gendaiseiji (Contemporary Korean Politics)*; Tokyo: Tokyodaigaku Shuppankai, 1998

Nihonbouekishinkoukai (JETRO): *Sekaito Nihonno Boueki (External Trade of the World and Japan)*, Tokyo, different years

Nihonkeizai Shimbun

OECD: *Historical Statistics 1960 – 1995*, Paris, 1997

OECD: *Research and Development in Industry Expenditure and Researchers, Scientists and Engineers 1975 – 1996*, Paris, 1998

OECD: *Science, Technology and Industry Outlook*, Paris, 1998

OECD: *Foreign Trade by Commodities 1992 – 1997*, Vol. 4, Paris, 1998

OECD: *National Accounts 1960 – 1997*, Paris, 1999

Park, Woo-hee: *KankokunoGijutsuhatten (Technological Development in Korea)*, Tokyo: Bunshindou, 1989

Soumuchou-Toukeikyoku (Management and Coordination Agency: Statistics Bureau): *Nihon-Toukeinenkan (Japan Statistical Yearbook)*, Tokyo, different years

Twu, Jaw-yann: *NICS*, Tokyo: Koudansha, 1988

The Asian Crisis: Its Causes, Course and Spread, and Stabilizing Options, from a German Perspective

Willy Kraus

Ruhr-Universität Bochum

1 Euphoric Praise of the Pacific Basin as the New Center of Gravity of the World Economy

For a long time the opinion was expressed both in Germany and in Europe as a whole that the Pacific Basin was developing into the center of gravity of the world economy. It was said that this region was about to replace in part the North Atlantic region (western Europe and North America), dominant for the past two centuries, as the driving force of technical progress and world economic development (See Willy Kraus, Wilfried Lütkenhorst, "Atlantische Gegenwart—Pazifische Zukunft? Anmerkungen zur wirtschafts- und außenpolitischen Orientierung der USA", in: *Asien, Deutsche Zeitschrift für Politik, Wirtschaft und Kultur*, January 1984, No. 10, pp. 5—21; Wilfried Lütkenhorst, *Konzepte einer wirtschaftlichen Kooperation zwischen Industrie- und Entwicklungsländern im pazifischen Raum,* Bochum: Institut für Entwicklungsforschung und Entwicklungspolitik, Materialien und kleine Schriften, Nr. 92, 1982). The Pacific region was said to be in any event on the point of overtaking Europe, to the extent that in certain areas this had not already occurred. The potent phrase about the coming of a Pacific Century was also repeatedly expressed, not infrequently with reference to Arnold Toynbee's prediction that from the twenty-first century on, a flourishing Asian civilization would arise.

To be sure, the dynamics of the Pacific Basin were for a long time given little attention in Europe. But in the 1980s, they all the more vehemently became a central topic in discussions of political economics (Lütkenhorst, p. 17f.). Discussions about the geographical requirements for inclusion in the Pacific center of gravity have been rather controversial. But at last a consensus has been achieved as to a plausible definition of the relevant areas. The following countries are included beyond any doubt:

-Japan, with its turbulent growth and breathtaking rise, achieved mainly through the political-economic principle that the increases in production required for expansion of the domestic product can only be expected if production processes are continually transferred to technically more developed areas and outmoded methods and declining branches are rigorously abandoned;

-the ASEAN nations Indonesia, Malaysia, the Philippines, Thailand, Singapore and Brunei, which set out early on the path towards a consistent orientation to world markets and have already cornered a high percentage of the exports in finished goods;

-the East Asian threshold nations other than ASEAN, meaning Taiwan, South Korea and Hong Kong, which account for well over 50% of all industrial exports in the entire Third World since the shift in orientation to exports;

-and finally, the People's Republic of China, whose need for ideology is dwindling and which increasingly ascribes to a market-economy-oriented pragmatism.

Reference has often been made to the efforts at cooperation in the Pacific region, as defined above, efforts first expressed in 1968 by Drysdale and Kojima at the Pacific Trade and Development Conference. But it was also clear that even at this time, there were in fact profound interconnections that might increase in breadth and depth by means of the right institutional superstructure. In any case, empirical investigations into the degree of interconnectedness in this region have revealed a remarkably large component of intra-trade (See Hermann Sautter, "Regionalisierungstendenzen im Welthandel zwischen 1938 und 1970", in: Giersch, H./Haas, H.-D., eds., *Probleme der weltwirtschaftlichen Arbeitsteilung*, Berlin 1974, p. 596ff.). This state of affairs was pointed out, and the progressive harmonization and integration of this region was noted (a comprehensive portrayal of the most varied concepts of cooperation can be found in Wilfried Lütkenhorst, *Konzepte einer wirtschaftlichen Kooperation*, op. cit.), quite independently of the fact that the members of the area of cooperation sometimes reproached each other for engaging in unfair trade practices, closing markets for certain types of commodities, carrying out open or concealed protectionist measures, violating GATT rules, and so on (see the *Report of the Advisory Group on Economic Structural Adjustment for International Harmony* [Maekawa-Report], submitted to the Japanese Prime Minister Yasuhiro Nakasone on April 7, 1986). Furthermore, despite all the processes of cultural and ethnic melding, there are still considerable differences in the fundamental religious and philosophical outlooks of the nations of the rim. But in our view, this heterogeneity has been drawn together by a number of supravening characteristics: a vital desire to learn, belief and pleasure in progress, willingness to communicate, and above all, the will to dynamism.

Along with the cultural factors of obvious and great importance, there were also high rates of savings and investments, as well as the systematic building of export markets. We should keep in mind that up until 1997 the East and Southeast Asian countries were the fastest growing in the world. "For almost two centuries gross domestic products of South Korea, Thailand, Hong Kong, Taiwan, Singapore, Malaysia and Indonesia increased at an average rate of 7-8%, compared to the average 3% for the countries of the developed world. Moreover, these countries, in spite of their growing populations, experienced a per capita growth in gross domestic product almost three times that of their developed, industrial rivals" (Stephan K. Green, "Die Asienkrise und ihre Bedeutung für die Weltwirtschaft", in: *Politische Studien*, Heft 366, 50. Jahrgang, July/August, 1999, p. 14). Whereas Asia's share of world income in 1950 was about 19%, by 1992 it had already climbed to 33% and has continued to increase ever since (Steven C. Radelet and Jeffrey D. Sachs, "Asia's Long Run Economic Growth and Development, *HIID Research Review*, Vol. XL, No. 3, Spring/Summer 1998, p. 1).

The Federal Republic of Germany and the entire European Union came to feel the power of East and Southeast Asian export offensives. Overall, the Japanese exports, enhanced by successive threshold countries from East and Southeast Asia, were concentrated on a few areas and therefore caused severe distress in major branches of European business. All this took place according to concepts designed for the long term and stubbornly enforced programs of efficient export marketing, but its prerequisite was cost-effective production. Such a conspicuous development of course contributed greatly to a further increase in "Pacific euphoria" in Europe, which was, by the way, not restricted to Europe. In an American publication of 1982, for instance, we read that "Pacific optimism has become a growth industry in the United States" (This is the evaluation of D. K. Emmerson, quoted in: *CAPS-Newsletter*, The Center for Asian and Pacific Studies at the University of Hawaii, Vol. 1, 1982, No. 2, p. 7). On March 27, 1980, Mike Mansfield declared in Hawaii: "We are convinced that the future is in the Pacific, just as it was in the Atlantic in the past." (*Tokyo Keizai* [Tokyo], June 14, 1980; *Jiyu* [Tokyo], June 1980).

To be sure, cautions were voiced early on in the face of the excessively euphoric mood, warning against taking only the exuberantly optimistic Pacific region into account and relegating all other regions to an age now regarded as passé or in decline. But the Asian-Pacific actors in the drama continued to perceive the great miracle more than the dangers and risks (see Paul Krugman, "The Myth of Asia's Miracle", in: *Foreign Affairs*, Vol. 73, 1994, p. 62ff.). Political and economic inadequacies were indeed noted, but they were often regarded as "growing pains" (Stephan K. Green, *Die Asienkrise und ihre Bedeutung für die Weltwirtschaft*), which would not hinder further growth. The profound and incessant so-called

Asian crisis therefore took us by surprise and triggered a widespread discussion, not only among the experts, but also in the general public.

2 Globalization and the Asian Crisis

The globalization debate, this wide-ranging discussion about the international integration of commodities, service and capital markets, i.e., about the increasing networking of economic activities (Jürgen Friedrichs, "Globalisierung—Begriff und grundlegende Annahmen," in: *Aus Politik und Zeitgeschichte,* August 8, 1997, p. 3), has added some harsh overtones to the discussions of the Asian crisis. There is surely no question about the fact that the degree of internationalization in national economies after 1945 has greatly increased, as it has become ever quicker and cheaper to cover physical distances, and that accordingly the international division of labour has spread and deepened immensely. Thanks to the technological means of lowering the costs of transactions, capital mobility has continually risen (Paul J. J. Welfens, "Soziale Marktwirtschaft und Globalisierung," in: *Orientierung zur Wirtschafts- und Gesellschaftspolitik,* Heft 74, December 1997, p. 11). Globalization is naturally connected with strong competitive pressure upon the commodities and service markets. It intensifies local competition, and it promotes international competition in taxation. It leads ultimately to numerous challenges requiring appropriate responses.

The opponents of globalization, and often even the proponents of the globalization debate, have produced any number of arguments against the increasing degree of internationalization. They point to the alleged "naked dominance of the markets," to the "unadulterated capitalism," to the difficulties of financing in resolving social questions, to the endangerment of the goals of environmental protection, to the pressures from imports upon domestic production and the resulting destruction of jobs, etc. This was certainly yet another essential argument of the proponents of Japanese trade restrictions against other countries, whether as part of a complaint about their dismantling, or as part of a plea for their reinstatement.

Critics of globalization in the meantime are even speaking of "crises of globalization," asserting that economic crisis situations are a direct manifestation of globalization. In the same vein, it is claimed that globalization, with its "unchecked flow of capital" into Asian countries, was the "trigger" of the Asian crisis (*Epi-Entwicklungspolitische Informationen*, 1-2/1999, p. 28.). The General Director of UNCTAD, Rubens Ricupero, stated in Geneva on September 20, 1999 that the turbulences in Asia, Russia and Latin America were crises of developmental policies and of globalization ("UNCTAD: Die Globalisierung nützt bisher vor allem den Reichen", in: *FAZ*, September 16, 1999 and September 21, 1999. Although in the mid-1990s UNCTAD believed that globalization offered a chance for the poor, its opinion now is that global integration is dashing the hopes of the developing nations.). We, however, have repeatedly taken the point of view that globalization does indeed demand a higher degree of flexibility and adaptability, but that under these conditions of "creative destruction," "creative restructuring" should follow from the introduction of foreign production and foreign services, and will create new possibilities for production and new jobs (Christian Watrin, "Die Herausforderung der Globalisierung: Chancen und Notwendigkeiten", in: Anton Rauscher, *Zukunftsfähige Gesellschaft. Beiträge zu Grundfragen der Wirtschafts- und Sozialpolitik*, Berlin, 1998, p. 69ff.). One is of course constrained to doubt whether such conditions generally exist in a well-developed form. Ultimately, however, globalization provides advantages for everybody, as long as the markets are functional over an extended period. UNCTAD, on the other hand, still adheres to the ideology that globalization primarily benefits the rich. And yet there is no mistaking the fact that globalization has contributed greatly to a basic improvement in the chances of developing countries to catch up. Whether they have known how to use the chances offered has of course always depended upon the domestic economic policy of the individual countries. There is no doubt that the developing nations of the Asian crisis region have been among the great beneficiaries of globalization. "Thailand, Malaysia, South Korea, Indonesia and Hong Kong have been the model pupils of globalization, and within a few decades they made the leap from poor developing countries to wealthy threshold nations" (Karl Zawadsky, "Globalisierungskrise", *Epi-Entwicklungspolitische Information*, 12/1997, p. 1.). In contrast to the losers, e.g., Subsaharan Africa, they have attached great importance to the creation of political and overall economic stability. They have invested heavily in human as well as material capital. And they have finally opened their markets, at least to a greater extent than before. They have obviously come into the full range of benefits of globalization, but they have not yet adequately performed the resulting new and comprehensive tasks involving basic adaptations. But it is the very nature of globalization that it imposes greater demands in terms of flexibility and adaptability, to say nothing of the fact that the traditional institutions too require thoroughgoing changes.

For many decades Japan was obviously exemplary in its domestic innovativeness, willingness to restructure and pioneering spirit, as it showed by following, as a rule, the signals of the market. But from our present perspective, doubts are justified as to whether it reacted overall with enough flexibility to the meteoric structural transformation of the most recent decades. There is no ignoring the fact that restrictions on imports in specific areas of production have largely been retained—to the particular dudgeon of the United States. And in Japan itself, institutional requirements have been put to a severe test in the train of the globalization process, e.g., the Japanese banking and financial systems. But we cannot find anything in this area which is a unique problem for Japan, past or present. In our own country, and in Europe as a whole, we have a great deal of catching up to do.

However, even the most euphoric proponents of globalization strategies with their wide-ranging goals for globalization will sense the attack on their conceptions mounted by the Asian crisis. They hope that globalization will not only lead to a strongly increasing interweaving of the world economy, a limitation and disciplining of the economic policies of individual states, and a worldwide diffusion and re-creation of technical knowledge (Dieter Bender, "Globalisierung: Risiken oder Chancen für eine zukunftsfähige Weltwirtschaft? Ordnungspolitische Grundlagen wohlstands- und entwicklungsfördernder weltwirtschaftlicher Strukturen", in: Paul Klemmer/Dorothee Becker-Soest/Rüdiger Wink, eds., *Liberale Grundrisse* einer zukunftsfähigen Gesellschaft, Baden-Baden, 1998, p. 245ff.), but ultimately an overcoming of regionalism as well, accompanied by an elimination of regional crises (Jozef van Brabant, "Is Regionalism Compatible with Global Integration? The Transition Economies," in: *Comparative Economic Studies*, Vol. XL, No. 4, Winter 1996.). Even so, one cannot ignore the fact that regionalization can be found everywhere in the world. Practically every nation in the world economy belongs to some trading block—not just the countries of East and Southeast Asia. (Norbert Lamar, "Globalisierung vs. Regionalisierung," in: Dieter Bender, Hans-Rimbert Hemmer, eds., *Entwicklungsländer im Zeitalter der Globalisierung*, Frankfurt/Giessen, 1999, p. 37f.).

3 Manifestations and Causes of the Asian Crisis

3.1 Some Facts about the Asian Crisis

On July 2, 1997, the Thai government decontrolled the exchange rate of the bath, which promptly lost 20% of its value against the dollar and bottomed out at 28.8 bath per dollar. The entire region was in fear of a knock-on effect. Interest rates were sharply raised to support the currency. There followed a period of turbulence and unrest, which extended beyond the borders of Thailand and especially affected Korea and Indonesia. It is however necessary to keep in mind that before the Thai bath was decontrolled, a number of events had already indicated that problems were looming:

As early as January 1997, Hanbo-Steel in Korea had collapsed. In February 1997, Thailand's Somprasong Concern had trouble meeting its obligations. In March of the same year, the Sammi Steel Concern in Korea went into receivership. In addition, a significant decrease in Korea's foreign currency reserves was noticeable. In March and April, the conditions for granting real-estate loans were tightened in Malaysia and Thailand. In May, a rapid fall in the yen was recorded in Japan. In June, the Thai Prime Minister, Chavalit Yongchaiyudh declared, despite all this, that the bath would never be devalued. (A comprehensive chronology of the Asian crisis can be found in Herbert Dieter, *Die Asienkrise. Ursachen, Konsequenzen und die Rolle des Internationalen Währungsfonds*, Marburg, 1999, p. 165ff. Also worthy of note is Hans Christoph Rieger's work, *Erscheinungsbild und Erklärungsmuster der asiatischen Wirtschaftskrise: Beitrag für die Jahrestagung des Ausschusses "Entwick*lungsländer" des *Vereins für Sozialpolitik in Halle am 4./5. Juni 1999.*) When the bath was, in fact, devalued, as noted above, international investors became nervous. The risks carried by firms and banks, which in many cases were also carrying loans in U.S. dollars, increased substantially. Moreover, the flaws and systemic weaknesses of the Asian economic systems were now manifest. "The result was the beginning of an erosive process which was to lead to a catastrophic situation" (Stephan K. Green, *Die Asienkrise und ihre Bedeutung für die Weltwirtschaft*, p. 16). The deciding factor was doubtless the loss of confidence arising from insufficient clarity about the actual situation of the financial sector and the connections among banks, industry and government" (Ibid., p. 17.).

The loss in confidence was accompanied by clear contractionary symptoms in the Asian financial markets. Local currencies and share prices went into decline. Loss in value of currencies was massive, e.g., 52.5% for the Indonesian rupee, 48% for the Korean won, 42% for the Thai bath, 33.5% for the Malaysian ringgit, 13.5% for the Singapore dollar, 30% for the Philippine peso and 14.2% for the Taiwanese dollar (against the U.S. dollar in all cases: *ibid.*, p. 17. The Indonesian rupee bottomed out with a loss of over 80% of its value against the U.S. dollar.). Foreign indebtedness, which was especially high in Indonesia, Thailand and the Philippines, rose alarmingly, expressed in domestic currency. Per capita income sank dramatically. The number of insolvencies increased greatly, combined with a disturbing degree of unemployment. Even so, the Korean won, the Thai bath, and the Indonesian rupee had recovered a good portion of their value by the middle of 1998. In view of the low exchange rates, export volumes remained fairly stable and renewed capital influx from abroad could be anticipated. A series of events at this juncture, however, dashed any hopes for a speedy recovery.

In August 1998, the Russian financial crisis shook the confidence of financial markets around the world, much more so, surely, than if East and Southeast Asia had not been racked by their own crisis. "It was a further ruinous blow for the confidence of investors in the 'emerging markets' and provided a new and powerful motive for the aversion to risk that spread over the world" (*ibid.*, p. 18). The contagious effects triggered in Asia ultimately reached all the markets of the developing nations. In Brazil, the government had great difficulty in stemming the outflow of capital, which finally led to real interest rates of over 15%. The IMF was finally moved to put together a financial aid package for Brazil amounting to over $40bn. In South Africa, the Rand lost about one-fourth of its value. And so the crisis intensified once again. One can surely say with confidence "that in the age of globalization, a crisis in one economic region can spread to completely different economic areas through contagious effects" ("Banken haben aus der Finanzmarktkrise gelernt": *Börsenzeitung*, Frankfurt/Main, September 9, 1999.). There were also those who spoke of the herd instinct of the players in the finance markets, which was alleged to have contributed to the expansion of the Asian crisis within a relatively short time to Southeast Asia, Latin America and Russia (*ibid.*). Nor did the states of the Western world remain unaffected by the Asian crisis. According to Ernst-Moritz Lipp, a member of the board of the Dresdner Bank, internationally active banks lost about $300-350bn, based on available estimates (*ibid.*). For all that, recovery set in East and Southeast Asia with surprising speed. Japan, the most important exporting and investing nation in this region, was most strongly affected. Its rise in exports leveled off, and in 1998 the export volume even decreased in absolute terms.

3.2 Alleged Causes

3.2.1 Inadequate Preparations for Crises

In Asia, too, people were not adequately prepared for possible manifestations of crisis. Instead, they lived in the euphoric sense that the great age of Asia had dawned and that Europe's exit from the stage was imminent. The unrestrained optimism radiated by the "Asian tigers" finally bedazzled even their foreign partners. There was therefore hardly any occasion for reservations about an Asian speculative bubble and the possible accompanying effects. Only a few observers, e.g., Paul Krugman ("The Myth of Asia's Miracle," loc. cit., p. 62ff.) and Walden Bello, expressed a certain skepticism about the Asian miracle, with general reference to the national economies of Korea, the Philippines, Malaysia, Indonesia, Singapore, Thailand, Hong Kong, China and Taiwan. But when the dominant mood is confidence that obviously nothing will or can ever go wrong that might stop a development decreed by fate, then risk factors will be ever more ignored. In such cases there is then little motive to think seriously about the need for restructuring or reforms.

3.2.2 Inadequacies of the World Finance System and Lack of World Currency Regulations

The world finance system and the lack of world currency regulations are held responsible for the Asian crisis. Milton Friedman is doubtless correct to point out that even today there are still only national finance systems—the British with the Bank of England, the European with the European Central Bank, the Japanese with the Bank of Japan, the Federal Reserve System in the United States, etc., which are connected through exchange rates and world trade. He also takes the view that the speculators have done no harm. "Thailand, for instance, pursued an unsound monetary policy, which was bound at some point to lead to a crash. If there had been no speculators, the crash would have come later, but then it would have been much worse" ("Milton Friedman über Finanzen, Spekulation, Steuern und das Ende der Staatsgewalt," in: *Vorhaben--Deutsche Bank* 24, No. 1, September 1, 1999, p. 12ff.). Furthermore, Friedman does not believe that there is any need for world currency regulations. What is important is that the separate monetary authorities ensure stability of prices in their realms, that the market forces take their effect, and finally that protectionism and trade barriers are avoided. However, the national bank systems of the Asian nations affected by the crisis are all the more criticized for their undercapitalization, their inadequate supervision of banks and the weak position of their central banks. In the declaration of the major industrial nations of Autumn 1998, the need for reform of the then world finance system was also emphasized.

3.2.3 Excessive Expansion of Credit and Unchecked Capital Influx

A gigantic expansion of credit, which led to considerable short-term growth rates, but was not sustainable in the long term, has been duly noted. This development was connected with high inflation rates and large deficits in the balance of payments and trade. The constantly increasing money supply further led to rapidly rising stock prices and truly explosive values on the real estate market. The relationship of credit volume to gross domestic product achieved exceptionally high figures when international comparisons were drawn (Lukas Menkhoff, "Die Rolle finanzieller Globalisierung in der Asienkrise," in: Dieter Bender and Hans-Rimbert Hemmer, eds., *Entwicklungsländer im Zeitalter der Globalisierung*, Frankfurt, 1999, p. 90.).

In many cases Asian currencies in the crisis area were pegged to the dollar. The weakness of the dollar against the yen, however, promoted the export viability of the Southeast Asian countries, but then in 1995, the dollar-yen relationship was reversed—combined with a decrease in competitiveness with regard to the United States and Japan. The rise of the American currency against the yen and most European currencies led to a considerable increase in the real external value of most Eastasian currencies with all the consequences in respect to exports and balance of payments (Erich T. Geis, "Globalisierungseffekte im Lichte der Asienkrise", in: Dieter Bender and Hans-Rimbert Hemmer, eds., *Entwicklungsländer im Zeitalter der Globalisierung*, Loc. cit., p. 108.). In any event, the so-called Currency Board, the pegging of a currency to a key currency, could not be sustained during the Asian crisis.[1]

---

1 But one should not overlook a fact to which Rüdiger Machetzki has justly called attention, "that thecurrently criticized pegging to the dollar functioned for over a decade as an important asset.": Rüdiger Machetzki, "Stimmen Asiens werden leiser", *FAZ*, September 10, 1997.

Attention has also been given to the foreign creditors and their role in the Asian crisis. They are reproached with having unleashed an unchecked flow of capital into the Asian nations afflicted by the crisis, capital only partially used to build up a working capital stock. Furthermore, it is said that this capital flow led to short-term, unrestrained investments in the finance system and on the real-estate market. "Explicitly or implicitly assumed state guarantees for the creditors increased the capital influx to domestic banks" (Rainer Klump, "Erscheinungsbild und Erklärungsmuster der asiatischen Wirtschaftskrise": *Beitrage für die Jahrestagung des Ausschusses 'Entwicklungsländer' des Vereins für Sozialpolitik in Halle am 4./5. Juni 1999*). Available data on private indebtedness in the debtor countries Indonesia, Malaysia, the Philippines, Thailand and South Korea show that the share of Japanese credits (according to a publication of the *Financial Times* of January 30, 1998) was especially high, at $97.2bn, and thus amounted to the entire sum of the claims of the other large creditor nations (Heribert Dieter, *Die Asienkrise, Ursachen und Konsequenzen*," loc. cit., p. 55.). Various writers have concluded from this that Japanese capital exports were an "essential contribution to the development of the Asian crisis" (*ibid*., p. 56.).

However, we are inclined to believe that the foreign creditors as a whole committed errors. Jeffrey Sachs expressed this as follows: "In all of the countries, international money market managers and investment banks went on a lending binge from 1993 to 1997" (Jeffrey Sachs, "The Wrong Medicine for Asia", in: *The New York Times*, November 3, 1997.). An additional factor was that a large number of these loans were short-term. The huge import of foreign capital into the region of the crisis was followed by an abrupt and panicky outflow of capital in 1997, and especially in 1998, which could only intensify the crisis.

3.2.4 Inadequate Management of Banks

The management of the banks was extensively castigated. Functioning supervisory bodies were often lacking, along with the willingness to supervise the banks efficiently. There was also a widespread conviction that trust was, after all, better than control. Everywhere the provisions for avoiding risk were rather superficial. Even in relatively small stock markets, derivatives were offered and hedge funds established, which led to a growing volume of uncollectable credit and finally placed the existence of the entire finance system in question. In addition, skepticism about the competence of the governments to solve problems increased. One should however note that the banking institutions under governmental control contributed significantly to the crisis. They had an especially strong inclination to misrepresent their solvency and to grant "rotten" loans.

3.2.5 The Urge to Expand of the Firms

Firms in the region of the crisis often gave free rein to their urge to expand without taking due account of the risks involved. This point of view is also placed in context with the policy of the IMF, which is said to have generally encouraged expansion with its way of granting credit. "International speculation is said to have been encouraged, because financial assistance is supposed to have enabled it to withdraw abruptly with limited losses in case of a crisis" (Philippe Delhaise, President of Thomson Bankwatch Asia, Hong Kong, at the East Asian Summit of the World Economic Forum in Singapore in October 1999, reported, *FAZ*, October 27, 1999.). Because the IMF propagated exchange rate peggings and a comprehensive liberalization in capital movement, it is said to have, firstly, offered stimuluses for speculative engagements, and, secondly, to have created better possibilities for a precipitate withdrawal" (Peter Nunnenkamp, "Der IWF als Krisenursache? IWF-Kredite, Moral Hazard und die Reform der internationalen Finanzarchitektur," Paper for the annual meeting of the committee "Entwicklungsländer" of the Society for Social Policy in Halle, June 4-5, 1999). According to this view, the IMF takes on "the role of an arsonist trying to put out a fire that he himself started" (Ibid.), a thesis which can hardly be maintained in such a radical form. But we should also not overlook the fact that the powerful and longlasting expansion prior to the Asian crisis led to a lack of qualified managers and other executive personnel who were able to see the approaching dangers and were also in a position to mount an effective form of crisis management. In addition, the industrial structure was unbalanced "because of an expansion of large enterprises and unfavourable conditions for large and medium-sized enterprises" (Günter Heiduk, Nicole Pohl, "Financing the Industrialization in Emerging Economies by Capital Inflows: A Matter of Regulation or Deregulation? Experiences from the Asian Countries": Manuscript, Gerhard Mercator University, Duisburg).

3.2.6 Bad Economic Decisions, Disruptive Political Factors and Interdependencies with Interest Groups

From our point of view, the Asian crisis clearly stems from a whole set of causes, partly monetary, partly non-monetary, and, not least, partly political in nature. In any case, it is our opinion that bad economic decisions and disruptive political factors played an important role, above all in their interaction. Overall, there were surely serious structural flaws at work, which were either perceived too late or redressed after excessive delays. A fatal factor in this situation was that given the corrupt entanglement of economics and politics, negative economic and political developments proceeded together and exacerbated the crisis as it progressed.

In many cases we have been able to determine that the political leadership was closely involved with interest groups, and that huge investment schemes served unproductive ends. In many cases the flow of capital was controlled not by prices and interest rates, but by nepotism and corruption, of which two former Korean presidents were found guilty in courts of law. In Indonesia, the Suharto Clan enriched itself enormously at the expense of the general population. "Courtesy banking" was widespread. The credibility of the governments decreased according to the circumstances and was a factor further exacerbating the crisis.

4 Stabilizing Policy Options of Leading Regional Powers

The individual countries of the region were affected by the Asian crisis to varying degrees, and the stabilizing policy options of the leading regional powers were accordingly very different. At present only Japan and China can be definitely regarded as leading regional powers.

4.1 The Role of China and Its Stabilizing Policy Options

As regards China, one cannot deny that this country too was affected by the Asian crisis. In 1994 the renminbi (RMB) was devalued, an act officially proclaimed not as a devaluation but as a "restructuring of the exchange-rate system" (Heribert Dieter, *Die Asienkrise*, p. 67.).

The previous rate, set at 5.7 renminbi per dollar, was now reduced to 8.7 renminbi per dollar, a devaluation of 52%. It was apparent that this move granted Chinese firms significant advantages over the other exporters of the region. It has also been claimed, based on this fact, that China thereby contributed to the Asian crisis.

But along with the devaluation of the renminbi came numerous deregulatory measures aimed at enforcing the highest economic and sociopolitical priority at the time, the promotion and securing of general prosperity. Between 1993 and 1995, real growth of the gross domestic product accordingly shows double-digit real rates, e.g., an increase of 12.6% in 1994. In the course of this development, however, rates of inflation also rose significantly and were sometimes over 20%, e.g., 21.7% in 1994. Ultimately it was possible to halt the breakdown of this runaway boom and to pursue a stable growth trend. But subsequently a steady downward trend was observable in China. After a period of declining rates in price increases, prices themselves began to drop in October 1997, along with falling growth rates in the gross domestic product. "Over the past two years, the Chinese central bank has lowered interest rates seven times, cut the cost of credit, and drastically reduced the interest on the Chinese people's savings accounts in order to entice money out of the banks and into circulation" (Markus Gärtner, "China hat seine Karten ausgereizt", *Handelsblatt*, June 18, 1999.).

Overall, the Asian crisis made itself felt in China through a slacking off in exporting activities and a decrease in direct investment from abroad. The nations of the crisis in the region were no longer in a position to absorb the previously normal quota of exports from the People's Republic of China. Hence, in the first three quarters of 1998, Chinese exports to the ASEAN countries dropped by 16.1%, to Japan by 6.5%, and to South Korea by 32.4% (Markus Taube, "Wirtschaftliche Entwicklung unter dem Einfluss von Asienkrise und Flutkatastrophe: VR China 1998", in: *Bochumer Jahrbuch zur Ostasienforschung*, Vol. 22, 1998, p. 111.). Furthermore, the massive devaluations in the region of the crisis led in effect to a real revaluation of the renminbi and limited China's competitiveness. Despite all this, China came out of the Asian crisis relatively unscathed. The gross domestic product continued to grow even at the nadir of the crisis. Foreign currency reserves have increased and at present amount to ca. $140bn.

A decisive contribution to the solution of the Asian crisis and to the economic stabilization of the region was surely that from the beginning it was emphatically stated that the renminbi would not be devalued. After many assurances that there was no intention to devalue, the president of the Chinese central bank himself declared at the APEC Conference in Auckland in September 1999 that there was no question of any devaluation of the renminbi. A devaluation race, triggered by a Chinese devaluation, would have been the worst possible disservice to the region of the crisis at this time. For the Chinese leadership, there were economic as well as political reasons for the refusal to devalue:

It was by no means clear that under the dominant conditions a devaluation would really lead to rises in exports. But it would make it more difficult to service China's foreign debt (*ibid.*, p. 112.). A devaluation would also have limited the importation of important components from Japan. It seems to us however that in this case there were political reasons which were even more important: If the renminbi had been devalued, the pegging of the Hong Kong dollar to the U.S. dollar could hardly have continued. The Chinese leadership implied that the pegging of the Hong Kong dollar must be maintained, if a serious loss of confidence was to be avoided (Markus Taube, op. cit., p. 113ff., gives a detailed account of the various measures.). Beijing clearly regards it as very important to act as a stabilizing force in the region and hence to demonstrate the political clout it has now acquired. In accord with this posture, China also took part in supportive measures during the Asian crisis, and made $1bn available to Thailand as an emergency measure.

Beijing also viewed its refusal to devalue as a measure calculated to strengthen its negotiating position for attaining membership in the WTO. Even so, China did not refrain from using a variety of fiscal measures and subsidies to compensate for not devaluing. Attempts are also being made to deal with the decrease in attractivity of direct investment in the People's Republic of China by appropriate measures, e.g., the reintroduction of duty-free imports for firms with foreign capital investment as of January 1, 1998. This will hardly be sufficient. The only real help will come from a general improvement in basic conditions, especially the improvement in guarantees of rights.

Within the framework of present course of action, the Chinese leadership does not have all too many stabilizing options. A further transformation of the system through a comprehensive reform of the state-owned enterprises, which has already resulted in numerous employees being laid off, is at present out of the question, given mass unemployment affecting 180-260m people, none of whom can be supported by a supraregional social security network The Central Office of Statistics in Beijing has in the meantime presented figures for the first three quarters of 1999. They indicate a rise of 7.4% in the GDP compared with the corresponding period in the previous year. On the other hand, exports in the first three quarters only increased by 2.1%. Foreign investments were down by 6.8%. The Central Office of Statistics also reported that the number of state-owned businesses, 56,100 at the end of 1998, was now only 48,200 as a result of closures and mergers (*FAZ*, October 21, 1999). The Chinese leadership has also perceived that the reform of the financial system provides an essential stabilizing effect. In an interview with the *Financial Times*, the Chinese Minister of Finance, Xiang Huaicheng, stated: "The Asian financial crisis has offered us a very good lesson. We did not realise how serious the problem of bad loans can be. They do not just upset banks, but they can upset governments too." (*Financial Times*, October 26, 1998, quoted by Markus Taube, op. cit., p. 122.). The general impression is that China made every effort during the Asian crisis to play the role of the emerging leading regional power that intends, come what may, to significantly lessen the lead of the dominant Japanese. "The Chinese domestic product (including Hong Kong's U.S.$1100bn) amounts at present to 30% of Japan's domestic product (compared with 15% in 1990)."

4.2 The Role of Japan and Its Stabilizing Policy Options

What view are we to take of the role played by Japan in the Asian crisis, and what stabilizing policy options has Japan, as the leading regional power, at its disposal?

4.2.1 Stabilizing and Destabilizing Elements

As in the other nations of the Asian crisis, a speculative boom on the real-estate and stock markets was set in motion in Japan. Starting as early as 1986, there was a "bubble economy" in Japan which did not burst until the nineties. From that point on, Japanese growth has continually declined and in 1998 even gone into minus numbers.

In our part of the world a distinction is often made between Japan's own crisis, from the beginning of the 1990s, and the actual Asian crisis, which started up in a concentrated form in 1997. Japan's great difficulties in halting its own downward slide, so the argument runs, subsequently led to a "deepening of the crisis in the region" (Heribert Dieter, *Die Asienkrise. Ursachen, Konsequenzen und die Rolle des Internationalen Währungsfonds*, loc. cit., p. 144.). The economic recovery programme set in motion in 1993 to the tune of $650bn contributed little, it is argued, to the economic recovery. On the contrary, it is noted, the total public indebtedness from 1991 to 1998 increased from 59 to 98%, and by now has risen to 117% of the GDP. In this context reference is made to the lessons learned from experience in Europe, namely, that the effectivity of state-financed economic recovery programmes has been greatly overestimated. Usually, the stimuli from such programmes ebb away quickly. Japan—so it is believed—has played its last hand and has "at present no further means of reacting appropriately and decisively to the crisis" (*ibid.*, p. 145.). According to this point of view, the options in economic policy are very limited, with regard both to individual national requirements and to the requirements of the entire region.

In November 1998, a poll of business leaders commissioned by the foundation *Industrieforschung* was conducted on the question, "How does German business really view Japan?" The conclusion was that German businesspeople are skeptical as to "whether the reforms will actually be carried through and whether they will really do any good" (Karl Lichtblau, "Japan-Experte im Institut der Deutschen Wirtschaft, Köln", in: *Japans Weg aus der Krise—eine Zwischenbilanz. Podiumsdiskussion*, March 23, 1999, Hotel Nikko, Düsseldorf, p. 17). The opinion is also expressed that Japan has contributed much more to destabilizing than to stabilizing the Asian region affected by the crisis. Whereas this region more than ever needs decisive political leadership, so the opinion, Japan has fallen into apathy. Such statements draw a special connection to the greatly increased public indebtedness, to considerable number of banks in distress, to the interest-rate policy of Japan's central bank, which lowered the discount rate in 1995 to 0.5%, to the generally necessary and long overdue restructuring of the Japanese economy, and, naturally, to Japan's unemployment rate, considered very high for that country.

4.2.2 Long-Term Proposals for Reform

In our country there are of course other, quite different, opinions. Still, there seems to be general agreement on one topic: The crisis in Japan, the worst recession of the postwar era, had different causes and must be differently categorized than the complex of phenomena known as the "Asian crisis". Differences of opinion are especially common in regard to the first grouping mentioned when Japan is said to have played its last hand and is incapable of appropriate responses in the present critical situation. We, at any rate, have formed the impression that Japan is now no longer satisfied with mere short-term crisis management, but is on the contrary making every effort "to use the critical situation to construct a 'new country'" (Kenji Tanaka, "Japan's Path out of the Crisis--An Interim Report", loc. cit., p. 8.). Hence there is already talk about the "New Japan". There are, consistent with this idea, a number of essential proposals and measure for reform which will naturally require time, in some cases a great deal of time, to be enacted (Kuniko Inoguchi, loc. cit., p. 11ff.):

- An administrative reform with the goal of "slender administration", which will simplify administrative processes and structure them in a clearer and more economical way;

-A thoroughgoing reform of the finance system;

-A rehabilitation of the banks through temporary state ownership, establishment of interim banks, strengthening of the equity base, etc.[2];

-Liberalization and opening of the markets, which, one must note, has been heralded for years now.

As to the pessimistic assessment of Japan's present situation, however, it is not enough to cite only the long-term character of Japanese reforms. One has also to note a whole series of immediate measures, enacted with great courage. Whether they will succeed remains to be seen:

---

2 In September 1999, for example, Y260bn (ca. DM4.3bn) were provided by the Financial Reconstruction Commission in Tokyo for strengthening the equity base of four regional banks. It is however questionable whether the great mergers have not already contributed to the rehabilitation. It was already known that the amount of emergency credit for the large banks had been set at Y20, 700 bn (Euro 167bn) and for the 64 main regional banks at Y17,200bn (Euro139bn). See *FAZ*, September 29, 1999. See also Helmut Becker, "Japans Banken brauchen Wachstum", in: *Börsenzeitung*, Frankfurt, Juni 25, 1999: "When one considers that Japan's commercial banks alone have up to now in this decade absorbed problem loans of about Y50bn (Euro 403bn), mainly through value adjustments and factorizations, e.g., to the CCPC, whose ultimate losses are carried by the banks, then it is clear how deeply dependent the banks are on prompt economic growth—and vice versa.

-The City of Tokyo, in expectation of a deficit in the fiscal year from April 1, 2000 to March 31, 2001, has gone so far as to cut the basic salaries of its employees by 4% and their bonuses by 10.5% for the next three fiscal years (*FAZ*, September 22, 1999.);

-The maximum inheritance tax is to be reduced as of April 1. The extremely high realty prices, which still apply, have led to special regulations for bequests of small businesses with plots of up to 330 square meters, as long as the business is carried on by the heirs;

-The government acted rapidly and decisively to deal with the difficulties of the Long Term Credit Bank;

-The Coupon Action, begun in February 1999, in which about a fourth of the population received coupons, each worth just about DM300, has in our view had little effect. No doubt the political benefit was greater than the economic.

4.2.3 Respect for the Interests of Neighbouring Countries

Even though it is often maintained that signs of a change in the trend in Japan are only in limited evidence, due to the many uncertainties, we still believe that there are many hopeful indications, despite the fact that improvement in the job market has yet to be seen:

-Inventories are being increasingly reduced;

-Construction of houses and apartments shows a strong increase;

-The comprehensive restructuring of individual firms, e.g., Sony, Honda, Matsushita, Mitsubishi Electric, etc., is now spreading to other companies. This applies to the entire banking business, which is now obviously on the way to changing into powerful groups of sole proprietors;

-The climate for business has improved, as the Bank of Japan announced in its Tanaka Report, published at the beginning of October;

-"The Japanese automobile manufacturers are once again expanding their production in the Southeast Asian countries appreciably in comparison with the previous year. Output in the region in the current year should again be between 700, 000 and 800 000 vehicles, as against 400, 000 in the previous year";

-The Nikkei share averages once again climbed to 17,000 for the first time in about 20 months;

-Gross domestic product rose between April and June by 0.2% compared with the first quarter;

-Naturally the high value of the yen is cause for concern[3]. Still, it is too simple to say that the strong yen is hindering the continuation of the economic upturn. "For Japan's neighbours the strength of the yen is a blessing, not a curse. For Korea's damaged exporting industries, e.g., which are often in direct competition with Japanese concerns, opportunities on foreign markets grow with each successive rise in the value of the yen. The rapid recovery in countries like Thailand or Malaysia we have observed in recent weeks would never have been possible if they had been locked in a race for devaluation with Japan."

It is bound to be in Japan's interest for its Asian neighbours to find their feet again. A good 30% of all Japanese exports go to these countries. Moreover, Japan also profits from the strength of the yen because of cheaper imports of raw materials. In discussions of the yen's rate of exchange and the problems of intervention by the central bank we should also keep in mind that Japan's dependence upon exports is much less than Germany's.

4.2.4 Making Up for Regulatory Neglect

Nor can we share the view that Japanese options in economic policy are extremely limited, if this is taken to mean that Japan's innovative potency has given way to lasting apathy and mediocrity. Obviously Japan is faced with two basic options:

---

3 The threshold of pain seems to be at an exchange rate of about Y118 per dollar. The lowest rate for the yen (after a period of eight years) came on August 11, 1946, when one dollar cost Y147.64.

Either to:

-powerfully revitalize its economy;

-basically reform its tax system;

-promote competition;

-rehabilitate its banking system appropriately to the system and structure an efficient supervision of its banks;

-create more transparency than has heretofore existed, i.e., to stabilize expectations through a policy of openness of information;

-carry on energetically with deregulation. "The Planning Office of the government estimates that the share of the domestic product in Japan produced in regulated sectors is still over 40%, which is just as high as in 1965" (Karl Lichtblau, Panel Discussion, loc. cit., p. 17.), and,

-undertake accommodation to international economic standards, e.g., even through mutual recognition of technical requirements.

Or to:

-further expand the public share of the GDP, as in past years;

-moderate the cutback in overcapacity;

-stop carrying distressed banks and unprofitable businesses at state expense;

-cease the immediate writing off of unrecoverable obligations, and instead spread the debt mass over fifteen years (Takenaka Heizo, "Aussichten für den japanischen Big Bang," *Japan Echo*, No. 2, 1997, p. 27.), and:

-continue to provide industry with capital influx at extremely low interest rates which do not even approximately correspond to true market conditions.

The impact of the events in Japan, as well as in the neighbouring countries shaken by the crisis, surely indicates clearly that the path to be followed consists in making up for neglect in regulatory policies with a view to the future. As Hirotaro Higuchi stated: "What Japan requires above all else is a forward-looking perspective". We would like to believe that only this path will allow Japan to recover its role as the political and economic model for East and Southeast Asia.

5 The Expansion of World Trade through Regional Blocks or through Unrestricted Global Competition

During the period of euphoria within the Pacific region about the desired Pacific age and the consequent boom in Pacific activities, the wish was often expressed for not just the formation of a Pacific sphere of cooperation, but for the construction of a powerful Pacific block. A great system of alliances of Pacific markets was supposed to arise, regionally oriented and facing the West as a partner not in cooperation, but at best in negotiation. In this context we should note the pithy comment of Malaysia's Prime Minister Mahatir: "For a long time we looked towards the West, but the West is no longer a suitable model" (Erhard Haubold, "Der Westen verliert Anziehungskraft", *FAZ*, February 22, 1998).

Kyoshi Kojima, one of the fathers of Pacific cooperation, took the point of view that "if there were no European Community, we would have no reason to contemplate an economic integration of the Pacific" (Kyoshi Kojima, *Economic Cooperation in a Pacific Community*, Tokyo: The Japan Institute of International Affairs, 1980, p. 10). In this vision, Pacific integration was a massive buffer, capable of defying the buffer constituted by the European block. Accordingly, the intention was also to strongly reduce dependence on Western markets. The foreign trade of the nations of the Pacific Basin was to be carried on as far as possible within the region, i.e., the aim was a powerful expansion of intra-trade. In this context people also spoke of the triangle of powers consisting of "Pacific Region, Europe, U.S.A.," whose member blocks were now to enter into competition with each other, thereby displacing the previous dominance of the West. But now we clearly see that in its time of testing, during the Asian crisis, the Asian-Pacific Economic Community (APEC) did not make the slightest contribution to a solution of these grave problems. It wrapped itself in silence and "due to its weak performance nearly died a quiet death" (*FAZ*, September 13, 1999).

Nowadays it is hardly possible to speak of a massive Asian-Pacific block. Adherence to the free market and to international exchanges during the postwar years and the following decades was a significant contribution to the widely admired revivals in Japan and the Federal Republic of Germany. Free markets, free access to markets and a free international order continue to constitute the best form of cooperation, not only for Japan and the Federal Republic, but also for relations among the other Asian-Pacific countries and the developing interior of Europe.

Competition should be carried on not among blocks, but among firms and consumers, and not only within a region but far beyond regional borders[4]. Let us keep in mind in this context that the Asian crisis, despite its many negative consequences, also produced benefits. We note, among others, a great increase in entrepreneurial activity throughout the Asian-Pacific region. Many unemployed people, especially from middle management, are no longer inclined simply to wait for job openings to come along, but instead have seized the initiative and started small businesses with their savings (Warapatr Todhanakasem, "Thanks for the Crisis", in: *Far Eastern Economic Review*, March 11, 1999, p. 34.). It is also indicative of the changed attitude towards economic policy that nearly all the nations of the region affected by the crisis have kept their markets open, reason enough to look with optimism—though not euphoria—to the Asian future.

---

4 This surely accords with the concept expressed by Kenichi Ohmae in his book *Macht der Triade*, Wiesbaden, 1985.

List of References

Asian Development Bank. Special Issue the Asian financial Crisis. Vol. 30, No. 4, 1998.

Crafts, N., East Asian Growth before and after the Crisis. *IMF Working Paper* 98/137, Washington D.C. Sept. 1998.

Diehl, M. and Schweickert, R., Currency Crisis: Is Asia different? *Kieler Diskussionsbeiträge* 309, Jan. 1998.

Dieter, H., Die Asienkrise. Ursachen, Konsequenzen und die Rolle des Internationalen Währungsfonds, Marburg 1999.

Fischer, St., The Asian Crisis and the Changing Role of the IMF. In: *Finance and Development*, June 1998.

Friedman, M., Über Finanzen, Spekulation, Steuern und das Ende der Staatsgewalt. In: *Vorhaben -Deutsche Bank 24*, Nr. 1. 1. Sept. 1999.

Geis, E., Globalisierungseffekte im Lichte der Asienkrise. In: Dieter Bender und Hans-Rimbert Hemmer (Hrsg.), *Entwicklungsländer im Zeitalter der Globalisierung*, Frankfurt/Main 1999.

Green, St. K., Die Asienkrise und ihre Bedeutung für die Weltwirtschaft. In: *Politische Studien*, Heft 366, 50. Jg. Juli/August 1999.

Harvard Institute for International Development. Special Issue: Asia's Emergence. Vol. XI, No. III, Spring/Summer 1998.

Kojima, K., Economic Cooperation in a Pacific Community. The Japan Institute for International Affairs, Tokyo 1980.

Kraus, W. und Lütkenhorst, W., Atlantische Gegenwart - Pazifische Zukunft? Anmerkungen zur wirtschafts- und außenpolitischen Orientierung der USA, In: *Asien. Deutsche Zeitschrift für Politik, Wirtschaft und Kultur*, Nr. 10, Jan. 1984.

Krugman, P., The Myth of Asia's Miracle. In: *Foreign Affairs*, Vol. 73, 1994.

Krugman, P. and Venables, A. J., Globalization and inequality. In: *Quarterly Journal of Economics* 1995.

Lane, T., The Asian Financial Crisis. What have we learned? *Finance and Development*, Sept. 1999.

Lütkenhorst, W., Konzepte einer wirtschaftlichen Kooperation zwischen Industrie- und Entwicklungsländern im pazifischen Raum. Institut für Entwicklungs-forschung und Entwicklungspolitik Universität Bochum, Bochum 1989.

Menkhoff, L., Die Rolle finanzieller Globalisierung in der Asienkrise. In: Dieter Bender und Hans-Rimbert Hemmer (Hrsg.), *Entwicklungsländer im Zeitalter der Globalisierung*, Frankfurt/Main 1999.

Menkhoff, L. und Reszat, B. (Hrsg.), Asian Financial Markets - Structures, Policy Issues, and Prospects, *Veröffentlichungen des HWWA*, Bd. 44, Baden-Baden 1998.

Nunnenkamp, P., Wirtschaftliche Aufholprozesse und „Globalisierungskrisen" in Entwicklungsländern, *Kieler Diskussionsbreiträge* Nr. 328.

Nunnenkamp, P., Dealing with the Asian Crisis. IMF Conditionality and Implications in Asia and Beyond Intereconomics, March/April 1998.

Sachs, J., The Wrong Medicine for Asia. In: *The New York Times*, 3.11.1997.

Taube, M., Wirtschaftliche Entwicklung unter dem Einfluß von Asienkrise und Flutkatastrophe: VR China 1998. In: *Bochumer Jahrbuch zur Ostasienforschung*, Bd. 22, 1998.

Rieger, H. Ch., Erscheinungsbild und Erklärungsmuster der asiatischen Wirt-schaftskrise. Beitrag für die Jahrestagung des Ausschusses „Entwicklungsländer" des Vereins für Socialpolitik in Halle am 4./5. Juni 1999.

Wolff, J. H., Ende des südostasiatischen Wirtschaftswunders? Vernachlässigte Wirtschaftsordnungspolitik und die Folgen. In: *Bochumer Jahrbuch zur Ostasienforschung*, Bd. 23, 1999.

The Strategies of the Japanese Government and Trade Associations

Michiteru Nagamine
Yokohama Commercial University

1 Globalization

Globalization has various aspects, including the social, economic, and historical. Human and social history is in general the history of the globalization of human and social activities in the world. Because of the fall of the system in Eastern Europe, the abolition of the East-West barrier throughout the world, and the liberalization of economic activities, the globalization of humankind has reached a new height. But if we want to be precise, the collapse of the centralized Soviet regime has merely created a new set of basic conditions for globalization. One of the most recent aspects of so-called globalization is the globalization of the financial world. This financial globalization has been too quickly and too one-sidedly promoted by technological advances, particularly in the area of the microelectronic revolution. One consequence of market fundamentalism and of the euphoria of the Western world was the Japanese "bubble". The peak year of the "bubble" was 1991. Two years after the fall of the Berlin Wall and immediately after the collapse of the Soviet Union, the Japanese overinvested. An overcapacity was produced in Japan, because the collapse itself created no large, adequate markets. This unilateral type of globalization is not successful. The victory of so-called global capitalism has lost its aura over the past several years. The collapse of the so-called "emerging markets" (arising or entering markets) and their repellant effect on advanced economies does not of course mean the end of globalization. But it is certainly the end of an era. Now it is necessary to steer the present type of globalization in a rational direction through international cooperation.

2 American Hegemony and Export Expansion in Asia

Since the fall of the Soviet and Eastern-European communist regimes, Washington has striven to push ahead with the transition to global capitalism in the American sense. America, in agreement with Europe and Japan, is supposed to guarantee security and arrange for accords affecting world trade and regional stability. But this procedure is too rapid and too one-sided, and therefore it is naturally failing. If the crisis is to be used creatively, it is necessary to create a sound and rational basis for globalization. America wanted global leadership cheaply and painlessly. As one critic of the IMF stated, the United States did not wish to be obliged to pay cash for a peaceful reconstruction of Russia, or to improve conditions of poverty and disease in Africa. Essentially, America has attempted to market its social ethos, meaning, the rich do not need to help the poor, since the poor can enjoy a rising standard of living and one day become rich themselves (http://www.stern.nyu.edu/~nroubini/asia/sachsECO.html.). But Washington's dream of a rapid movement towards global financial liberalization has been dashed. It is hard to believe that a mere two years ago the IMF was heralding unhindered flows of capital. Practically all observers now concede that the premature liberalization of capital markets in the Asian nations, often under pressure from the IMF itself, was a cause of the Asian economic crisis (ibid.). The United States wants to continue to play the role of the sole dominating power in Asia. By means of the "New Guideline" between the USA and Japan, the Japanese government intends to continue the military alliance under the leadership of the USA, while concentrating its own energies on the economic sphere. But international trade relationships are also vital for American interests. In order to encourage the boom of the 1990s at home and abroad, the Americans wish to reinforce open and competitive trade. As in the mid-nineteenth century, when England wanted unconditional free trade around the world on the basis of its industrial and financial predominance, the Americans on the threshold of the twenty-first century enjoy unconditional free trade and a deregulated world economy. The Americans want to sell more goods and services on Asian markets and establish or further strengthen their financial dominance. Despite the economic difficulties in many Asian countries, the Americans believed that there would continue to be good export opportunities for US suppliers. President Clinton encouraged American firms to seize these opportunities (http://www.marshall.usc.edu/ibear/iep/apbo/index.html.). In the spring of 1999, the United States sent Presidential Business Missions to China and Korea (http://204.193.246.62/public.nsf/docs/asia-trade-mission-visit-ar2399.). But before US imports to many Asian countries can be increased, the gigantic economic crisis must first be overcome, a new financial crisis must be avoided, and a stable financial structure along with the conditions for a sound economic structure must have taken shape.

3 The Economic Crisis in East and Southeast Asia as a Consequence of Globalization

There are multiple causes of economic and financial crisis in Asia. The Japanese economy has suffered from a high level of non-performing real property and a large shortfall in productivity. The most serious cause of the Asian crisis is, as so often noted, the activities of the American hedge funds. The developing nations of Asia used short-term loans for long-term projects and investments. As the report to President Clinton in April of the present year ("Hedge Funds, Leverge, and the Lessons of Long-Term Capital Management: Report of the President's Working Group on Financial Markets") confirms, excessive leverage was the most important cause of the crisis. The Working Group accordingly proposed a series of measures to constrain the excessive leverage of the hedge funds. It seems that the hedge funds and the American government have learned from the Asian crisis. Because of its long-lasting period of high business activity, the United States was able to recover quickly from the fiasco of the LTCM. But basic conditions in the Asian developing countries are quite different. Because of the economic crisis, especially the reduction of official expenditures for vital services such as health care and education, the social plight of many of these countries became even more desperate. Individual incomes dropped, many people lost their jobs, wages were lowered. In the short term, poor nutrition and even starvation will continue to spread. Contagious diseases are rampant and children are no longer receiving schooling. There is complete incapacity to act in the public health and education systems. These institutions, in existence long before the crisis, have now been exposed. In the long term, the poor health situation and inadequate nutrition will influence the productivity of the workforce, reduce future growth, and delay recover. The effects of poor nutrition and lack of schooling will be especially hard on children, who may suffer from stunted growth and cognitive underdevelopment in consequence (http://www.worldbank.org/poverty/eacrisis /whatis/htm.). The dependence of the four ASEAN nations upon exports is too high. For ten years now, the economic development of these countries has been export oriented. The overcapacity of the export industries was financed by direct, short-term foreign investments. The events in Thailand, Korea and Indonesia did not stem from profligate governmental policies. Rather, they came from weakness in the financial sector. These three countries were especially vulnerable due to their massive short-term foreign loans. But structural weakness is at the core of the crisis. A reorientation of the economy is necessary. Increasing expenditures for the social security net, to soften the effects of the crisis on the weakest members of society, would also be an important goal. Structural reform in the major sectors is a central concern. It will extend to reconstruction of insolvent financial institutions, promotion of competition in the domestic economy, improvement of "corporate governance", as well as transparency, modernization of the legal and regulatory framework, and, not least, the strengthening of the social security net (http://www.imf.org/external/np/speeches/1999/012299.HTM.).

4 Demands of the Japanese Trade Associations / Keidanren (Japanese Federation of Economic Organizations)

http://www.keidanren.or.jp/english/policy/pol084.html

The main and most fundamental role of Japan ist the fastest possible revitalization of its own domestic economy. The result of a series of economic emergency measures by the Japanese government was the comprehensive package from April of last year dealing with public construction projects, further tax cuts, etc. Even so, a successful restabilization of the national financial system remains fundamentally necessary for a restoration of faith in the future of the Japanese economy (ibid.). In response to the regional crisis, Japan has already provided various forms of financial aid. One of the important areas of Japanese cooperation is the preservation of the level of economic activity through expansion of the so-called yen loans and credits from the Export-Import Bank of Japan. The Japanese associations of large businesses want to improve the access to Japanese markets through deregulation, simplification of quarantine procedures, improvement of the tax system, etc. Their proposal to the government is that "Japan should open up Japanese markets, in order to increase imports of agricultural, forestry and fishery products from other Asian countries. Japan should examine its system of preferential taxation, with a view to making exports from the Asian countries easier" (ibid.). The Japanese trade associations (Central Association of Japanese Industry and Trade, or Keidanren) as well as individual Japanese firms are demanding to continue their operations in Asia, so as to demonstrate their steadfastness in cooperating with their host countries. Japanese economic circles want to perform services along with the government to bolster the development of human resources and the growth of the "supporting industries" (ibid.). To support the continued economic development of Asian nations over the medium to long term, it is absolutely necessary to foster the growth of the supporting industries, particularly small- and medium-sized enterprises, upon which export industries depend. Needed measures include technical cooperation, yen loans, and investment loans by the Export-Import Bank (ibid.). To support development of human resources, funding for human resource training should be increased, more Japanese specialists should be dispatched abroad, and more persons should be invited to Japan for training programmes. To ensure that these latter two activities can be carried out smoothly, existing programmes should be improved and executed more flexibly to develop organic coordination among different programmes. (A number of different programmes are now run by different government agencies, and they are generally not well coordinated with each other.) Workers should be invited to Japan for job training. Visa requirements for such persons should be relaxed, and application procedures should be simplified. The government should provide more support for foreign students in Japan to help them continue their studies in Japan (ibid.). The Japanese economic community (the Central Organisation of Economic Associations, or Keidanren) remains convinced that the Asian economy has great potential for economic growth, and that once it has overcome the present difficulties, it faces a promising future. For the good of the long-term development in Asia, it is important for the nations of the region to adhere to the agenda for liberalization of trade and investments. This agenda has already been adopted by the Asian-Pacific Economic Cooperation (APEC) and by other regional forums. The member nations of the Association of Southeast Asian Nations (ASEAN) must continue to strengthen their solidarity, expand the ASEAN Industrial Cooperation Scheme (AICO) and make the ASEAN Free Trade Area (AFTA) a reality. In order to urge the other countries of Asia to liberalize further, Japan's Keidanren intends to set a good example by freeing further sectors of the Japanese economy from protective tarifs (ibid.). Stability of currency is an important prerequisite for the progress of liberalization within the ASEAN region. In connection with this topic, the Japanese economic community means to expand the internationalization of the yen, as it has done up to now. Japan needs to develop its short-term financial markets in order to create an increasing attractivity of the yen as an international currency. Japanese firms want to make every effort to promote the use of the yen in their international dealings. In particular, they want a secondary market for short-term government loans (ibid.).

5 The New Miyazawa Initiative to Overcome the Asian Currency Crisis

In order to help the Asian countries get a grip on their economic difficulties and to contribute to the stabilization of the international financial markets, Japan's government is prepared to provide a package of supportive measures in the amount of $30bn, of which $15bn is intended for mid- to long-term financial aids to financial recovery in the Asian countries, and another $15bn for possible short-term capital requirements during the process of carrying out economic reforms (http://www.mof.go.jp/english/if/ele042.htm). To cover this mid- to long-term capital requirement on the part of the Asian nations, the Japanese government means to grant assistance to these countries. The Japanese government hopes that this necessary solicitude will pay off in terms of a better use of the Tokyo markets. The following specific aid measures are planned: 1) Provision of direct financial assistance, consisting of i) extending Export-Import Bank of Japan (JEXIM) loans to Asian countries, ii) acquiring of sovereign bonds issued by Asian countries by the JEXIM, iii) extending ODA yen loans to Asian countries; 2) Supporting Asian countries in raising funds from international financial markets, comprising i) use of guarantee mechanisms, i.e., a) utilizing the guarantee functions of the JEXIM, b) providing export insurance to bank loans to Asian countries, c) requesting the World Bank and the Asian Development Bank to step up their efforts to provide guarantees for bank loans and bond issues by Asian countries, d) the establishment, it is hoped, in the long run of an international guaranteeing institution with a prime focus on Asian countries, still to be considered; 3) Financial support in the form of co-financing with multilateral development banks; 4) Technical assistance: the World Bank and the Asian Development Bank will be requested to proved necessary technical assistance through Japanese special funds to Asian countries intended to implement a comprehensive approach to address the issue of corporate debt restructuring and the restoration of the financial system. Japan is prepared to contribute in providing technical assistance to these Asian countries, taking into account their individual situations.

6 Resource Mobilization Plan for Asia: The Second State of the New Miyazawa Initiative

NIES and the ASEAN countries have made it through the first stage of the currency and economic crisis. The next stage is to prevent a further stagnation of the economy. The Asian economies have now entered a new stage of cooperation for the construction of a more stable and powerful economic system. Through it they can regain their strong economies and also sustain them. The urgent capital requirements of the individual Asian countries have been covered by means of the New Miyazawa Initiative and other public forms of assistance, and the Asian economies are now beginning the long march back up from their lowest point. The economies of Southeast Asia have bounced back due to the export-led recovery. This revitalization has been fostered by increased public expenditures and domestic consumption as well as by low interest rates and weak currencies. Export growth has been fueled primarily by Asia. Asia itself has absorbed the largest portion of the exports from Southeast Asia and hence played a key role in the recovery. A national economist from Singapore once said that the United States had contributed "nothing" to the export growth of Singapore, which came largely from Japan and other Asian countries. To achieve a really strong recovery in these countries, it is now necessary to mobilize private funds both at home and abroad. Measures towards a full use of the vast and extensive savings in Japan are indispensable. Such efforts can contribute to the internationalization of the yen and an even more active use of the Tokyo market.

7 The Responsibility of the Developed Nations

The industrialized nations must work even harder for this development, according to the 1999 report of UNCTAD (United Nations Conference of Trade and Development: http://www.unctad.org/en/press/pr2817en.htm.). Although the worst fears of a global recession have receded, the prospects for the world economy are still discouraging. In 1999, the world economy will merely repeat the poor performance of the preceding year. According to UNCTAD; Neither a return to stability in the buffeted Asian economies, nor the apparent containment of the Brazilian crisis should hide the immediate downside risks facing the global economy over the near future. The report warns that a stabilization of the conditions in the so-called "emerging markets" does not mean that the underlying problems have disappeared; There is no ground for complacency, since the systemic forces responsible for the recent turmoil are still present. The continuing dependence of many developing countries upon highly ephemeral capital penetration is one of the main reasons for the concern expressed in the UNCTAD report (http://www.unctad.org/en/press/pr2816en.htm.). There is also reason for doubt about the ability of the United States economy to adapt smoothly towards a more sustainable growth rate, and the ability of the EU and Japan to achieve a stable recovery. We will have to keep working, and harder.

The US Dollar, the Euro, and the Yen: An Evaluation of Their Present and Future Status as International Currencies

Rainer Beckmann, Jürgen Born and Wim Kösters

Ruhr-Universität Bochum

1 Introduction

During the entire post-World War II period the international monetary and financial system has been shaped to a significant degree by the United States of America having the status of the leading economic power. An impressive indication of this superiority is the fact that the US dollar is acting as the only currency of outstanding international importance. Despite the fact that the Deutsche mark and the Japanese yen internationally gained ground in the course of the last two decades, the US dollar was ahead by a wide margin, and the US acted as the only economy that had to a considerable degree to cope with both the beneficial and the disadvantageous effects emanating from the issuance of an international currency. The process of European integration and especially the introduction of the euro as the single currency for the 12 present member countries of the EU in 1999 may alter this clear currency hierarchy. The euro area is comparable in size to the US with respect to GDP and even exceeds the US regarding the share in world trade. Thus questions arise of whether the international monetary system will turn out to be bipolar in the long run or whether the yen can also play its part.

No accepted theoretical framework has yet been developed to clarify which conditions will be sufficient to secure for a currency a status of a major importance. Traditionally, trade relations and GDP but also inertia with respect to the use of a certain currency as a medium of exchange and store of value have been mentioned as factors to explain the international role of a currency. In view of globalization with capital flows almost completely liberalized worldwide, liquid and sophisticated financial markets are now overwhelmingly seen as yet another crucial precondition for a currency to play a significant international role. This is especially important after the start of the EMU, making the US and the euro area economies of comparable economic size. A deeper look at the developments of European financial markets is then indispensable, since their pure aggregation may be deceptive in the light of still prevailing barriers to truly integrated financial markets in Europe.

The paper proceeds as follows. In section 2 the functions, benefits, and costs of a leading international currency are discussed. In section 3 key determinants for the continuous dominance of the US dollar are analysed in order to assess the sustainability of this regime. Since it turns out that highly developed financial markets are of special importance, section 4 takes a closer look at the integration of European financial markets emphasizing the enormous structural changes that have come about since the euro was established in 1999. The comparatively weak international status of the yen, currently ranked third, is briefly sketched in section 5. In the last section we sum up our findings by trying to assess how the future currency regime most probably will look.

2 Functions, Benefits and Risks of an International Currency

A sound institutional frame allowing for a dynamic development of international financial markets in the future requires an appropriate design of the underlying currency regime. Under the Bretton Woods system fixed exchange rates to be defended within narrow limits caused monetary authorities and national governments to play a dominant role. Today, in a world of almost completely free international capital movements and exceptionally high turnovers on foreign exchange markets that add up to a daily average of 1.5 trillion dollars (BIS, 1999), central banks may no longer be capable of successfully intervening on these markets. In a study of the continuously decreasing success of foreign exchange market interventions by central banks Anna J. Schwartz states: "Experience has disillusioned them" (Schwartz, 2000, p. 1). Billions of dollars are A sound institutional frame allowing for a dynamic development of international financial markets in the future requires an appropriate design of the underlying currency regime. Under the Bretton Woods system fixed exchange rates to be defended within narrow limits caused monetary authorities and national governments to play a dominant role. Today, in a world of almost completely free international capital movements and exceptionally high turnovers on foreign exchange markets that add up to a daily average of 1.5 trillion dollar (BIS, 1999), central banks may no longer be capable of successfully intervening on these markets. In a study on the continuously decreasing success of foreign exchange market interventions by central rapidly moved and removed from one place to another. Countries particularly dependent on (short-term) foreign capital can easily be faced with drastic (long-term) economic consequences.

Especially short-term-oriented investors who are repeatedly blamed for their alleged destabilizing speculation may withdraw their capital as soon as possible if expected risk-adjusted returns fall in one country and rise somewhere else. Governments, therefore, are forced to adjust their economic policy to avoid a sudden outflow of foreign capital resulting from unsustainable policies in the respective country.[2] In this sphere of the "new structure of power" (Cohen, 1998) governments have to share their monetary power with international financial markets, the latter now serving as a strong monitor for national economic policies and reducing their range of activities.[3]

2.1 Functions of an International Currency

The change in the international financial framework sketched above calls for a more detailed analysis. In particular, the decisions of participants in international markets to use a certain currency are of interest. In Table 1 three key functions of the use of a currency outside the issuing country are presented. The functions of an international currency correspond to the classical functions of (national) money: medium of exchange, unit of account, and measure of value. In addition, the private use of money can be distinguished from its official use.

Table 1: Functions of an International Currency

Function	Private use	Official use
Medium of exchange	Vehicle currency	Intervention currency
Unit of account	Quotation currency	Pegging currency
Store of value	Investment/ Financing currency	Reserve currency

Source: Hartmann (1998) and Detken and Hartmann (2000).

Hartmann (1998) defines a currency as international if private or official agents that reside abroad make significant use of at least one out of the six functions in Table 1. To get an overall view of a currency's degree of internationalisation one could be tempted to analyse each of the functions given in Table 1. But in this paper we focus on private currency use, since on foreign exchange markets power has shifted away from official action towards international market forces. So we

---

2 During the 1997/98 currency crisis, for instance, Asia had to undergo this. Some Southeast Asian countries, though, recovered in terms of GDP growth rates in 1999 and 2000.

3 Cohen adds to his view of a shifting structure of power that cross-border competition has not so much *diminished* as *transformed* the role of the state (Cohen, 1998, chapter 7).

primarily deal with the vehicle, the quotation, and the investment/financing functions of international currencies. The functions of a currency are of course intertwined rather than distinctively separated. Therefore, it is not sufficient to purely analyse each for the sake of completeness. Instead, the different functions concerning the private use of international currencies are selectively taken up during the discussion in sections 3 to 5 when the respective roles of the dollar, the euro, and the yen are discussed.[4]

2.2 Benefits

One major, direct and indisputable economic benefit of the widespread international use of a currency in favour of the issuing country is international seigniorage. As soon as foreigners are willing to hold an international currency for transaction and portfolio purposes, they exchange no interest-bearing money for their own interest-bearing securities, so that a net gain for the issuing central bank occurs.[5] For the US this gain is estimated to amount to about 0.1% of GDP per year.

Another economic benefit is a liquidity premium on interest rates, which Portes and Rey (1998, p. 309) call "another, often neglected source of seigniorage." .According to them the comparatively high share of US government securities held by non-residents denotes a disproportionate international demand for dollar-denominated US debt. Because the US dollar serves as an international investment currency, interest payments for outstanding debt are lower. Portes' econometric work as well as estimates from market participants show that the interest rate liquidity premium amounts to at least 25 basis points adding another estimated yearly flow of 0.1% of GDP to the seigniorage mentioned above (Portes, 2000).

Further efficiency gains result from liquid and sophisticated financial markets in the domain of the currency predominantly used. In that case transaction costs in foreign exchange and securities markets tend to be lower, and, in addition, a broad maturity spectrum and a wide array of innovative financial products improve the risk-management and the unbundling of risks for private actors. In their „big euro" scenario Portes and Rey (1998) expect the benefits for the euro area resulting from a reduction of transaction costs to be equal to the combined gains of seigniorage and "liquidity discount," amounting to a further 0.2% of GDP.[6] Added together, annual benefits of 0.4% of GDP may solely be attributed to the fact that a currency

---

4 For a detailed investigation of each function see Hartmann (1998).

5 The use of Deutsche mark for example is presently widespread all over Middle- and Eastern Europe. It serves as a second national currency in Bosnia and Montenegro. Therefore, the *Deutsche Bundesbank* earned parts of its profit abroad.

6 In the "big euro" scenario the US dollar only dominates the dollar-yen market, whereas the euro is dominant on the euro-yen and the euro-dollar markets.

plays an outstanding international role (corresponding to a "big dollar" or "big euro" scenario).

Some examples may illustrate these gains. Within the country that issues an international currency consumers pay lower transaction costs for exchanging cash due to relatively narrow bid-ask spreads. Companies gain from a widely accepted invoicing currency by reducing their costs of currency conversion and exchange rate risk management. Hedging costs deriving from foreign exchange exposures (claims and liabilities) have then to be borne by their counterparts residing in countries having no international currency. A well known example is the disadvantage of Airbus Industries with respect to Boeing in this field. Existing market rules force Airbus Industries to invoice its products in US dollars whereas its costs are mainly denominated in euros. Unanticipated fluctuations in the euro-dollar rate thus inevitably lead to volatility of Airbus profits since the dollar proceeds have to be exchanged for euros. Therefore, risk exposure or hedging costs are solely the problem of Airbus Industries - a clear competitive advantage for Boeing.

Another example relates to the competitive position of the financial services industry. Here microeconomic benefits result from the privilege of large international investment banks to be located in a country having an international currency. Empirical evidence shows that financial institutions residing within the country that issues an international currency dominate the international primary bond market. The Bank for International Settlement (BIS) presents market shares of bookrunners whose nationality matches the currency of issue and compares these figures with the market shares of bookrunners that share the nationality with the borrower, both for the EU-11 and the US. The results for 1996-98 reveal that "historically the nationality of the underwriter of an international bond has been more closely associated with the currency in which the bond is issued than with the nationality of the borrower" (BIS, 2000, p. 131). Again, this means a competitive advantage for the US, i.e., for its corporate financial services industry. According to Steinherr, "in no other industry has the United States been as resolutely superior as in the financial industry" (Steinherr, 1998, p. 29).

However, trying to quantitatively assess these indirect economic benefits is very difficult. Similar to the role of English as a lingua franca, the widespread use of the US dollar as an international vehicle, quotation, and investment currency contributes to the worldwide establishment of American business practices, capital market rules and accounting standards. Feldstein holds the view that "the Anglo-American common law rules, corporate governance principles and accounting standards improve the efficiency with which capital is invested." (Feldstein, 2000a, p. 1). As a consequence of the growing acceptance of America's leading position, other countries trying to set their own rules might soon be confronted with penalties from foreign investors, since their regulations are not in line with international, i.e., American arrangements. Therefore, the role of the dollar as the dominant international currency helps the US to turn their own regulations into international economic standards, while the costs of adjusting to these rules are imposed on all other countries.

2.3 Risks

If we consider the risk side of having an international currency, two main issues emerge. First, negative welfare effects of supplying an international currency may arise if the national central bank comes under pressure to serve as an international lender of last resort. For the provider of reserves to the international financial system the prevention of a collapse of a major single bank or a crisis of the whole banking system may turn out to be costly. At the same time, however, this confers political power on the international lender as shown e.g. by the "key role of the US Treasury alongside the IMF in the Mexican crisis, the Asian crisis, and Brazil" (Portes, 2000, p. 2).

Second, the large quantity of an international currency held outside the country of issuance may blur domestic monetary policy. In 1995, for instance, 70% of total dollar cash (outside banks) vs. 20% of total Deutsche mark cash was held abroad (Rogoff, 1998). The demand for money by non-residents, originating, e.g., from dollarized economies in Latin America like Brazil or Argentina, is potentially more unstable than the domestic money demand. Monetary strategies of many central banks (among them the ECB) put strong emphasis on a reliable forecast of monetary aggregates. Shifts in and out of an international currency mainly by non-residents will bring about a higher volatility of shifts in the quantity of money and thus cause problems for the implementation of a monetary policy oriented towards price level stability. It has been exactly for this reason that the Deutsche Bundesbank and the Bank of Japan were hesitant to allow for a wider international use of their currencies. The Bundesbank was afraid of inflationary potentials that could unfold in a scenario of a depreciating Deutsche mark in the wake of strong and abrupt sales of this currency. Under such circumstances monetary policy decisions may become unintentionally affected by the need to discourage abrupt switches into other currencies.

Yet, from a political perspective, the omnipresence of the dollar creates indisputable benefits for the US, besides the purely symbolic and psychological significance of possessing a world currency. Several further political repercussions are pointed out by Cohen: "Domestically, the hegemon is better insulated from outside influence or coercion in formulating and implementing policy. Abroad, it is better able to pursue foreign objectives without constraint as well as to exercise a degree of influence or coercion to others" (Cohen, 1998, p. 128f).

To sum up, the status of an international currency is indeed of great importance. Significant, not negligible gains have to be balanced against potentially small, more indeterminate losses. Recent policy clearly confirms that the US wants to preserve its dominant position while the EU and East-Asia have made a political effort, especially with respect to financial market liberalization and economic integration, to make the euro or the yen more competitive with the dollar. In Japan, for instance, even an official „Study Group for the Promotion of the Internationalization of the Yen“ was formed in September 1999. Apparently, in the view of political authorities the potential gains would outweigh potential losses.

3 The Status Quo: Factors Determining the Dominance of the US Dollar

From a historical perspective the dominance of the US dollar today can partly be explained by accommodating institutional settlements made in earlier periods. The transition from pound sterling to the US dollar as the leading international currency in the first half of the last century took place rather slowly and was finally pushed by the creation of the Bretton Woods System in 1944. Rey (1999) shows that pound sterling remained the dominant international currency as long as the volume of Great Britain's foreign trade exceeded that of the US. Despite the fact that in 1870 the US had already surpassed the UK in terms of economic size (measured by GDP), it took the dollar more than half a century to replace the pound as the international key currency. "Only after World War II did the exports of the US overtake significantly the exports of the UK. These data are consistent with our result that trade flows are the key determinants of internationalisation of currencies, as opposed to economic size" (Rey, 1999, p. 26f).

According to Kindleberger (1973) the long transition period in which the pound started to lose its dominant role as international currency without being instantly replaced by the US dollar caused a vacuum of international leadership in the wake of the Great Depression in 1929. Neither the Bank of England nor the US Federal Reserve assumed the responsibility needed to fight instability on international financial markets. Not before the end of World War II did the US have the power and the political will to design a new international financial order that eventually paved the way for an era of unprecedented economic growth.[7]

The Bretton Woods System institutionalised the role of the US dollar as the major international currency. In order to reduce financial instability as experienced during the Great Depression, the classic Gold Standard was replaced by a fixed exchange rate regime pegging all currencies to the dollar and installing a dollar-gold link. Such regulations were perfectly in line with the widely accepted

---

7 Kunz (1995) points out that "geopolitical power depends on financial power, each of which supports the other." This interdependency has to be kept in mind when discussing the economics of international monetary and currency regimes.

view that an institutional settlement allowing for active intervention would be most efficient to control volatile and erratic moves of markets. But the envisaged stabilizing effect of fixed exchange rates turned out to be a problem when rapid economic recovery in West Germany and Japan would have required consecutive devaluations of the US dollar. Because international coordination about adequate realignments failed due to diverging economic interests, the sustainability of that regime was undermined. When the Bretton Woods system finally broke down in 1972, the new regime of floating exchange rates seemed to put an end to the privileged position of the US dollar. But even though the Deutsche mark and to a lesser extent the yen started to take over a few international currency functions (Table 1), they never really threatened the widespread dominance of the US dollar in this respect.

3.1 Size, Trade, and Invoicing

According to Rey's (1999) aforementioned argument, the high share in worldwide exports which Britain once had, rather than its GDP, accounted in great part for the international success of the pound sterling before World War II. But such a finding must be examined carefully before deriving general conclusions. If we take a look at economic size and the share in international trade in 1999 (Table 2), it stands out that the US share of world GDP (20.8%) is larger than the respective numbers of the euro area (15.5%) and Japan (7.5%), whereas the euro area has a considerably higher share of world trade (19.5%, excluding intra-European trade) than the US (15%) as well as Japan (8.5%). These trade figures are underlined by the fact that the euro area is more open (17%) than the US (11%) and Japan (9%).

Table 2: Economic Size, International Trade, and Openness, 1999

	Share of world GDP in %	Share of world exports in %	Openness: Exports[a)]/ Imports[a)]
EU-11	15.5	19.5[b)]	17[b)] / 15[b)]
USA	20.8	15	11 / 13
Japan	7.5	8.5	9 / 8

Source: ECB (2000). a) As % of GDP, averages 1997-99; b) Relating to extra-area trade trade flows.

Table 3: Invoicing of International Trade

	1980	1992	CI[b)] 1992
EMS-5[a)]	31	33	-
Deutsche Mark	14	15	1.4
US Dollar	56	48	3.6
Japanese yen	2	5	0.6

Source: McCauley (1997); more recent figures are currently not available.
a) EMS-5: DEM, FRF, GBP, ITL, NLG; b) CI (coefficient of internationalisation) = trade invoiced in currency x, divided by trade of country with currency x as legal tender.

Assuming that these relations remain rather stable over time and in line with Rey's assessment that trade flows are most important, one might suggest that we are on the verge of a switch from the US dollar to the euro as the leading international currency. But a completely different story is told by the invoicing practices of participants in international trade (Table 3).

To reach an agreement about the unit of account used for an international transaction trade partners have three choices at their disposal: payment is carried out in the exporter's, the importer's or a third (vehicle) currency. If Grassman's Law (Grassman, 1973) applied fully, i.e., trade tends to be invoiced in the exporter's currency, and if exports and imports were balanced, different currencies should reveal a similar coefficient of internationalisation (CI). However, the CI column of Table 3 reveals huge differences: In 1992 the US dollar was used to denominate trade 3.6 times the value of US trade, whereas the corresponding factor for the Deutsche mark was 1.4 and that for the yen far below. One has to concede that between 1980 and 1992 the estimated share of world trade invoiced in US dollar declined significantly, but to a certain extent this can be explained by the drop in oil prices.[8] Nevertheless, dollar invoicing remained on a high level of 48% for the last decade.

Up to now a high percentage of trade between the EU-11 and non-European countries has been invoiced in US dollars. A lot of raw materials like oil are traded almost exclusively in US dollars regardless of the nationality of buyers and sellers. The relatively high share of US-dollar-invoiced trade implies that the use of the dollar in international trade does not reflect the foreign demand for US goods. Thus, a first important outcome of our analysis is that neither a country's absolute size nor its share of world trade are indicators *sufficient* to determine the international performance of its currency.

---

8 See McCauley (1997). For a more detailed analysis of the patterns of invoicing see Krugman (1992) and Cohen (1998).

3.2 Interaction on Foreign Exchange and Securities Markets

In order to make the explanation of the US dollar's supremacy more precise, Alogouskoufis, Portes, and Rey (1997) developed an innovative theoretical framework by incorporating the structure of international financial markets into the analysis. They approached the invoicing puzzle sketched above for the most part from the perspective of transaction costs, accentuating the interaction between private market participants on foreign exchange (forex) and securities markets. International financial markets have been subject to rapid changes in recent decades. Technological progress, financial innovations (partly due to improved theoretical models of finance, e.g., the theory of option pricing by Black and Scholes, 1973) and above all reduced regulations have led to an upsurge in the transaction volumes of financial markets. Therefore, synergy effects between securities and forex markets have increased. Within this framework official actions such as the management of currency reserves or the choice of a certain currency regime (Table 1), e.g., exchange rate pegging, are of secondary importance.

On foreign exchange markets the US dollar has adopted the role of a global vehicle currency, i.e., it serves as the prevalent international medium of exchange. Table 4 shows that the US dollar accounted for more than 80% of the turnover on international foreign exchange markets in 1992 and extended this lead to 87% in 1998 with the Deutsche mark and the Japanese yen following by a share of 30% and 21%, respectively (all figures based on 200%, see note in Table 4). Even all EMS currencies taken together accounted for a turnover considerably less than the dollar. These figures become even more impressive when intra-European forex transactions are excluded: McCauley (1997) estimates that the share of the US dollar would rise under the assumption of European Monetary Union from 83% to 92% in 1995 whereas the EMS currencies would drop from 70% to 56%.

Table 4: Turnover on International Foreign Exchange Markets in %

	April 1992	April 1995	April 1998
EMS	70	70 / 56*	63
Deutsche Mark	40	37 / 31*	30
US dollar	82	83 / 92*	87
Japanese yen	23	24 / 26*	21

Source: BIS (1999); *corrected for intra-EMS turnover, McCauley (1997); own calculations. Because two currencies are involved in each transaction, the total of shares adds up to 200%.

This pattern of disproportionately high dollar shares on foreign exchange markets (similar in magnitude to the aforementioned invoicing figures) favours the trading of financial assets denominated in the "privileged" currency. In turn, a more liquid US-dollar securities market strengthens the role of the US dollar as a vehicle currency. Thus, a circular effect arises and enhances the liquidity of both the foreign exchange and the securities markets. A drop in transaction costs is the major result but simultaneously also the ultimate cause for these feedback dynamics. Alogoskoufis, Portes, and Rey (1997) developed an approach to analyse the potential of the euro in challenging the dollar's international supremacy. The nucleus of their influential analysis consists of financial market considerations emphasizing the interaction between foreign exchange and securities markets, while private invoicing practices, official reserve management, and currency pegging decisions are forced to adjust. A network of financial relations is then crucial in explaining the strong dollar shares. In a similar framework, special features of the "new economy" are analysed by Shapiro and Varian: "The value of connecting to a network depends on the number of other people already connected to it" (Shapiro and Varian, 1999, p. 174). These network externalities or demand-side economies of scale can only occur as long as a huge share of all transactions on foreign exchange markets is intermediated through one single currency (the dollar). Otherwise, it is hard to reach a critical degree of liquidity which is necessary to realize the desired advantages in cost reduction.

3.3 Financial Market Liquidity

The continuous strength of the dollar has been primarily based on the superior efficiency and liquidity of US dollar financial markets that long were able to develop before the European and Asian markets. They provide narrow bid-ask spreads, the ability to buy or sell larger amounts showing no price effects, a rich array of instruments and deep repurchase markets. To assess the competitiveness of different financial markets, Alogouskoufis, Portes, and Rey (1997, p. 27) compare bid-ask spreads of benchmark government bonds (10-years to maturity). They conclude that transaction costs between the US and European markets differ by a factor of at least two in favour of the US. Another helpful indicator to evaluate the liquidity of financial markets is the ratio of turnover versus the amount of outstanding bonds traded on secondary markets. On US government bond markets in 1995 this ratio (14.0) was significantly higher than the equivalent ratios for Europe (9.9) and Japan (6.2).

Similarly, as soon as the focus shifts to private equity and corporate bond markets, an unambiguous story is told. Here US markets turn out to be impressively ahead in every respect. The volume of issuance of commercial papers and daily trade volumes of stocks listed at the NYSE are several times higher than in the euro area. A good example to illustrate the international standing of US dollar financial markets is the auction of UMTS licenses in

Germany in August 2000 (Frankfurter Allgemeine Zeitung, August 14, 2000). All companies trying to obtain one of the few "third-generation" licenses offered by the government were soon faced with a rapidly rising need for funds they had to pay in euros immediately after the auction. With the total amount adding up to about 50 billion euros, some of the companies announced the intention to finance a part of their bill by issuing corporate bonds. Because euro corporate bond markets were only moderately developed, however, they had to decide to issue the major portion of the bonds in dollars and exchange them thereafter for euros. Thus, only US dollar markets could offer the depth and breadth necessary to avoid price distortions and, hence, continuously rising capital costs. To sum up, the US dollar financial markets provide a unique degree of cost efficiency and liquidity attractive to both investors and issuers worldwide.

3.4 Risk Factors and the Diminishing Dominance of the US Dollar

The conclusions reached so far have stressed size factors like real activity (GDP, trade) and financial liquidity (inseparably connected with the transaction-cost argument) as economic determinants for the international role of a currency. However, a convincing financial market perspective has to be complemented by considering risk factors that mainly involve monetary stability, financial market volatility, and cross-country asset correlations (Detken and Hartmann, 2000). International investors, whether they are central banks or private agents, are seeking to reduce risk by diversifying their portfolios. In a world of imperfectly correlated interest rates and equity returns, the rationale of portfolio diversification paves the way for one currency to become the single international currency. Though transaction costs might be lowest when investing and financing concentrates on only one currency, investors and borrowers strive to optimize the structure of their portfolios with respect to risk-return considerations. Via this risk effect the centripetal forces of dollar liquidity are countered to some extent. Standard portfolio models of capital market theory compute an extensive degree of diversification relating to international portfolios. In reality, however, a strong home-bias "puzzle" has to be resolved (i.e., the unexpected empirical evidence suggests that international, cross-border diversification remains below optimal levels).[9]

Another factor potentially limiting the dominance of the US dollar relates to the stability in monetary conditions. At the beginning of the 1980s a severe economic crisis accompanied by historically high rates of expected inflation in the US diminished the attractiveness of the dollar as an international investment currency.

---

9 See Tesar and Werner (1995) for a discussion and Danthine, Giavazzi, and von Thadden (2000) for current figures concerning the home-bias puzzle.

At this time it was on the verge of not fulfilling the store of value function any more. Comparatively low inflation rates in Germany associated with expectations of a further appreciation of the Deutsche mark were the result of the stability orientation and the unique reputation of the Deutsche Bundesbank. The mark became a "safe-haven" currency for investors to reduce their dependency on the US dollar. To a lesser extent the same applied to the yen. As a consequence, capital inflows enhanced the liquidity on German bond markets and finally led to spill-over effects on German financial markets. In order to cope with the enormous demand for assets denominated in Deutsche mark new financial instruments and services were introduced to the markets. Such measures brought a rise in efficiency on financial markets, making the Deutsche mark an even more attractive international investment currency. Within a few years the mark adopted the role of a junior international currency, ranging far ahead of the yen and other currencies, though still well behind the dollar.

Due to reduced needs for intervention and a rising exchange rate volatility after the break-down of the Bretton Woods system, changes in the central bank's reserve management occurred, too. Parts of their foreign reserve portfolios were shifted away from US dollar assets and gold towards other foreign exchange reserves. European central banks linked their monetary policies to that of the Deutsche Bundesbank. In that way the (unofficial) role of the anchor currency of the European Monetary System (EMS) accrued to the Deutsche mark, simultaneously fostering its role as the second international currency. The dollar's presence, in particular, as a vehicle currency intermediating between European currencies diminished in favour of the Deutsche mark.

In this section it has been pointed out that the US dollar serves as by far the most important international currency primarily because of the efficiency and liquidity of US dollar financial markets. The prevailing regime will most probably continue at least as long as European and other markets cannot fully compete in this respect. This is all the more important the less size differences in the real sector matter. Particularly with reference to a possible catching up of the euro with the dollar, economists like Portes and Rey (1998), Eichengreen (2000) and Wyplosz (1999) formed a financial market perspective or adopted it. When analysing transaction costs on financial markets, Wyplosz puts his view as follows: "Of all characteristics of an international currency, the existence of wide and deep markets with low transaction costs seems to be the most crucial" (Wyplosz, 1999, p. 95).[10] To evaluate the potentials of the only serious aspirants, the euro and the yen, to challenge the position of the dollar, the effects of European monetary and financial integration and the prospects of the yen will now be examined.

---

10 Further fundamental work with respect to the euro's impact on European and international financial markets has been done by McCauley (1997), McCauley and White (1997) and Prati and Schinasi (1997).

4 Catching Up: The Euro's Impact via European Financial Market Integration

Most international economists see the launch of the euro in 1999 as one of the most important events in the post-World War II international monetary and financial system besides the creation of the Bretton Woods System and its collapse in the early 1970s (Bergsten, 1997, p. 17). Twelve members of the European Union (Greece joined at the beginning of 2001) abolished their national currencies and delegated their monetary policy to a supranational and independent authority, the European Central Bank (ECB). Although the circulation of euro notes and coins will start only at the beginning of 2002, the new currency completely replaced the legacy currencies from the outset.

In this section we deal with the question of the extent to which the euro has already helped European financial markets to overcome their historically generated segmentation and develop truly unified markets. Although mainly confined to intra-European markets, this investigation is undertaken against the background of the future international potential of the euro. Evidence from the first two years of the euro's existence regarding key segments of European financial markets (i.e. money, bond, equity markets) lead observers to speak of a "revolution in European finance" (Eichengreen, 2000, p. 356). In the following remarks the available evidence is reviewed.

Before going into details three caveats should be pointed out. First, in analysing the forces at work that develop and integrate European financial markets, problems arise about how to distinguish between effects resulting purely from the introduction of the euro and those which would have occurred regardless of its launch. Nonetheless, one can agree that the new currency works at least as a catalyst for European financial market developments with the "precise role of EMU difficult to quantify" (Danthine et. al., 2000, p. 3). Second, due to the East Asian financial crisis starting in 1997, the Russian sovereign default, and the crash of the Long Term Capital Management hedge fund (LTCM), both occurring during autumn 1998, international investors returned to a 'safe haven' strategy focussing mainly on dollar investments. In contrast, international and European borrowers issued large volumes of euro-denominated bonds in the first year after the introduction of the euro. However, strong one-off effects played their part, since large companies intended to establish a benchmark position within the highly underdeveloped European corporate bond market (Bayle et al., 2000, p. 42ff). Third, a long-term slump of the euro against the dollar (and the yen) occurred and did not come to an end until October 2000, after a depreciation of about 35% since its introduction. This unfavourable development most probably impeded the attraction of funds to European financial markets. Danthine et al. (2000, p. 4), however, in attesting European financial markets an "excellent performance...despite the depreciation," play down the importance of this issue.

Most recent BIS data on international debt securities markets show that the dollar has re-established its leading position on international bond markets. While throughout 1999 the euro had a slightly higher share of international debt issues ($571 vs. $545bn), the dollar clearly surpassed the euro by 29% during the first three quarters of 2000 (BIS, 2000b, p. 24). Bearing in mind these caveats, we will attempt to give a careful interpretation of the prevailing evidence in the following remarks.

4.1 Money Markets

European money markets rapidly expanded and established a high degree of integration subsequent to the adoption of the euro and the concurrent implementation of a single monetary policy. The run-up to EMU already showed a considerable convergence of money market rates ("convergence trading"). Quite important, though, for the two most significant segments of the euro money markets, the secured (repo) and the unsecured segment, a distinction has to be made with reference to their individual integration progress.[11]

While the repo market demands collateralization in addition to the exchange of short-term liquidity, the unsecured interbank market just involves the latter. National differences in procedures used across the numerous securities trading platforms, clearing houses, and securities settlement systems are the most impeding factors (OECD, 2000, p. 64) for a single repo market. By contrast, unsecured money markets solely require a payment system (a cash "leg") but no additional securities "leg" (ECB, 2000, p. 53).[12] Two main sources are held responsible for the speed and the high degree of integration with respect to this segment. First, after minor initial operational problems, TARGET, the major settlement system for large-value payments in the euro area, functions smoothly and plays a key role in facilitating the redistribution of liquidity across the euro area.[13] The domestic share of money market activity of the largest market participants therefore diminished from 54% in 1998 to 40% in 1999 (ECB, 2000, p. 18). In addition, via this trouble-free cross-border payment facility, price differentials in the prevailing national segments of the money market throughout the euro area have been offset by arbitrage operations. Second, two benchmark indices, EONIA (euro overnight index average) and EURIBOR (euro area interbank offered rate), have been placed in the field of the euro area money market. Immediately after the start of the euro they were "broadly accepted by all market participants" (ECB, 2000, p. 24) and for that reason created a single money

---

11 The secured and unsecured segments show a combined share of 77% of euro money market activity in 1999 (ECB, 2000, p.15).

12 These infrastructural problems on European securities markets are taken up below.

13 TARGET stands for the Trans-European Automated Real-time Gross settlement Express Transfer system.

market reference yield curve acting also as the backbone for the booming derivative market activities. In this money market "network" derivative markets generate a positive feedback into the spot money markets. Turnover in both segments boomed, a self-reinforcing process of liquidity calling forth liquidity emerged.

An appropriate indicator for this development can be found in the form of a decline in money market transaction costs. For the three-month segment continuously dropping bid-ask spreads of annually 10% have been observable since 1996. A comparison with the corresponding US segment shows approximately identical transaction costs of about 9 basis points in 1999 (BIS, 2000, p. 124).

With regard to the unsecured and the swap segments, the TARGET system in conjunction with the rapidly established euro area indices enabled market participants to play in a melted single market. Taken together, integration and standardisation of all segments of European money markets are not yet complete. Especially in the case of the repo market further evolutions can be expected in order to come closer to US dimensions.

4.2 Bond Markets

Extensive as well as unexpected changes came about on European bond markets, especially concerning the corporate bond sector. The euro changeover period was characterised by the smooth redenomination of government bonds formerly denominated in the euro legacy currencies into euro-denominated bonds. New debt since then has been exclusively issued in euros. Bonds have also been reconventioned.[14] The fundamental element of change was the removal of currency risk. Thus an equal risk base emerged throughout the euro area. Both investors and borrowers had to attune to a broader set of feasible transactions, thereby increasing demand- and supply-side potentials of EMU bond markets (Danthine et al., 2000, p. 17ff). Former constraints to investment on a cross-border scale, such as currency matching rules applying to insurance companies and pension funds, disappeared. Previous to EMU, life insurance companies in Germany, the Netherlands, Spain, and Italy, for instance, were obliged to invest at least 80% of their total assets in their respective home currency. Moreover, commercial banks' requirements for raising central bank credits through repurchase agreements were without exception based on national collateral. With these restrictions eliminated, the focus of market participants gradually could shift from currency risk to other risk characteristics, such as credit and liquidity risk. A

14 The reconventioning encompasses, for instance, standardized rules concerning the pay and calculation of interest, thereby turning these bonds into more comparable and substitutable assets. Most private issuers adapted to these rules.

new need for portfolio diversification resulted from this shift, which is expected to lead to the reduction of the euro area home-country bias in investing and financing. This prediction definitely holds not only for European bond markets but also for European asset markets in general.

4.3 Government bond markets

In analysing government bond markets in the euro area, the main item is the convergence of yield differentials across participating economies. Is it a realistic appraisal to expect yield differentials to vanish completely and a truly integrated market to emerge that treats, e.g., Spanish and French bonds as perfect substitutes for one another? To tackle this question one has to examine the major risk components that are the reason for spreads in bond markets: fundamental (default or credit) risk, currency risk, and liquidity risk. Previous to monetary union, existing spreads mainly reflected the currency risk component of bonds issued by countries that have been more inflation-prone than stability-oriented Germany. Once the irrevocable fixing of the euro area exchange rates was announced in May 1998, currency risk vanished and therefore the decline in yield spreads already observable prior to that announcement accelerated to amounts below 40 basis points for bonds of two- to ten-year maturity (BIS, 2000, p. 126). In the preceding years spreads between 200 and 400 basis points had been common. However, it is striking that many issuing governments even now have to pay a premium compared to German issues, especially for the German 10-year bond representing the key segment of the yield curve. Now that the bulk of issuance is denominated in euros, other factors must explain interest rate spreads in the euro area.

At first glance one might suppose fundamental risk to be responsible for remaining spreads, primarily because the Maastricht Treaty, by means of the "no-bail-out“ clause (Article 104b), prohibits any shared liability for debt of single EMU member countries. Yet, technical reasons as well as matters related to liquidity, rather than the risk of default by a member state, have been identified by market observers.[15] In consequence, liquidity risk remains the key factor in determining the prevailing yield spreads even though differences in credit risk are by no means abolished.

An outstanding element of the European financial market's new landscape that explains the liquidity risk component is the enhanced competition of public debt issuers. Each government attempts to minimise their debt-servicing costs by attracting the demand side of the market. National debt management agencies are forced to acknowledge investors' desire for portfolio diversification and therefore are afraid of losing their traditional "home base." Moreover, the current low-yield environment, together with the absence of exchange rate risk, forced European

---

[15] See BIS (2000) and Danthine et al. (2000) for details.

investors to diversify not only geographically but also into the corporate debt segment, which offers higher risk-return combinations. These competitive circumstances forced national Treasuries to start a "race to the benchmark yield curve" (Danthine et al., 2000, p. 19), providing a considerable "built-in liquidity" advantage for large sovereign issuers like Germany, France, and Italy. Especially the smaller issuers (e.g., Ireland and the Netherlands) currently undertake benchmark policies to foster certain maturities or innovative products (niches) since their total amount of government debt is too small to ensure sufficient liquidity through the whole yield curve. However, big volumes of outstanding and newly issued debt alone cannot account for a benchmark status. Issuance has to be supplemented by specific issuance procedures, market transparency as well as secondary and derivative market liquidity. For instance, within the two- and the ten-year sector, German bonds are the benchmark in the latter case, mutually reinforced by the turnover of the Bund future contract in effect at a given time at Eurex, Frankfurt's Swiss-German derivatives exchange. France, conversely, sets the benchmark in the intermediate five- to seven-year range and for maturities of over ten years (ECB, 2000, p. 39).

On the one hand the observable rivalry and the diverging issuance strategies lead to innovative and transparent market practices. On the other hand idiosyncratic national debt management cannot exploit the potential economies of scale only a unified market structure could offer and therefore will remain more costly than the US Treasury's debt management. While the US Treasury serves as a centre of gravity, a central euro issuer is lacking. Furthermore, there are drawbacks for other financial market segments. A well-defined government ("risk-free") yield curve is lacking, so that the pricing of corporate bonds does not have a generally accepted floor. In addition the market for secured short-term deposits (repo market) suffers because bond market conventions are only insufficiently harmonized.

To summarize, the competition for liquidity and differences in credit risk are the consequences of a non-unique government yield curve. Furthermore, a truly unified market in this field is hardly to be expected in the near future. As the BIS puts it in its last annual report: "Any argument based on the economic benefits of greater coordination has to be carefully weighed against the further erosion of national independence“ (BIS, 2000, p. 127). Additionally, according to a recent report prepared for the European Commission by the Giovannini Group (2000), "co-ordination involving a joint or single debt instrument was not regarded as a practical option for the euro area as a whole." This allows for a preliminary conclusion to be drawn on the competition between the dollar and the euro concerning their international roles - the disadvantage for the euro is clearly evident.

4.4 Corporate Bond Markets

Right along with the launch of the euro, huge changes evolved for the previously underdeveloped European corporate bond markets and put them into a "new dimension" (ECB, 2000, p. 47). The first three quarters of 1999 saw a stunning increase in euro-denominated corporate bond issues (i.e. global issuance) by 390% compared to 1998.[16] The doubling of the average size of individual corporate bond issues is also evidence of the soaring liquidity. Along with this increase of market depth the breadth of the market grew, too. Baa-rated bond issuance boomed by 529%, starting however from a very low level, while bonds rated AA or A still rose by 55% and 122% respectively (ECB 2000, p. 39). Consequently, average credit ratings of companies that tap the bond market have fallen, a clear move towards US American conditions.

Yet, one should bear in mind two important facts to qualify these figures. First, European private non-corporate debt issuers (i.e., banks and other financial intermediaries) in 1999 still outperformed corporate issuers by a factor bigger than 4 (ECB, 2000, Chart 16). Second, the size of the European corporate bond market, measured by market value of outstanding issues, still is merely one-fifth that of its US counterpart (ECB, 2000, p. 48). Nevertheless, a further expansion of the European corporate bond markets is to be expected. Gros and Lannoo (2000) present several arguments contributing to this favourable outlook:

- A smaller growth of the government debt market due to the Stability and Growth Pact,
- historically low yields of government debt,
- no constraints by formerly (bad) credit ratings of the issuers' country[17], and
- lower issuing costs resulting from stiffer competition between market intermediaries in a more liquid euro market.

Moreover, the merger and acquisition boom in many sectors, especially in the telecommunication sector, amplifies the financing needs for companies. Finally, demand-side effects are also significant. Investors have more capital at their disposal, for instance due to gradually supplementing the pay-as-you-go pension systems by a capital pillar in Germany and elsewhere. Even more important, as has been mentioned above, investors show a readiness to diversify on a geographical (cross-border) scale as well as into riskier asset classes.

---

16 The exact figures are ?117 vs. ?30 billion. See Eichengreen (2000, p. 363).

17 Solvent companies may have a better rating than their central government.

To sum up, in contrast to the sovereign debt market, European corporate bond markets were largely underdeveloped prior to EMU. The evidence mentioned reveals an astonishing boom that appears to have overcome the critical mass effect. "A broader used currency and more liquid capital market could attract more issues than the sum of the component currencies before, as seems to be the case so far in the first months of EMU" (Gros and Lannoo, 2000, p. 44).

Nonetheless, even considering all these factors, it might take a decade for the corporate capital markets in Europe to be comparable in size with its US equivalent.[18]

4.5 Equity Markets and Securities Market Infrastructure

The integration of European equity markets presents an ambivalent picture. The pure magnitude, measured, e.g., as turnover on primary and secondary markets in 1999, has grown rapidly along various dimensions, including the successful development of high-tech sectors like the German *Neuer Markt*.[19] A more efficient organization of the market structure and initiatives to integrate European equity markets, however, turned out to be less successful, as the failed merger of the London Stock Exchange and the Deutsche Börse has illustrated. The latter problem, though, applies to the European securities markets in general, because the trading, clearing, and settlement infrastructure still contains huge efficiency potentials.

Against this background, the question arises as to whether the euro can promote the geographical diversification away from nationally oriented equity portfolios. Prior to EMU, it was generally expected that structural changes in equity flows would decrease the enormous equity home-bias. According to that logic, national impacts on share prices should diminish since now it is less probable that shocks will emanate from national macroeconomic policies. Monetary policy is conducted by the ECB, fiscal policy is restricted due to the Stability and Growth Pact and currency risk has been eliminated. Hence, (macroeconomic) country risk would converge and thus the widespread strategy of managing a portfolio country-by-country should be abandoned in favour of a sector-by-sector view throughout the euro-area. In fact, to some extent this behavioural switch has already materialized as indicated by the appearance of pan-European or euro-area stock market indices (e.g., Stoxx-50 and Euro-Stoxx 50). The available evidence relating to a shrinking home-bias, however, is still rather unconvincing. Danthine

---

18 Other segments of European bond markets, e.g. the asset-backed securities market and the bond-related derivatives market, grew strongly, too. Especially, the German "Pfandbriefe" market established a high acceptance on a European scale; see ECB (2000, p. 48f).

19 Figures for 1999 show a 66% increase in euro equity issues and a 42% increase in European equity trading volume. See Danthine et al. (2000, footnote 36).

et al. (2000) in their thorough analysis present figures that show a tendency toward a slow portfolio rebalancing across euro-area sectors. At the same time, however, the Bank for International Settlement claims that "prices continue to be driven principally by local investors with a considerable geographical portfolio bias" (BIS, 2000, p. 133).

Besides hesitant reactions, the basic issue at stake is the problem of the complex European trading, clearing, and settlement infrastructure.[20] Notwithstanding the aforementioned mixed evidence regarding first steps towards portfolio rebalancing, a broad consensus exists with respect to the still massive (i.e., expensive) barriers to cross-border portfolio investment in the euro area. This fragmentation is significant since it limits further integration and portfolio diversification and thereby impedes the development of a unified European capital market. Transaction costs resulting from inefficient structures impose a type of tax on trading and thus prevent investors from achieving optimum portfolios (ECB, 2000, p. 41; Gros and Lannoo, 2000, p. 67ff).

The fact that European stock exchanges strive for alliances or cooperation serves to illustrate this difficulty. Overly optimistic, the Bank of England said in June 2000: "The proposed merger between the London Stock Exchange (LSE) and Deutsche Börse [...] is a key step in the consolidation of the European exchange infrastructure, and likely to encourage further consolidation of clearing and settlement services" (Bank of England, 2000, p. 7). Yet, due to several unsettled problems and finally motivated by fears that the hostile bid of OM, a Swedish technology company, could be successful, the LSE withdrew from their plan to merge the two biggest European exchanges into iX (International Exchanges) in September 2000. Meanwhile, another alliance was successfully founded in September 2000: Euronext, the merged Paris, Brussels, and Amsterdam exchange, is going to start business in summer 2001. These events reflect the competitive pressures traditional exchanges are exposed to. They are not only alarmed about (un)friendly takeover strategies by established exchanges but also feel challenged by newly emerging electronic platforms like virt-X or Jiway (The Economist, 2000).

Apart from the lack of integration in securities trading, in particular segmented European clearing and settlement systems are regarded as being too expensive compared to US structures. Standardized trading of securities requires not only a trading platform in the form of electronic or traditional exchanges, but also the settlement of cash and securities through clearing houses and securities settlement systems. Previous to EMU, these systems were organized nationally. Moreover, in the case of monetary and fiscal relations, the pre-EMU legal environment was mainly based upon national peculiarities. Market and central bank practises

---

20 For a detailed description of the different components of the European financial infrastructure, see ECB (2000, p. 53ff).

together with tax and accounting regimes differed to a large extent. The mere introduction of the euro hardly changed this situation. Although the European Commission issued directives relating directly to legal issues (e.g., Investment Services Directive, Capital Adequacy Directive and Settlement Finality Directive), a lot of differences still exist. In particular, little progress has been made concerning such key areas as taxing and accounting (ECB, 2000, p. 57ff).

The overall picture shows that the structure of European stock exchanges is still fragmented with no single pan-European exchange in sight. The same holds true for the complete range of European securities infrastructure (trading, clearing, and settling). Economies of scale would call for merging the multiple clearing houses and securities settlement systems into one central agency because "settlement is the most expensive part of cross-border trading, and can cost up to ten times as much as in America" (The Economist, 2000).

The main conclusions drawn so far in section 4 may best be summarized by the following statement: "Even after the introduction of the euro capital markets will retain a strong national flavour. 1999 will thus see the start of a process of unification, rather than its completion" (Gros, 1998, p. 26f.). With hindsight, this forecast for the most part has been corroborated as the above presentation of actual developments shows. However, it should be kept in mind that different segments of European financial markets differ with respect to their pace of integration.

4.6 European Monetary Policy

Besides financial market integration, a sound design of European monetary policy is an indispensable issue involving the future international role of the euro. A crucial factor leading to a good performance of an international currency is whether monetary policy will be dedicated to achieving price stability and therefore will gain the confidence of international investors and borrowers. With respect to the euro area, the independence of the European Central Bank (ECB), as well as its obligation to strive first and foremost for price stability and the prohibition against financing public budget deficits, both stipulations laid down by the Maastricht Treaty, are necessary conditions in this respect. Equally important is the validity of the Stability and Growth Pact, the purpose of which is to ensure a permanent upper limitation of public debt and deficits and which even provides sanctions in the event that these conditions are not fulfilled. Only a sustained acceptance of these clear conditions will support an increasing international role for the euro.

However, a political void exists concerning the responsibility for exchange rate policy. Only the European Council of Ministers (and not the ECB) is authorized to initiate international agreements on fixed exchange rates and target zones for exchange rates (Maastricht Treaty: art. 109); this potentially undermines efforts made by the ECB to defend price level stability. Moreover, the reputation of the ECB hinges on a convincing explanation of its monetary strategy to the actors on international financial markets and the general public. Deficits in this field together with debates about an appropriate degree of transparency of the ECB's policy decisions arose during the first two years of EMU.[21]

4.7 Inertia

The analysis carried out so far suggests that the euro could catch up with the dollar in the long run. But forecasts about the speed of adjustment are very difficult to obtain and are likely to be of only questionable accuracy. Empirical knowledge tells us that economic agents are risk-averse and that it is only with great caution that they adjust their traditional behaviour to structural changes. Inertia is a reasonable assumption in the light of uncertainty. Though the competition between the US dollar and the euro is going to be finally decided on international financial markets, inertia in the reactions of economic agents supports the argumentation that the euro could be quite slow to catch up, even though the majority of economic indicators might point in another direction. It is important to note that no sufficient condition exists for a currency to achieve world status. Even in the situation of equal transaction costs, though, a switch from one currency to another could be delayed because uncertainty leads to hesitant reactions. A dependency on tradition and convention therefore is of greater significance than automatism. One clearly has to distinguish between laying the institutional, economic, and political foundations on the one hand and convincing market participants to effectively change their behaviour on the other.

Consequently, it seems to be almost impossible to make an assessment about a plausible time frame as long as it remains uncertain whether a shift will occur at all. However, Portes still insists on linking the possible international role of the euro directly to progress made on European financial markets: "The time frame of the analysis [the euro catching up with the dollar, authors' comment] is that of the integration of euro-area financial markets - say five to ten years" (Portes, 2000, p. 7). This assessment should be altered to the extent that it refers to a realistic time frame for attaining the quantifiable *preconditions* for a leading international currency. More prudently, we adhere to the opinion expressed by Wyplosz: "Finally, we are looking at a very slow process. The virtuous cycle of declining costs and growing market size is unlikely to unfold fast. The time-scale is measured in decades not in months" (Wyplosz, 1999, pp. 88, 95).

---

21 Problems in the broader field of macroeconomic policy are not to be discussed in this paper. One should, however, bear in mind that structural reforms on labour markets and the restructuring of existing pay-as-you-go pension schemes should be of first priority in most continental European countries.

5 The Position of the Yen: Insufficient Political Backing

After having evaluated the prospects of the euro as an international currency, we should add a few remarks to sketch the dismal prospects the yen has of joining the euro in potentially competing with the dollar. Initially and most crucially, political conditions in Japan and East Asia are absolutely different from those prevailing in the European Union. Critics of the process of European integration argue that a lack of political unity in Europe works against a sustainable EMU.[22] If one attaches importance to this reasoning, there is practically no way for Japan to further promote the role of the yen because of serious political obstacles that might arise in the attempt to form an East-Asian economic bloc comparable to the EU in this region. Due to historical burdens stemming from Japans' occupations of other Asian countries in the first half of the 20th century, cooperation between Japan, Southeast Asian countries, and perhaps China to push a pan-Asian currency (presumably the yen) must be regarded as exceptionally unlikely to succeed. Against this background it is all the more astonishing that in Japan the internationalization of the yen is announced as an explicit political target. These ambitions are indicated by the appointment of a "Study Group for the Promotion of the Internationalization of the Yen" in 1999 (Japanese Ministry of Finance, 2000).

On purely economic grounds and commensurate with its clout in terms of GDP and technological sophistication, Japan, the second-largest world economy, should perform the role of an obvious regional leader. However, an "unresolved issue of leadership" exists, as Grenville, the Deputy Governor of the Reserve Bank of Australia, states when considering the possibilities of regional financial arrangements in East-Asia. For this reason the yen hardly has a chance to catch up with the dollar or the euro. A thorough analysis of Japanese and Asian financial markets therefore is not useful in this context.[23]

The figures presented in Section 3 (Tables 2-4) as well as recent economic conditions in Japan and Southeast Asia substantiate our continues view of the yen's international prospects. It is worth reconsidering the 0.6 value for the yen's coefficient of internationalization (Table 3). This means that in 1992 the yen was used to denominate trade by far less than the value of combined Japanese imports and exports. The corresponding numbers for the US dollar and the Deutsche mark are 3.6 and 1.4, respectively. This implies that concerning the patterns of invoicing , the yen is significantly underrepresented compared to Japan's potency in world trade. Moreover, relatively intense US trade with East Asia, together with the

---

22 Most prominent among them is Feldstein (2000b).

23 A thorough and refined analysis of the yen as an international currency has been worked out by Strube (2001).

tendency of Southeast Asian countries to peg their currency to the dollar even after the currency crisis in 1997/98, prevents the yen from being the natural regional currency even in its "own" area. Likewise, figures on economic size, openness (Table 2), and turnover on foreign exchange markets (Table 4) strongly underscore the weak position of the yen, compared with the dollar and the euro (or its predecessor currencies).

Additionally, deteriorations in the region's economic performance in recent years should be noted. Japan and Southeast Asia still suffer from the consequences subsequent to the financial and economic crisis at the end of the 1990s. Furthermore, Japan so far has not overcome all the problems caused by the burst of the bubble economy in the early 1990s. The growing indebtedness of the Japanese government (130% of GDP in 2000) due to extensive public spending is commonly seen as another striking problem. On this account, yen-denominated Japanese government bonds were downgraded in September 2000 by Moody's (Financial Times, 2000). Overall, in the foreseeable future the yen most probably cannot establish functions of an international currency comparable to the dollar or the euro. Even a regional dominance of the yen in East Asia must not be taken for granted.

6 Outlook for the Future International Currency Regime

The present currency regime makes it likely that the US will reap most extra benefits since it is the issuer of the leading international currency. Today the euro can be considered the only currency to have the potential to threaten the dominance of the dollar. In thinking ahead to what the international currency system could look like in the future it is useful to briefly reconsider the most prominent characteristics making a currency preferable on a world-wide level:

1. *real activity*: size of output (internal market) and trade (share in world trade),
2. *liquidity*: size and sophistication of financial markets,
3. *risk factors:* monetary and exchange rate stability, stability of economic policy, and
4. *inertia* (dependency on tradition and institutional settlements).

While real activity in terms of GDP and share in world trade does not clearly privilege any of the economic blocs in question, an analysis of financial liquidity seems to be a more promising field of study. It has been shown in more detail that Europe is on the verge of moving towards highly developed financial markets, whereas Japan is limited to its narrow domestic markets with no political perspectives to establish a unified Asian market. Should the UK join EMU in the near future, the European integration could ultimately accelerate. The prospects for providing financial liquidity in Europe are fostered by the irrevocable process of political integration. In the end, Europe might emerge as a political unity comparable to the US with the ability to guarantee a degree of stability necessary to satisfy the demands of market participants. In this respect, Japan has to face clear political disadvantages that will finally obstruct all efforts undertaken to promote the yen as an international currency. Despite great opportunities for the euro to compete favourably with the dollar in terms of size, sophistication of financial markets and political stability, inertia in combination with switching costs is likely to retard a catching up of the euro for decades. We assume that the previous historical experience of only gradually changing supremacy of international currencies still applies. However, the possibility must not be excluded that unexpected shocks may completely change the scenario outlined above.

List of References

Bank for International Settlement (2000a): *70th Annual Report*, Basel.

Bank for International Settlement (2000b): *International Banking and Financial market Developments*, November 2000, Basel.

Bank for International Settlement (1999): *Central Bank Survey of Foreign Exchange and Derivatives Market Activity* 1998, Basel.

Bank of England (2000): Practical Issues Arising from the Euro, June 2000.

Bayle, M., Santillán, J., and Thygesen, C. (2000): The impact of the euro on money and bond markets, *ECB Occasional Paper* 1.

Berger, A. N., DeYoung, R., and Udell, G. F. (2000): Efficiency barriers to the consolidation of the European financial services industry, *European Financial Management* 6.

Bergsten, C. F. (1997): The impact of the euro on exchange rates and international policy cooperation, in: Krueger, T. H., Masson, P. R., and Turtelboom, B. G. (eds.), *EMU and the International Monetary System*, IMF, Washington, DC.

Black, F., and Scholes, M. (1973): The pricing of options and corporate liabilities, *Journal of Political Economy* 81, 637-659.

Cohen, B. (1998), *The Geography of Money*, Cornell: Cornell University Press.

Danthine, J.-P., Giavazzi, F., and von Thadden, E.-L. (2000): European financial markets after EMU: A first assessment, paper presented at the Bundesbank/BIS conference on „Recent Developments in Financial Systems and their Challenges for Economic Policy: a European Perspective", Frankfurt 28/29 September.

De Grauwe, P. (2000): The euro dollar exchange rate in search of fundamentals, mimeo.

Detken, C., and Hartmann, P. (2000): The euro and international capital markets, *ECB Working Paper* 19.

Economist, The (2000): European stock exchanges - Two into three, July 22.

Eichengreen, B. (2000): The euro one year on, *Journal of Policy Modeling*, 22(3), 355-368.

European Central Bank (2000): The external trade of the euro area economy: Stylised facts and recent trends, *ECB Monthly Bulletin* August 2000.

European Central Bank (1999): The international role of the euro, *ECB Monthly Bulletin* August 1999.

European Commission (2000): Report on co-ordinated issuance of public debt in the euro area. Report of the Giovannini Group, http://europa.eu.int/comm/economy_finance/ document/ euro/giovannini1100_en.htm

Emerson, M., Gros, D., Italianer, A., Pisani-Ferry, J., and Reichenbach, H.: (1991): *One Market, One Money*, Oxford: Oxford University Press.

Feldstein, M. (2000a): Aspects of global economic integration: Outlook for the future, *NBER Working Paper* 7899.

Feldstein, M. (2000b): The European Central Bank and the euro: The first year, *Journal of Policy Modeling*, 22(3), 345-354.

Financial Times (2000): Japan's credit rating downgraded by Moody's, September 8.

Frankfurter Allgemeine Zeitung (2000): Vor einer Flut von Telekom-Anleihen, August 14.

Grassman, S. (1973): A fundamental symmetry in international payment patterns, *Journal of International Economics* 3, 105-116.

Grenville, S. A. (2000): Notes on East Asian financial cooperation, speech reprinted in: *BIS Review* 68, 2000.

Gros, D., and Lannoo, K. (2000): *The Euro Capital Market*, Chichester: Wiley.

Gros, D. (1998): *EMU and Capital Markets - The Institutional Framework*, Brussels.

Hartmann, P. (1998): *Currency Competition and Foreign Exchange Markets: the Dollar, the Yen and the Euro*, Cambridge: Cambridge University Press.

International Monetary Fund (2000): *Annual Report*, Washington DC.

Japanese Ministry of Finance (2000): Interim Summarization (June 30, 2000) of the Study Group for the Promotion of the Internationalization of the Yen (Provisional Translation), http://www.mof.go.jp/English/if/if025b.htm.

Kindleberger, C. P. (1973): *The World in Depression, 1929-1939*, Berkeley: University of California Press.

Krugman, P. (1999): *The Return of Depression Economics*, New York: Norton.

Krugman, P (1992): *Currencies and Crisis*, Cambridge: MIT Press.

Kunz, D (1995), The fall of the dollar order: The world the United States is losing, *Foreign Affairs* 74, 4.

McCauley, R. N. (1997): The euro and the dollar, *BIS Working Paper* 50.

McCauley, R. N. and White, W. R. (1997): The euro and European financial markets, BIS Working Paper 41.

Portes, R. (2000): The role of the euro in the world: Past developments and future perspectives, presented at the Bundesbank/BIS conference on „Recent Developments in Financial Systems and their Challenges for Economic Policy: a European Perspective", Frankfurt 28/29 September.

Portes, R., and Rey, H. (1998): The emergence of the euro as an international currency, *Economic Policy*, 26, 307-343.

Prati, A., and Schinasi, G. J. (1997): European monetary union and international capital markets: Structural implications and risks, *IMF Working Paper* 62.

Rey, H. (1999): International trade and currency exchange, *CEPR Discussion Paper* 2226.

Rogoff, K. (1998): Blessing or curse? Foreign and underground demand for euro notes, *Economic Policy*, Vol. 26, 263-303.

Schwartz, A. J. (2000): The rise and fall of foreign exchange market intervention, *NBER Working Paper* 7751.

Shapiro, C., and Varian, H. R. (1999): *Information Rules: A Strategic Guide to the Network Economy*, Boston, Mass., Harvard Business School Press.

Steinherr, A. (1998): *Derivatives, the Wild Beast of Finance*, Chichester, Wiley.

Strube, J. (2001): *Der japanische Yen als internationale Währung – Voraussetzungen, funktionale Interdependenzen und Motive der Währungswahl*, mimeo, Ruhr-Universität Bochum.

Summers, Lawrence H. (1999): Economic engagement: The risk of malign neglect, speech, http://www.ustreas.gov/press/releases/ps179.htm.

Tesar, L., and Werner, I. (1995): Home bias and high turnover, *Journal of International Money and Finance* 14, 467-492.

Wyplosz, C. (1999): An international role for the euro?, in: Dermine, J. and Hillion, P. (eds.:), *European Capital Markets with a Single Currency*, 76-104, Oxford: Oxford University Press.

Effects of Globalization and Crisis upon Competitive and Cooperative Relationships in Asia: The Example of the Japanese and East Asian Electronics Industries

Sachio Imakubo

Graduate School of Economics

Kyoto University

1 Introduction

It is my task to report on the "Effects of Globalization and Crisis upon Competitive and Cooperative Relationships in Asia" from the Japanese perspective. Since I find this topic far too broad, I should like to limit myself to one example, the electronics industries in Japan and in East Asia. By East Asia I mean not only Northeast but also Southeast Asia. The electronics industry, one of the main driving forces behind the "East Asian Miracle," is playing the leading role in the revival of productivity after the recovery from the Asian Crisis. In other words, it is functioning as one of the most important factors in the recovery from the crisis and the stabilization of the economy. Within the framework of the globalization of this industry up to the 1990s, an international system for the division of labour in East Asia arose, which had its centre in Japan, and which is closely involved with the competitive and cooperative relationships of the electronics industry in this region. The Asian Crisis and the long-lasting weakness in the business cycle of the Japanese economy are also having severe effects as destabilizing elements within this system of division of labour upon the structure hitherto found in the electronics industries of Japan and East Asia. Thus viewed, the electronics industry offers some helpful illustrations for our topic.

2 Development of the Electronics Industries of East Asia and Japan

2.1 Development of the Electronics Industry of East Asia in Cooperation and in Competition

The East Asian electronics industry developed very rapidly and nowadays has reached such a level that Asia is called the "world factory for electronics products." (Takeuchi, 1999, p. 180) The following indicators document this fact: Due to this headlong development, the electronics industry in nine Asian countries and regions achieved a total production volume of ca. $223.1bn in 1996, almost equal to Japan's production of $245bn (Yearbook of World Electronics Data, 1998, Takeuchi, 1999, p. 190). Especially in the production of semiconductors, East Asia after 1995 had the highest share (34%) in the group of world regions, a share it increased to 36% in 1998 (Table 1). Of the worldwide capital investment in semiconductors, just about 40%, estimated, worth over $10bn, is accounted for by East Asia, making this region far and away the frontrunner for such capital investments (1999 nendoban, 1999, p. 7). East Asia's share in the worldwide export market for electronic goods grew from 14.5% in 1986 to 33.1% in 1995 (1996 International Trade Statistics Yearbook, 1997; Taiwan Boeki, 1997, p. 191). In 1986 the shares of the world regions in the semiconductor market were: Europe ca. 20%, America ca. 33%. Japan ca. 39%, and Asia and the Pacific region ca. 8%. By 1998 the Asian-Pacific region had expanded its market share enormously: Europe 23.4%, America 33%, Japan 20.6%, and Asia and the Pacific region 23%. Japan had obviously been overtaken by this region (WSTS, 1999). All these indicators would also seem to show that the developmental trend of the electronics industry in East Asia is still continuing.

The reasons for the rapid development in East Asia are, for one thing, that American, Japanese and European electronics firms followed the trend of globalization and located strategic production sites in the region, and, for another, that the East Asian countries pursued a hightech and export-oriented strategy of industrialization with the help of foreign capital. On the other hand, East Asian electronics firms, especially in the NIES countries (Samsung Electronics, Taiwan Semiconductor Manufacturing, etc.), have grown considerably in the meantime. Among the globalization strategies of the American, Japanese and European electrical engineering and electronics firms, the geographical concentration of strategic production sites of the Japanese firms in East Asian is conspicuous. Of a total 1274 production sites of Japanese firms abroad in June 1998, there are 223 in North America, 145 in Europe, and 873, i.e., a sizeable majority of 68.5%, in Asia (Table 2). Of the total 973.000 employees in these foreign production sites, Asia's share of 740.000 (76%) is the largest. North America's share of slightly over 140.000 and Europe's of 70.000 are relatively minor (Nihon no denshikogyo 1999,

p. 12; 1998 nenniokeru, 1999, p. 4). Furthermore, Japanese firms are nowadays the most strongly committed to the East Asian electronics industry through direct investments (Heisei 11 nenban, 1999; Tsusansho, 1999, p. 118 - 123; Ajia no keizaikiki, April 1998, p. 35 - 39). The immediate perception from these facts is that in the area of investments the East Asian and Japanese electronics industries are most closely allied with each other.

The direct investments also exert an influence upon trade. According to Fig. 1, the share of imports of electrical engineering and electronic appliances from Asia to the West up to 1997 was higher than in Japan. Japan, however, had a very high share of the exports to Asia (Fig. 2). The most important products in these cases were electronic parts and components (Nihon no denshikogyo, 1999, p. 12). In other words, Japan exports mainly intermediate goods and capital assets to Asia, where they are used to make finished products. Asia then exports these finished products to the West, primarily to the USA. This trade structure, which supported the development of the electronics industry in the NIES countries during the 1980s, was expanded to include all of East Asia. Among the production sites in Asia there are of course also non-Japanese and indigenous firms, but the localized Japanese firms are the centre of gravity. They are the main mediators of this trade structure. Figure 1 also shows the rising trend in exports from East Asia to Japan in the 1990s (the slow growth in 1997 was doubtless due to the Asian Crisis and the slump in Japan's business cycle). This change in the trade structure was brought about by the increase in procurements from East Asia by Japanese firms during the 1990s, in order to reduce material and parts costs (said to constitute 70-80% of the production costs of finished products) and to avoid the risks of exchange rate fluctuations, such as a strengthening of the yen. The increase in imports of products with high price competitiveness, e.g., consumer electronics, is another contributing factor (Takeuchi, 1999, p. 191 – 193). The decreasing special rate on exports from 1990 to 1997, responsible to a high degree for the export to Asia of certain Japanese products such as electronic parts (e.g., semiconductors), telecommunications appliances, electronic gauges and AV appliances, also plays a part in this change in trade structure (Ajia keizai, March 1998, p. 9). The localized Japanese firms make a great contribution to this trade between East Asia and Japan. Hence the production sites of Japanese firms in East Asia also have the characteristics of sites for exports to Japan.

Thus the Japanese and East Asian electronics industries are allied with each other by means of direct investments and trade relationships, with the local Japanese production sites playing a mediating role. This alliance reflects the fact that in East Asia a system of division of labour based mainly upon internal trade among groups of companies is being formed, expanded and deepened. But international division of labour also takes place between Western and East Asian firms, as well as within East Asian firms that involve themselves in the system of division of labour between Japan and East Asia.

Until the 1990s, internal trade among groups of companies arose in this region under Japanese influence, as the result of various forms of the division of labour: a) between the parent company in Japan and the Japanese groups of companies in East Asia, and b) within the Japanese groups of companies in East Asia, taking place internally, within the industry, the firms, and among various processes and products. The division of labour in b) made a great contribution to the expansion of trade within East Asia. Along with the internal trade of the company groups, there exists an intra-industrial division of labour, in which the localized Japanese firms play a role: c) division of labour and trade between Japanese firms in East Asia and indigenous firms, as well as d) division of labour and trade between Japanese and indigenous firms (including production to order by semiconductor foundry manufacturers in Taiwan for Japanese firms). Finally, e) international cooperation by large firms (e.g., NEC with Hyundai Electronics) counts as international division of labour between Japan and East Asia in the broader sense.

In the 1980s, the expansion of the acquisition of complementary parts from the region became unavoidable, and on the other hand the further reduction of production costs in the Japanese production sites in East Asia seemed to be reaching its limits. At this point, large Japanese firms called IPOs (international procurement offices) opened up in cities like Singapore, Hong Kong and Taipei. The IPOs played an important part in the aforementioned international system of division of labour, for their function was primarily to acquire parts and materials from local firms (see c), above), and to supply them to Japanese firms in East Asia or Japan (see a) and b), above). They additionally functioned as mediators for the division of labour, as in d). The IPOs also deliver parts and materials to Japanese firms in Europe and America, and thus they coordinate the acquisitions of these firms. Accordingly, they are at the very centre of the global acquisitions system within the global production strategy of the Japanese electronics firms.

This development of the East Asian electronics industry, which originally spread out from the NIEs across ASEAN in the second half of the 1980s and reached China in the 1990s, describes a peak development like a "flight of geese" of the local industry and at the same time another "flight of geese" international displacement of the industry. Apart from the displacement of the American electronics firms to East Asia in order to secure their "offshore" production sites, whose influence on this development was not inconsiderable, the development arose because Japanese firms in the region which had developed earlier readjusted to higher-quality production due to the increased factor costs there, and transferred their older production, on account of more favourable factor costs, to a region which had developed later. Table 2 clearly shows the process of this "sequential redeployment of production."(Shimada et. al., 1997, p. 35 – 36).

The NIEs firms also followed this pattern in the second half of the 1980s, because of reduced competitive advantages stemming from their stronger currencies, rising payroll costs, more rigorous measures to protect the environment, etc. The changes in the functions or locations of the IPOs, to be discussed in detail below, result from the fact that IPOs in East Asia contributed to the buildup of the supportive and complementary industrial branches of the East Asian electronics industry which were redeploying according to the "flying geese" pattern.

The bond based on division of labour—that is, the cooperative and complementary relationships—between the Japanese and East Asian electronics industry were closely connected with the "flying geese" peak development and redeployment of the industry. This peak development and redeployment led however throughout the entire East Asian region to a multilevel local competition, because it drove the development of the electronics industry and with it economic growth in East Asia forward and simultaneously brought about a continual creation in the sequence "industrial substitution, boomerang phenomenon, reimportation, industrial adaptation." (Tran Van Tho, March/April 1999, p. 33).

Thus we have within the region: a) NIEs against ASEAN, b) NIEs against China, c) the NIEs countries or regions competing among each other, and d) ASEAN against China. These competitive relationships will be clarified here only with reference to those IPOs which have to do with the development of the supporting industries. As an example of the competition in a), Singapore will serve. In the 1990s, Singapore gradually lost its cost advantages through expanded local procurement and rising costs in infrastructure and wages. At the same time, the sub-contracting industry in the ASEAN countries developed to the extent that the Japanese production sites there were able to assume the function of an IPO in place of the factory-IPO (i.e., by purchasing factories; in Malaysia by an IPC, or International Purchasing Centre). The IPO in Singapore will either have to take on a new function as a "developmental purchase," that is, by opening up new regions for procurement, or reduce its size (1996 nen tonanajia, 1996, p. 51; 1998 Kaigai denshikogyo, 1998, p. 13, 53). In Malaysia, Japanese manufacturers of appliances have expanded their R&D function against the background of the IPO-supportive policy of the government adopted in 1996. To be sure, the development of the basic technology remains in Japan, but a more cost-effective construction, adapted to the buying country, is to be achieved locally through a reduction of the total number of parts and of the parts from Japan, as well as through examination of standards of quality and safety, and is to be produced in the ASEAN countries. Malaysia will take over the job of a factory-IPO: it will supervise and support the production from the technical and procurement side. An example of b): since the second half of the 1980s, numerous production sites have moved from Hong Kong to Kwangtung in China because of lower costs, leading to a weakening of the foundation in the electronics industry. An example of c): as an IPO, Hong Kong nonetheless gains in importance as a juncture to China, in contrast to Singapore. An example of d): the competition between ASEAN and China arose mainly through the redeployment of investments of foreign firms, i.e., from overseas Chinese in the

ASEAN countries to China. Through the founding of NAFTA, Mexico also emerges as a new competitor of East Asia in local competition (1996 nen tonanajia, 1996, p. 48; Kadensangyo, June 1997, p. 62 – 67). Initially, Japanese manufacturers of parts followed their Japanese manufacturers of appliances to East Asia when the latter redeployed their operations there in order to keep them supplied. Because of the effects of exchange rates and the establishment of "East Asian prices," their profit situation worsened, and gradually they lost their competitiveness to local parts producers. A problem was also posed by the transplantation of Japanese elements such as the production system and relationships among firms, which had yielded competitive advantages in Japan, to East Asia. Insufficient penetration meant that they did not necessarily lead to the same advantages in their new locations (Itagaki, 1997). The local competitive effect of the "flying geese"-shaped redeployment of production upon the electronics industry of Japan will be discussed below.

2.2 Effects of the Development of the East Asian Electronics Industry and Global Competition upon the Electronics Industry in Japan

In 1997, the investments of overseas subsidiaries of the Japanese electrical engineering and electronics industry were 62.5% of domestic investments, and the share of employees abroad was 46.4% of all the employees of Japanese firms (Ueda, May 1998, p. 12; Nihon no denshikogyo, p. 3 – 4). The foreign share of production in this industry rose from 7.4% in 1985 to 19.7% in 1996, an almost three-fold increase, and among firms with their production sites abroad it rose to 33.1% in 1995.[1] Because of the redeployment of production for products and parts both for domestic and foreign markets and the increase in procurement abroad, the Japanese electronics industry, too, was confronted with local competition. Under the added influence of the cooling off of the developed domestic market, the redeployment of production led to a diminution of production and deployment in Japan, as well as to an erosion of the supportive industries. For the domestic market for household appliances and home entertainment electronics was in any case rather too saturated to be able to absorb foreign products as a substitute for imports or reimports from East Asian firms. Domestic production of household appliances and consumer electronics was especially hard hit, as this had already been redeployed abroad to a great extent. It was further greatly diminished by closings and downsizings of businesses, etc. (The share of the electronics industry shrank from 34% in 1978 to 9% in 1996.) The number of steady employees in the electronics industry was reduced over a

---

1 In 1984, before the conclusion of the Plaza-Accord, the export proportion of colour televisions was more than 40%. In 1988 the production abroad was higher than the domestic production, it increased further to 87,1%. (Takeuchi, 1999, p. 182)

period of five years, from 474 000 in 1991 to 425 000 in 1996. The reduction of employees in the household and consumer appliance sectors is also considerable (1997 nen ni okeru, p. 3, table 1). The redeployment of production of Japanese parts manufacturers abroad is a terrible blow for the supportive domestic industries, which carried the competitive advantages of the Japanese electronics industry up to now, especially since domestic appliance manufacturers increasingly opt for internal production and select their own suppliers. This leads to an erosion of the supportive industries (in the 1980s these were smaller firms in the countryside, in the 1990s also firms in the big cities). If this situation continues, entrepreneurs will have difficulty finding successor technologies of their own, successors who grew out of the industrial agglomeration of the small businesses. The competitive advantages of the Japanese electronics industry would thereby be further weakened. Because competition in costs is becoming more severe, costs rather than quality are now in the forefront, and appliance manufacturers are increasingly changing over to parts made abroad, which are used directly for domestic production. The traditional guarantee of quality and after-sales service (elements of the traditional competitive advantages) no longer works as it used to, and in the NIEs countries, frequency of flawed products is rising (Mitarai, 1995; Satake, 1994; Shinshuntaidan, 1997, p. 5). What is striking is the decreasing competitiveness of large Japanese firms compared with East Asian and Western firms. In the past, Japanese household appliances were far out in front, but after the region (Korea, Taiwan, etc.) had developed, they had to give up their market shares in the sectors of small appliances, standard appliances, etc., to these competitors. In 1988, Japan's worldwide share in semiconductor production was 51%, but in the 1990s it dropped. At the same time, the shares of Europe and East Asia (e.g., Singapore, Korea and Taiwan) greatly increased (Sangyogakkai, 1995, p. 366; Amano, 1999,). Apart from the redeployment of production to Asia, the following reasons for the decline in the Japanese semiconductor industry can be noted: the rise of specialized semiconductor firms in Europe, America and East Asia, progress in international horizontal division of labour in the form of production to order and cooperation among these firms, decline in investments of Japanese firms, and the weakening of the competitiveness along with the shrinking of the market in the general memory chip sector. These problems all derive, no doubt, from the failure of Japanese semiconductor firms, which have driven the strategy of vertical integration or diversification forward and thereby followed the model laid down by American computer business, to react in a timely and appropriate fashion to the structural change in the semiconductor business. This structural change is one of the major aspects of the tendency to change of the leading sectors within the electronics industry, namely, from the computer sector to the sectors of networking, and consumer and household appliances with digital information technology (Amano, 1999, p. 24).

This problem is closely bound up with another aspect of the change in competitiveness of the Japanese electronics industry: on the one hand, it was of strategic importance in this industry to quickly establish de-facto world standards during the global competition of the 1990s. But the constantly rising development costs could no longer be borne by individual firms, and so the de-facto world standards were frequently achieved by non-Japanese firms or by groups in strategic alliances. On the other hand, the enormous development costs led even large firms to split their technological sectors, in which their strength lay, resulting in a segmentation of the markets. This strong competition, encompassing both technology and market structure, is partly the product of the "flight of geese"-shaped development in East Asia. However, the competition is not based upon the geographical concentration of the electronics industry, as it was in the Japanese electronics industry until the 1980s, but now takes place globally, and not always homogeneously. This explains the fact that the importance of the competitive advantages of the traditional Japanese electronics industry, based on a homogeneous competition among large Japanese firms, is now greatly diminishing (Hiramoto, 1996). It is an expression of this fact, and a clear sign of the tardy reaction of Japanese firms to global competition, that first the USA and then Korea overtook Japan in the semiconductor market.

3 The Electronics Industry in the Asian Crisis and in the Japanese Recession

3.1 Backgrounds of the Asian Crisis and the Japanese Recession and Their Influence upon the Electronics Industry

It cannot be said that the process of industrialization in East Asia in itself was the direct or fundamental cause of the Asian monetary and economic crisis that began in July 1997. Nonetheless, the Asian Crisis had to do with problems inherent in this industrialization. In other words, the strategy of export-oriented industrialization followed by various East Asian countries formed a general, industrial-economic background to the Crisis. The following accompanying problems may be cited: 1) the gradual loss of cost-induced competitive advantages over the course of the economic development; 2) the limitation of economies of scale in the export markets (hence the expansion in production capacity of multinational firms exceeded the growth in demand of the industrial countries, causing more intense competition); 3) the slow buildup of national technological bases (technology transfers were restricted to the investing firms); 4) the formation of economic enclaves (the setting up of industrial districts for export purposes, the rise of export-oriented foreign processing and assembly operations and parts manufacturers which only networked slightly with local firms); and 5) dependence upon imports of parts (and therefore expansion of the trade deficit) (Mishima, 1998; Ajia no jidai, 1998, p. 6).

There are disagreements about Krugman's assertion that the economic growth of East Asia was realized by adding production factors and that total factor productivity had little to do with it (Krugman, 1994). Be that as it may, the background referred to above would seem to show that the delay in the formation of productive capacity through the buildup of independent technologies in East Asia was no less important than the industrial-economic background to the Asian Crisis.

As regards the East Asian electronics industry, we can observe two distinct situations, that of the development started mainly by the introduction of production factors, and that of the development arising both from the introduction of production factors and from the increase in productivity according to individual countries and sectors (Suehiro, 1995). From this perspective, Krugman's claim is not always completely accurate with regard to the electronics industry. Even so, one must concede that the above-mentioned problems of delay in the formation of productive capacity as an industrial-economic background to the crisis are partly applicable to the East Asian electronics industry.

The business slump in Japan since the beginning of the 1990s enters into this question, even if it is not a direct factor in the crisis. The connection, apart from the influence of foreign competition, consists in the previously mentioned redeployment of production of the Japanese electronics industry (for the Japanese national economy this is considered part of the outfall of productive capital) and the resulting stronger link to East Asia, as well as in the changes, also mentioned, in the structure of production, trade and employment in the electronics industry. The Asian Crisis and the downturn in the business cycle in Japan have caused a further acceleration of the structural changes described above and have confronted the East Asian and Japanese electronics industry with even more difficult challenges.

The Asian Crisis and the currency decline in East Asia have led to an overall drop in production of the main electronic appliances in East Asia. However, the impact has had a double aspect, according to country and demand structure. An investigative report of the Organization of the Japanese Electronics Industry from 1998 presents this situation as follows: In China the growth in colour TVs, VCRs and household applicances, including domestic production, has leveled off. In the southern Chinese region, including Hong Kong, production has fallen for the first time in 30 years. In Korea the decline in value of the won has inflated the dollar obligations of the large electronics firms and dragged their financing structures along into serious trouble. Under the monitoring by the IMF, capital procurement became difficult. Investments in the semiconductor sector dropped by 41% and 51% in 1997 and 1998, respectively. Recovery is still not in sight: In Taiwan mobile telephones and computer peripherals have been doing well, which however has less to do with domestic production and more with the shift of production to the Chinese mainland. The production of AV devices has stagnated. DRAM production had a bad year in 1998. The utilization rate in the semiconductor "foundry" factories has sunk rapidly due to the market imbalance. In Singapore, too, semiconductor production has decreased, although to a lesser degree. By contrast, in Malaysia, where the domestic parts industry was relatively well developed, the electronics industry has profited nicely from the currency crash. Due to its orientation to the European and American markets, the household appliances sector in particular was little affected by the slump on the Asian markets. On the contrary, its competitiveness with exports compared with China and other countries even increased, which gave it "tailwind." (1998 Kaigai denshikogyo, p. 9 – 54).

Apart from Korea, where the chaebols have a stronger capital foundation than the other countries and regions in East Asia, the dependence upon foreign investors is very high. If we consider the effects of the Asian Crisis on the Japanese firms in the ASEAN countries from this perspective, then we find yet another double aspect. Japanese firms producing for the local market suffered from the slump in demand on the various domestic markets. For example, the audio-video market in Thailand dropped 30% from the beginning of the slump. In Indonesia, the decline in the case of household appliances was as much as 60% to 80%. In many places the utilization rate of production capacity sank to 20% or 30%. The entry prices of imported raw and other materials rose steeply because of the currency crisis, which necessarily caused a corresponding rise in the domestic sales prices. The domestic sales volume therefore decreased even further, so that there were additional losses in profit. All this can be traced to the weakness in the supporting industries, or, in other words, to the deceleration of the "flying-geese pattern" of industrial peak development in East Asia. Japanese firms in East Asia geared to production for export were, by contrast, little touched by the currency crisis, or even profited from the currency devaluations in various countries. Most of these firms thereby gained in international competitiveness. To be sure, the decline in demand in Asia and the recorded drop in exports to Japan also caused problems for these firms (Ajia no keizaikiki, p. 59; Ajia no okeru, 1999, p. 37; Amano, 1999, p. 27 - 52). A further consequence of the currency crisis is revealed in the realization of foreign exchange risks. Quite a few Japanese firms had neglected to provide for a serious hedging of foreign exchange risks entailed by debts recorded in dollars and yen when financing their investments and suffered substantial losses in foreign exchange.[2] Of course, the production sites of Japanese firms in the ASEAN, including those for semiconductor products, import or purchase their preliminary products, raw and other materials on a dollar basis, and the same applies to their exports and sales to

---

[2] Many electronics companies, e.g. Hitachi and Toshiba, sustained heavy foreign exchange losses. These were booked in the balance of 1997 under special losses (Ajia no kaizaikiki, p. 57)

domestic branches of foreign firms. In such a structure, the influence of exchange rate fluctuations is limited (Ajia no keizaikiki, p. 81).

The Russian crisis triggered by the devaluation of the rouble in August 1998 was a blow to the Japanese production sites in ASEAN for AV equipment, which they supplied to the Russian market by way of the Middle East and Near East or Eastern Europe. The expected weakening of the business cycle in the USA was the occasion for these plants to downsize their production plans for the US market. The worsening of the business cycle in China and in Central and South America, the persistent recession in Japan, and the cyclical slump in Britain fueled rumours about a worldwide recession and further worsened the climate for the exporting locations in Asia. Hence, the Japanese electronics producers in ASEAN also had a difficult situation, and in October many of them in some cases reduced their volume-of-sales predictions for the second compared to the first half of the year by over 20% (Furukawa, 1998, p. 37).

Hence the direct involvements of Japanese firms after the Asian Crisis and under the influence of the Japanese recession have sharply declined. The fact that less capital flowed from the main provider nation, Japan, might have had serious consequences for East Asia's electronics industry, with its dependence upon foreign capital, and at the time this was a source of considerable concern to the various East Asian governments.

As regards the business cycle of the electronics industry in Japan, growth in production flattened out due to the weak domestic phase and the economic turmoil in Asia in the second half of 1997, and then dropped into negative figures from November of that year (Denshikogyo, 1999, p. 39). In 1998, gross production value and exports in the electronics industry showed negative figures for the first time in five years, as did imports for the first time in six years. The reasons were the continuing weak cycle in Japan, the upward revaluation of the yen, and the Asian recession. As a result, employment in the electronics industry in the sixth year went into decline. The number of employees was only 87.4% compared to 1992. Direct investments of the electrotechnical and electronics industry in the first half of fiscal 1998 did manage to retain their top position in Japan's manufacturing industry, but in comparison to the previous year they only reached a level of 51.3%, whereas total direct investments in the manufacturing industry reached 74.5% (1999 nen ni okeru, p. 1 – 4). In the case of the semiconductor industry, the basis of the whole electronics industry, a definite worsening of the market situation set in. The world market share of the Japanese semiconductor industry, which had still been at 39% in 1991, had shrunk to 22% by 1998 (Table 1). Between 1996 and 1998, i.e., over a period of three years, the Japanese semiconductor market recorded negative growth. As already mentioned, Japan's share of the world market for semiconductors up to 1991 was higher than those of the USA, Europe or the total shares of the other Asian countries. The USA was the first to surpass Japan, in 1992. In 1998, Japan for the first time came in last, behind Europe and Asia, with 20.6%.[3] The reasons behind this are to be found in the competitive situation, intensified by the Asian Crisis, the worsening of the export environment, and the stagnation of the Japanese economy. Hence the devaluations of the Korean and Taiwanese currencies caused by the Asian Crisis unleashed a competition in low prices, in consequence of which the Japanese semiconductor market was also depressed and the profit picture of the Japanese firms worsened. Due to the rise in consumer taxes and the uncertainties in the financial system, the demand of private households decreased, leading to a slump in production of electronics appliances for this sector. The gloomy cyclical outlook of the firms, another result of the uncertainties of the financial system, dampened investments in equipment and also led to a slump in the products of the electronics industry intended for this area. Because of the persistent sinking prices, semiconductor production noticeably declined as well. For this reason, the five Electro-Universal firms, accounting for a good 60% of the entire Japanese semiconductor production, recorded losses in 1998. Taken together with losses in the area of household appliances, this fact meant a worsening of their entire business performance for these large manufacturers. If we consider only the big firms which also deal in household appliances, we see that Matsushita, Sony, Toshiba and Sanyo, on a consolidated basis, recorded setbacks in their turnovers and profits, and that Hitachi and Mitsubishi suffered losses and reductions in turnover. Therefore Japan's firms had to substantially reduce their investments in equipment (in 1998, a mere half of the amount in 1995 was invested). On the other hand, firms like the US semiconductor company Micron Technology, as well as Korean and Taiwanese outfits, made large-scale investments, and European firms too showed growth in the area of semiconductors (Amano, 1999, p. 14; Heisei 11 nenban, 1999, p. 69; Nihon keizai shinbun, February 7, 1999).

The semiconductor sector expanded its share from 9.8% of the Japanese electrotechnical and electronics industry in 1985 to 15.1% in 1995. This fact reveals not only the substantial rise in volume of production, but also the extent of the effects exerted in the period between these years by profit fluctuations in the semiconductor sector upon the entire industry. In this case, a clearly increased instability in the profit picture became evident for the big Japanese Electro-Universal firms. The profit slump in the semiconductor sector already referred to and the decline in earnings in other segments (household appliances, computer peripherals, communications devices, heavy electrotechnical equipment) added up to a historical low point in total earnings of 0.4% (Illustration 3). In contrast to the previous cycles in silicon, this present outcome is closely connected to the worsened competitive position of Japanese firms in the semiconductor sector. There seemed to be a danger that the previous structural strength of Japanese firms in compensating for problems in low-yield sectors through high-yield or stable

---

3 The figures for the US in 1998 was 33% (WSTS, 1999).

ones would be lost (Amano, 1999, p. 19 – 21; Nihon no kikaikogyo, p. 69; Nihon keizai shinbun, February 21st, 1999).

The bad shape that the large firms got into, one after the other, shows what a crisis the entire Japanese electronics industry was in. Up to this point, the frequently stressed erosion of this industry had not been coupled with a crisis in the large, multinational Japanese firms, but now the two things were proceeding hand in hand.

It is hardly necessary to emphasize that the extent of the erosion, triggered primarily by the displacement of production to foreign countries, was significantly expanded by the difficult situation in the small and middle-sized firms of the electronics industry. The assessment of the business cycle from 1997 to 1998 also worsened for these small and middle-sized firms of the electronics industry. This was shown by the setback in production caused by the worsening of cyclical prospects and by the notably reduced investments in equipment, as well as by the decline in direct and indirect exports to Southeast Asia (Heisei 11 nendoban, 1999, p. 340 – 404). Nor was this the end of the consequences brought by the Asian Crisis and the unfavourable business cycle in the home country. On the contrary, in this case as well structural instabilities emerged which the Japanese electronics industry and electronics firms had to bear until the summer of 1997. Here we perceive that there was an existential crisis in the large firms, apparently the first ever suffered by the Japanese electronics industry.

A basic cause of this existential crisis was that the Electro-Universal firms had not adequately analyzed the earning potential of their individual branches. Above all, in the semiconductor branch, where as noted above the Japanese industry, following in the traces of the Americans, the leaders in the computer industry, had emphasized general computer memory chips, the Japanese firms, in comparison to their American, European and Asian competitors, neglected to strengthen and concentrate on new areas of specialization. The line of products was more typical of a department store, and there was a high degree of vertical integration. There was also a closely connected tendency to take into account narrower customer demands, both from one's own departments or from allied firms. Business was accordingly developed internally, i.e., directed towards one's own group. (The Japanese semiconductor manufacturers have, right down to the present, regarded the Asian firms in Korea and Taiwan as their competitors and only reluctantly formed alliances with European and American firms; in production and distribution they have always been fixated on the domestic market.) The structural change towards orientation to the outside world, and to a division of labour that spans both firms and groupings got off to a late start (Amano, 1999, p. 55; Nihon keizai shinbun, February 21st, 1999). The current crisis of the firms has revealed that the preparations of Japanese firms for global competition were inadequate through the mid-1990s.

The example of Matsushita reveals the inadequate and tardy preparations of the Japanese Electro-Universal firms for global competition from another perspective. This firm had the longest experience with globalization and at present has the largest number of foreign subsidiaries. Its organization resembled a matrix structure containing six regional headquarters. Its management is trying hard to move from its centralization in Japan through decentralization to a global form of management. There were, to be sure, many difficulties in realizing this company policy, once it was postulated, and because of this, the firm did not succeed in its responses to the violent exchange rate fluctuations in 1997. The investment earnings of the 211 foreign subsidiaries were extremely poor. To respond flexibly to such fluctuations, it was necessary to keep local inventories low and to cut down lead times. That is, the point was taken that a global information system was necessary for this, but Matsushita had no such system in place. The firm was not in a position to grasp, quickly and correctly, the situation regarding distribution in the firms of the group, which were spread all over the world. If this was true of Matsushita, one can imagine what things were like in the other Japanese firms (with the exception of Sony) (Matsushitadenki, 1997). With reference to the main theme of my paper, it should be noted that the deepening of cooperation, complementarity and mutual dependence between Japan and East Asia means that the mutual influence exerted by the capital provider nation and the capital receiver nation on each other's economies is being reinforced. Thus the period of peak growth in East Asia until 1996 constituted a highly positive environmental factor for the Japanese economy, which was suffering from the bursting of the bubble economy. But when the currency and economic crisis broke out in July 1997, this mutual influence turned negative (Heisei 11 nendoban, 1999, p. 115). A typical example of this is the way the Japanese Electro-Universal firms throttled their direct investments in the East Asian electronics industry because of their own existential crisis. Moreover, this circumstance helped bring to an end the ability of the Japanese parent companies to support money-losing subsidiaries in the USA and Europe, as they had done earlier.

3.2 Reactions of the Electronics Industry to Globalization Processes, the Asian Crisis and the Recession in Japan

Of the various strategies used by the East Asian electronics industry as a reaction to the Asian Crisis, measures taken by the various governments are the first thing one is struck by: a) The Thai government accepted the depreciation of its currency with the aim of reviving its economy through exports. To strengthen its competitiveness in the export markets, the duties on imported capital assets were lowered. These are typical examples of the deregulation of rules about foreign capital and in the trade and currency systems which was undertaken in various countries and regions as a consequence of the currency crisis. b) In Korea the government led the reform targeted on the conglomerates of firms, the chaebols.

In this context the attempt was made to strengthen the semiconductor sector by the merger of Hyundai Electronics and LG Electronics. As in Silicon Valley, a Media-Valley-Plan was developed. Singapore is also striving for the agglomeration of peripheral industries with its "Industry 21" concept, developed in 1998. High-tech venture business firms will be located in areas designated as the "Science Hub," in the framework of a policy aimed at developing intensively value-enhancing high-tech industries. Factory parks specializing in lead-time manufacturing stages, so-called Wafer Fab Parks, were established, thereby signalling the aim of mergers of the firms with European, American and Japanese firms. In addition there are measures of the government intended to acquire and develop operational headquarters and to import advanced production technologies. The large-scale Chinese state project, Plan 909, intended to develop Chinese semiconductor production, had a symbolic character in this project as well. With government support, the industries upstream of semiconductor production will also be strengthened. c) To develop the division of labour with ASEAN, AFTA was agreed as a duty-free zone. By 2002 the six main member nations will have declared duty-free status for 60% of commodities, and by 2015, they are to eliminate all customs duties, with this policy applying to all the members by 2018 (1998 Kaigai, p. 9 – 11; 1999 Tonanajia, 1999, p. 8 – 39; Amano, 1999; Nihon keizai shinbun, September 30, 1999 and October 8, 1999).

Naturally one should not overlook the entrepreneurial and private-business areas. In Taiwan and Singapore, firms are taking up strategies to enhance their self-producing capacity in major components and are also forming alliances with major foreign companies. Equipment manufacturers (electronics manufacturing services firms, or EMSs), design firms and high-tech venture firms are also in the offing. In China the big state firms are establishing themselves as producers of general household appliances and improving their competitiveness. Firms originating in Taiwan and Hong Kong are opening up fields for business as equipment manufacturers (EMSs) for themselves (1999 Tonanajia, 1999). Of course the strategies cited for developing primary industries and strengthening high technologies in the wider sphere of semiconductors, which are directed both publicly and privately, also have the goal of regaining the foreign capital that stayed away during the Asian Crisis. But these are not merely short-term countermeasures. They are striving for a mid- and long-term strengthening of their own industrial base and a continuing development of the electronics industry in areas with high value creation. In so doing, they are simultaneously tackling the structural problems that have hitherto beset the East Asian electronics industry in the wake of the globalization processes affecting it.

As regards the local Japanese firms, many of them that formerly aimed their production at the regional market have now lowered their rate of utilization, let go redundant personnel, undertaken rationalizations to intensify investment capital and made every effort to reconfigure their marketing strategy for exports. Japanese parent firms gave their East Asian subsidiaries a certain amount of capital assistance to compensate for their losses in foreign exchange during the currency crisis. On the basis of the liberalization of the regulations affecting foreign capital, the capital share in joint stock firms was unilaterally pumped up by the Japanese. Further short-term countermeasures were the opening of new export markets in the Near and Middle East and in Vietnam. To increase the local quota of procurements, local parts manufacturers were given technological support. The same goal was behind the tailoring of product design to the potential of local manufacturers. With a view to further liberalization of trade in the ASEAN region in the manner of AICO (the ASEAN Industry Cooperation Plan) or AFTA, Japanese firms have used the economic crisis and pushed ahead with the construction of a system of horizontal division of labour in this region. The production sites in ASEAN and China established for exports to Japan, Europe and the USA have already been able to improve their competitiveness due to the currency depreciation, and many firms have expanded their production capacities. Currency depreciation and recession have depressed real estate prices, personnel costs and other production costs in the ASEAN nations, so that outsourcings of production from Japan with the goal of lowering production costs are taking place as they did previously. Quite a few firms are undertaking new investments, because in their assessment, ASEAN and China will continue to be production sites for the world market (Ajia no keizaikiki, p. 61 – 92).

In the case of semiconductor production, local Japanese factories will not be dismantled, on the contrary, additional investments succeeded in bringing about the expansion of production in downstream stages. A poll of the Japanese KMUs asked the firms, among other questions, whether they would withdraw from Asia because of the poor prospects due to the Asian Crisis. No Japanese KMU in the ASEAN nations answered yes, and in Taiwan, an NIEs country, there was only one yes from a Japanese KMU. Over half the local KMUs, 56%, want to maintain their present involvements. The same proportion of the KMUs, 56%, also think that Thailand will continue to gain importance as an industrial and exporting site, which places it at the top in their assessment. For the ASEAN nations overall, 44% shared this opinion, and among the NIEs the figure was 30% (Higashiajia, 1999, p. 37). The typical observation about the Japanese semiconductor producers, that they are dismantling their production sites in Europe and the USA, goes together with these positive assessments of the Asian sites (1999 nendoban, p. 375). There are of course voices that regard these closures as a step back in the process of globalization (Amano, 1999, p. 11 – 12 and 53), but one should rather see in these strategies the efforts of the large Japanese firms and KMUs to form globally optimized production and procurement systems robust enough to withstand exchange rate fluctuations. And so, as a consequence of the Asian Crisis, and in the midst of the Japanese recession, the firms are increasingly concentrating upon the Asian region (Heisei 11 nihon no kikaikokyo, p. 97; Ajia no keizaikiki, p. 93). Of course this does not contribute to a solution of the problem of the erosion of the electronics industry in Japan. In fact, these strategies are even leading in part to an intensification of the problem.

The big electronics and electrotechnical firms have truly seized upon drastic restructuring measures, among them hefty cutbacks in personnel as well as the conversion of central administrative buildings into securities (practically speaking, the sale of the buildings), as in the case of NEC (Nichibei no daikigyo, 1999, p. 86).[4] As to mid- and long-term strategies, interest is focussed on the restructuring of every business sector, with the new ordering of the semiconductor industry at the centre. For this sector the following strategies can be listed: First, withdrawal from the general DRAM sector, which has become a factor dragging down earnings, and instead increased use of "intellectual property" in the design and awarding of production commissions to the foundry firms in Taiwan. Second, reinforcement of cutting-edge technology for memory chips through comprehensive alliances among big Japanese firms, or, in the case of NEC, through the passing on of important technology to Korean firms, all with the aim of spreading the risk. Third, the strengthening of the business areas (including every kind of alliance) of system LSI and logic chips, which are required in the fast-growth digital household and AV appliances and in mobile communication devices. Fourth, strengthening of the business areas of software and problem-solving schemes. Fifth, further strengthening of precision production technology. Sixth, revision of the vertically integrated organizational form through the introduction of the concept of the "firm within the firm," and with the goal of accelerating decision-making processes. The strategies for strengthening business fields subsume areas other than semiconductors, including specialties of the individual large firms, so that one cannot describe them as unified strategies.

These are all no more or less than the restructuring processes of the Japanese firms, in order to revise the business structure based mainly on the computer area and to place the emphasis in business on the areas with a future, such as information networks, digital household appliances and AV devices, software and problem-solving applications. The KMUs are also taking on many various strategies of adaptation and restoration. Here we should take special note of the increasing foundation of venture firms, such as the emergence of production-lot semiconductor firms (1999 nendoban, p. 3 – 7; Nihon no kikaikogyo, p. 97 – 100). As regards business with foreign countries, the already mentioned firm Matsushita-Panasonic will put its multi-netting system, connecting five regions of Japan, USA, Europe, Hong Kong and Asia with each other, into operation from April 2000, in order to lower the accounting costs of the concern through international equalization, or by accounting for credits and debits arising from trade within the ,firms of the group around the world. To this end, the business department is trying to design electronic parts and devices of the firm, including the Global Information System, by fiscal 2000, for a worldwide network of information delivery, so as to reduce its inventory by 50% and be able to react much more quickly to scheduling changes by customers. All these measures can

4 Until the year 2000 NEC has tried to dismiss almost 25.000 employees.

be seen as the hitherto delayed reaction of the Matsushita Concern to the ever advancing globalization processes of the world electronics industry. But one can also say that the Asian Crisis and the recession in Japan were their direct cause (Nihon keizai shinbun, May 29, 1998, April, 28, 2000; Nikkei sangyo shibun, February 3, 2000).

Finally, one is struck by various measures of the Japanese government, for instance, the support of restructuring measures within the framework of the law on special measures for the new ordering of industrial activity, or programmes in the so-called Millenium Project, which attempts a revitalization of the economy through the development of small and middle-sized firms, and also of research, development and information. The large firms are at present applying for these programmes. We can see in this an alliance of industry, bureaucracy and science as a response to the crisis of the entire Japanese electronics industry (Nihon keizai shinbun, July 22, August 3, November 3, 1999).[5]

4 Prospects

In the strategies resorted to as a response to globalization, as a reaction to the Asian Crisis and to the Japanese recession, the tendency can be found that East Asia has not only asserted its position as a site for mass production for the electronics industry and as an international procurement base within (although not exclusively) the European, American, Japanese and Asian groups of firms, but will continue to expand and develop it. Japanese, American and European multinational firms will rapidly transfer to Asia not only the mass production of standard products, but also new products, incorporating new stages of development and design, now that they are capable of mass production on the basis of their internal division of labour. Depending on the product, it is also possible that R&D as well as central administrative functions will be transferred. Nothing essential will change in the classical international transferral of industries according to the observable pattern of the flight of wild geese. Many Japanese electronics firms intend, once the currency crisis is over, to use Asia as a production and exporting site even more intensively in this regard. Japanese firms that go abroad increasingly show the tendency to concentrate on Asia. This tendency expresses their reaction to the potential of Asia, which exists just as it did before the Crisis, to continue to grow as a gigantic market of the electronics industry. To realize this potential, primary industries must be developed, the high-tech sector of firms must grow, and intraregional local competition must be regulated, which is surely no simple matter. Even so, it can be expected that the

5 Without exception, other Japanese firms also try to implement similar measures (Amano, 1999, p. 59 – 61).

East Asian electronics industry will develop over the long term in the direction described.

In the Japanese electronics industry the various firms are planning their flight from the Crisis, which has affected the entire industry. The Universal firms, active in global competition, are expanding their special sectors, forming alliances at home and abroad, and are decentralizing and slimming down their organizations. Venture firms are being founded and supported. All these measures are no doubt indispensable. However, they will not lead to any fundamental change in the structure of the Japanese electronics industry. Japanese firms, unlike their powerful American competitors, certainly were not able to grasp in a goal-directed way the demand for semiconductors growing out of the development of the computer industry. The sector of digital household appliances and AV information devices, seen today as having growth potential, is nevertheless a specialty of the Japanese electronics industry. The Electro-Universal firms will in all probability be able to exert their international competitiveness, if they use further improved information transfers between the semiconductor and appliances sectors, so that they can quickly and purposefully grasp the mutual requirements involved. A general competitive advantage of the Universal firm will continue to be sustainable, according to sector. In particular, the investments of the overseas Japanese firms will by no means lead to a loss of quality in the shopfloor-based Japanese production technology (development and production systems). True, in the area of supporting industries, the problem of erosion has in some cases worsened, but as a leading industrial nation, Japan has at its disposal its own agglomeration, an advantage which it still appears to be preserving (Amano, 1999, p. 55; Chosahokoku, July 1999).

As to the future development, the Japanese electronics industry will shape its own hybrid structures. The Universal firm, with its decentralized organization, will form the axis. Venture firms, connected by horizontal division of labour, and which are already appearing, will also form a part of it. The industrial structure will be held up by a broad fundament of supporting industries and industrial agglomerations. Every firm and every business sector within this fundament will have to develop its own globalization strategies. On the basis of the hybrid structure the attempt will be made to gain new competitive advantages. One such, not the least, will be founded on advances in the as yet relatively weak sector of software-based technologies and network technologies. But some time will still have to pass before the hybrid structure takes on specific form.

As to the relationship between the Japanese and the East Asian electronics industries, it appears that the Japanese electronics industry, with its comprehensive and varied developmental potential and agglomeration, will, at least for the present, be in the leading position in East Asia, and that therefore the cooperative and competitive relations of the electronics industries of Japan and of East Asia will continue in this sense (Takami, 1999, p. 20 – 27). It goes without saying that these findings cannot be generalized. They are limited to the electronics industries which were chosen as example for demonstrating the effects for globalization and crisis. Competitive and cooperative relationships in other sectors, however, might be quite differently effected.

Table 1: Proportion of worldwide semiconductor production by region

In US$, (%)

	1991	1992	1993	1994	1995	1996	1997	1998
Japan	28.774 (39)	27.070 (35.2)	31.961 (36)	39.465 (33.3)	50.931 (31.5)	43.747 (28.4)	39.332 (24.6)	33.259 (21.8)
North America	19.917 (27)	21.682 (28.2)	24.481 (27.6)	33.143 (27.6)	42.231 (26.2)	43.507 (28.3)	46.691 (29.2)	50.030 (32.8)
Europe	6.621 (9)	6.907 (9)	7.592 (8.6)	9.372 (7.9)	13.133 (8.1)	12.865 (8.4)	13.570 (8.5)	14.475 (9.5)
Asia	18.467 (25)	21.290 (27.6)	24.604 (27.6)	36.659 (30.9)	55.280 (34.2)	53.643 (34.9)	60.230 (37.7)	54.831 (35.9)
Sum	73.779 (100)	76.949 (100)	88.638 (100)	118.639 (100)	161.575 (100)	153.762 (100)	159.823 (100)	152.595 (100)

Source: Denshi-Journal (Electronics-Journal): Handoutai (Semiconductor) Data Book from 1993 to 1998

Table 2: Number of japanese production subsidiaries abroad (1998)

Product	NIEs	ASEAN4	China	Asia	World
Consumer Goods	50	105	76	245	357
Industrial Products	39	55	55	157	266
Components	166	237	144	556	757
Year					
Before 1978	117	29	0	149	230
1979-1973	20	17	2	42	86
1984-1988	56	96	18	148	297
1989-1993	32	142	84	233	354
1994-1998	14	103	169	301	379
Sum	231	351	258	873	1.274

Source: Electronics Industries Association of Japan (ed,): Kaigai Hojin (List of Japanese Foreign Corporations), and Elctronics Industries Association of Japan (ed.): Nippon no Densi Kogyo 1999 (Japanese Electronics Industry 1999)

Figure 1: Value of Imports of Electrical Appliances and Electronic Machinery from East Asia

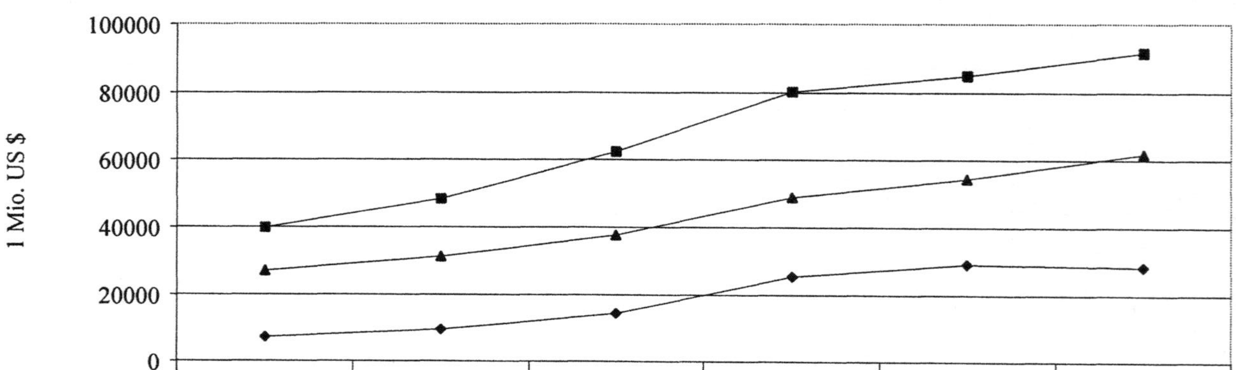

	1992	1993	1994	1995	1996	1997
Japan	7262,624	9560,348	14474,83	25383,34	29066,62	28315,77
USA	39765,82	48432,91	62393,34	80288,63	85007,75	91625,01
Europe	26878,56	31155,74	37585,96	48995,07	54518,61	61788,98

Source: Foreign Trade by Commodities 1992 – 1997,

Note: "Electrical Appliances and Electronic Machinery" here means 75 office machines & automatic data processing machines, 76 telecommunication & sound recording apparatus and 77 electrical machinery & appliances.

Figure 2: Value of Exports of Electrical Appliances and Electronic machinery to East Asia

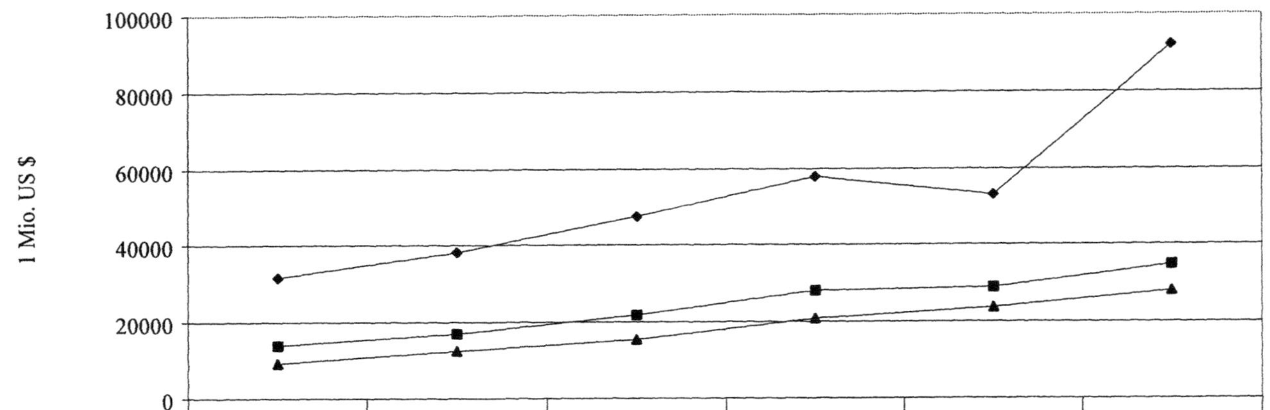

	1992	1993	1994	1995	1996	1997
Japan	31612,63	38133,78	47533,71	57958,34	53126,83	91995,76
USA	13837,99	16917,08	21793,91	28044,29	28915,83	34761,01
Europe	9120,363	12351,31	15354,6	20812,13	23693,48	27992,9

Source: Foreign Trade by Commodities 1992-1997, OECD, 1999

Figure 3: Developments in the Consolidated Operating Profits / Losses of the Big Five Japanese Electronics Companies*

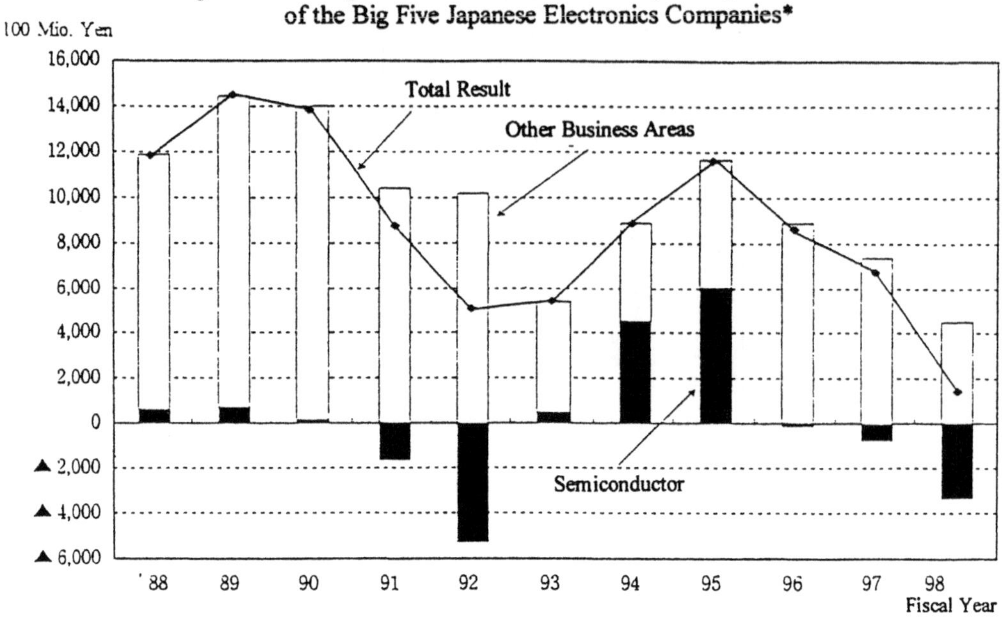

Source: Amano, Kyoko: Wagakuni Handotaisangyo ni okeru kigyo senryaku (Business Strategy in the Japanese Semiconductor Industry), in: Chosa (JDB Research Report), No. 259, ed. By Nihon Kaihatsu Ginko (Japan Development Bank), August 1999, S. 19.

Note : * NEC, Toshiba, Hitachi, Fujitsu and Mitsubishi Electric.

List of References

Ajia keizai no doyo ga nihon ni ataeru eikyo (Influence of the Disturbance in Asian Economy on Japan), in: Dai-ichi-kangin soken rebu, March 1998

Ajia ni okeru kaigaichokusetsutoshi (Foreign Direct Investment in Asia), in: *Ekonomikku Risachi* (Economic Research), March, 1999

Ajia no jidai ni okeru shitauke chushokigyo no sapotingu indasutori senryaku (The Strategy of Industrial Support by the Middle and Small Subcontracting Business), Kikaishinkokyokai keizai-kenkyujo, 1998

Ajia no keizaikiki to nihon kigyo (Asian Crisis and Japanese Enterprises), in: *Dai-ichi-kangin soken rebu* (Research Review of the Dai-ichi-Kangyo Bank), April 1998

Amano, Kyoko: Wagakuni handotaisangyo ni okeru kigyo senryaku –ajia sho-koku no doko kara no kosatsu (Business Strategy in Japanese Semiconductor Industry – View from the Trend in Asian Countries), in: *Chosa* (JDB Research Report), No. 259, Nihonkaihatsuginko (Japan Development Bank), August 1999, p. 10 – 26

Chosahokoku chusho kigyo man surii (Monthly Research Report on Middle and Small Business), July 1999

Dai 27 kai wagakuni kigyo no kaigaijigyo katsudo (27. Research on the Foreign Business of the Japanese Enterprises), Tsusansho (MITI), 1999

Denshikogyo nenkan 1999 (Yearbook on the Electronics Industry 1999), Denpa shinbunsha, 1999

Furukawa, Keiji: Sekidoajia no hikari to kage (Light and Darkness of the Equator-Asia), in: *Denshi* (Electronics), Shadanhojin nihondenshikikai gyokai, December 1998

Heisei 11 nenban nihon no kikaikogyo (The Japanese Machinery Industry 1999), Zaidanhojin kikaishinkokyokai keizaikenkyujo, 1999

Heisei 11 nenban tsusho hakusho (White Book of Trade 1999)

Heisei 11 nendoban chushokigyo hakusho (White Book on the Middle and Small Business, 1999), Chushokigyocho, 1999, p. 340 – 404

Higashiajia no keizaikiki no norikiru nikkeichushokigyo (Fighting against the East Asian Economic Crisis: Japanese Middle and Small Business in East Asia), Chushokigyo kin'yukoko chosabu, 1999

Hiramoto, Atsushi: Nihon no terebisangyo (The Japanese Television Industry), Minerva-shobo, 1996

Itagaki, Hiroshi (ed.): Nihonteki keiei seisan shisutemu to higashiajia (Japanese Business and Production System and East Asia), Minerva-shobo, 1997, p. 189 – 305

Kadensangyo ni okeru wagakuni to asean no aratana bungyo seisantaisei no ko-chiku (Formation of the New Division of Labor System between Japan and ASEAN Electrical and Electronics Appliance Industrie), Chushokigyo kinyuko chosabu, June, 1997

Krugman, Paul: The Myth of Asia's Miracle, in: *Foreign Affairs*, Nov./Dec., 1994

Matsushitadenki no kaigaikeiei (Foreign Business of Matsushita Electric Company), Matsushitadenki kabushikigaisha kaigaikikakushitsu, 1997

Mishima, Kazuo: Higashiajia ni okeru sangyokodoka no kadai – erekutoronikusu sangyo no chushin ni (The Challenge of the Advanced Industrial Structure in East Asia – in Focus on the Electronics Industry), in: Japan Research Review, Kabu-shikigaisha Nihon sogokenkyujo, Vol. 8, 12, December 1998

Mitarai, HISAMI: Higashiajia no denshibuhinsangyo to nihon no sangyo chosei (The East Asian Electronics Parts Industry and the Industrial Restructuring in Japan), in: Kitamura, Kayoko (ed.): Higashiajia no kogyoka to nihon sangyo no shinkokusaika-senryaku (The Industrialization in East Asia and the Strategy of New Industrialization of the Japanese Industry), Ajiakeizai kenkyujo, 1995, p. 237 – 243

Nichibei no daikigyo ni yoru jin 'insakugen no doko (Trend on the Personnel Reduction by the Big Business in Japan and USA), in: Dai-ichi-kangin soken rebu, No. 2, 1999

Nihon keizai shinbun (The Japanese Economic Newspaper),

Nihon no denshikogyo 1999 (The Japanese Electronics Industry), Shadanhojin nihon denshikikai kogyokai, 1999

Nikkei sangyo shinbun (Nikkei Industrial Daily), February 3, 2000

Sangyogakkai (ed.): Sengo nihon sangyo (The Development of Japanese Industry after the World War II), Toyokeizai shinposha, 1995

Satake, Noriaki: Kaigai-seisanshifuto ni tomonau shinkeieisutairu no tsuikyu (The Qest for New Business Style under the Trend of Production Shift to Overseas), in: *Nomura Research*, November 1994

Shimada, Katsumi, Fujii, Mitsuo and Kobayashi, Eiji (eds.): Gendai ajia no sangyo hatten to kokusai bungyo (Industrial Development in Modern Asia and the International Division of Labor), Mineruvashobo, 1997

Shinshuntaidan atarashii chushokigyo ga 21 seiki o kirihiraku (New Years Talk. New Middle and Small Business Open up the 21 Century), in: *Chosageppo* (Monthly Research Report), Kokumin kin'yukoko, January 1997, No. 429

Suehiro, Akira: Dynamism of the Industrialization in Asia, in: Kudo, Akira (ed.): *Twentieth Century Capitalism II*, University of Tokyo Press, 1995

Takeuchi, Junko: Erekutoronikusu sangyo no ajia tenkai (Development of Electronics Industry in Asia), in: *Ajia no keizaihatten to chusho-kigyo* (Asian Economy and Middle and Small Business), Sakura Sogo Kenkyujo Kantaiheiyo Kenkyu Center, Nihonhyoronsha, 1999

Takami, Koji: Den kikikai sangyo no kokusai tenkai (Internationalization of the Electrotechnical Industry), in: *Sangy ricchi* (The Industrial Location), June 1999, p. 20 - 27

Tran Yan Tho: Ajia no sangyo hatten to takokusekikigyo (Industrial Development in Asai and Multinational Enterprises), in: *Kaigaitoshi kenkyuho* (Report of the Institute for Foreign Investment Research), Nihon yushutsunyu ginko, March – April, 1999.

Ueda, Kazuo: Ajia kiki no keikenshite (The Experience of Asian Crisis), in: *Kaigai toshi kenyuho*, May, 1998

WSTS 1999 Shuki handotaishijo yosokukekka (WSTS 1999 Spring-Edition of the Semiconductor Market Estimation, IDC, Japan, July 1999

Yearbook of World Electronics Data 1998, Tokyo, 1999

1996 International Trade Statistics Yearbook, United Nations, New York, 1997

1996 nen tonanajia denshikogyo no dokochosa hokokusho (Research Report on the Trend of the Electronics Industry in South-East Asia, 1996), Shadanhojin nihondenshikikai kogyokai, 1996

1998 Kaigai denshikogyo no doko chosa hokokusho (Research Report on the Trend of the Electronics Industry Overseas), Shadanhojin nihondenshikikai kogyokai 1998

1998 nen ni okeru denshikogyo no doko (Trend of Electronics Industry 1998, 1999)

1999 nendoban handotai sangyokeikaku soran (1999 Yearbook of Business Plan of Semiconductor Industry), Sangyotaimuzusha, 1999

1999 Tonanajia denshikogyo no dokochosa hokokusho (Research Report on the Trend of the Electronics Industry in South-East Asia), Shadanhojin nihondenshikikai kogyokai, 1999, p. 8 – 39

Globalization and Crisis and Their Effects upon Japan and China – Judged by Assessing Their Regional Positioning and Foreign Mergers and Acquisitions

Wolfgang Klenner

Ruhr-Universität Bochum

1 Introduction

China, as well as Japan, is increasingly regarded as one of the dominant national economies in the East and Southeast Asian region. Japan, which produces about 70% of the entire GDP of Asia (computed in U.S. dollars), possesses the highest savings in the world, and stands at the pinnacle of technology, tends, to be sure, to exercise restraint and prefer subtle methods in extending its influence beyond its borders. China, on the other hand, has adopted an ambitious posture, considering its present economic power, and is unmistakably pressing its claim to be a leader. In any case, both these national economies belong to countries which have the basic ability, in their own opinion and that of their partners and competitors around the world, to position themselves to their best economic advantage and to take on important economic leadership functions. To what extent this will actually happen depends not least upon how they come to terms with the symptoms of crisis of recent years and with the challenges of increasing globalization processes. The following comments will deal with these questions.

2 Clarification of Concepts and Preliminary Considerations

A few clarifications of concepts and preliminary considerations are in order: The positionings of Japan and China will be examined mainly with regard to their willingness and ability to take on leadership functions in the broadest sense. Among the pertinent topics are stabilization of their own economies and those of their partner nations, the provision of stimuli for growth, and responsible monetary policies.

Globalization is defined as two related developments. One is the set of processes of the last decade embodying the specific characteristic of "borderless" activities by firms. For example, firms are by now able to acquire their necessary capital in Japan and their raw materials from Africa or Australia, carry out production in China or even in Burma or North Korea, do research in Switzerland, develop designs in Hong Kong, plan their marketing strategies in the USA, and finally sell all over the world. The driving force behind this development is the set of worldwide connections provided by physical, but primarily virtual, networks. It both enables and demands cross-border expansion, means that hardly a single country is now out beyond the pale of information, saves on transaction costs, forces business into global locational competition as well as into a new international division of labour in consequence of the overcoming of temporal and spatial constraints, and ultimately disciplines the concepts and methods of national economic policies, especially regulatory policies. The other pertinent topic, at least at present, is the worldwide spread of concepts about regulatory policies, approaches to organisational solutions, economic patterns of behaviour, accounting regulations, etc., mainly in the forms developed in the Anglo-American realm. The consequence of this may be that the manufacturing concerns and financing institutions which adapt most quickly to corresponding norms and behaviours will gain considerable competitive advantages. Certainly the individual economic results achieved need not necessarily be "better" from a national-economic or societal point of view. They may even, if we take as examples the goals of Germany's social market economy or the social order in Japan, which is more strongly fixated on consensus, be evaluated as "worse." But apart from this, a country with a high "degree of globalization" seems to offer its firms better preconditions for survival in international competition and for building advantageous forms of cooperation than a national economy resistant to globalizing tendencies.

Globalizing processes are marked by many different indicators. They include quantitative units of measurement such as the dimensions of international trade patterns, financial investments, and direct investments. Because globalizing processes cause qualitative changes, qualitative indicators are also suitable, such as the degree of the spread of internationally common accounting guidlines, increasingly important at present, or the orientation of business decisions towards shareholder value. In the following comments, a quantitative indicator will mainly be referred to in order to assess the globalizing processes in Japan and China, namely, the extent in both countries of ongoing foreign mergers and acquisitions. Mergers are unifications of economic units in such a way that only one of them survives and then takes on all the assets and obligations of the others. Acquisitions are defined as the acquisition of all or part of the assets of a firm, which continues to exist as an economic unit. Mergers and acquisitions have been common in the West for many decades, but have become significant in Japan and China only in recent years. They therefore seem an appropriate indicator for this study, because they lead much more intensively to confrontations with regulatory structures and with organisational and technical standards and behaviours than international commodity movements and financial investments and the like, and even more intensively than new formations of international joint ventures or straight subsidiaries of foreign firms, and because they exert great pressure on the "weaker" partner to adapt. To this extent, they can be seen as the result of ongoing globalizing processes and at the same time as stimuli for even further globalizing processes.

3 On the Positioning of Japan and China during the Financial Crisis

As a result of the Asian financial crisis, changes in the regional and world economic positioning of individual nation economies can be observed. Sustained economic successes and the efficient performance of world-economic leadership functions have strengthened the position of the United States even further. On the other hand, weaknesses in the Asian region among several national economies have triggered a definite negative snowballing effect. The positioning of Japan and China in particular has been transformed.

3.1 Japan

Japan suffered setbacks on two fronts. It was not possible to overcome the domestic economic problems caused at the end of the 1980s by an inappropriate expansionist monetary policy (see C.F. Bergsten, C.R. Henning, *Global Economic Leadership and the Group of Seven*). Despite all the economic stimuli, including the lowering of interest rates to a worldwide almost unprecedented degree, extensive fiscal-policy programmes raising the share of state debt in the GDP to over 130%, and finally the distribution of consumer vouchers, once the speculative bubble burst and during the course of the Asian crisis, there was no stopping ever larger sectors of the economy from being dragged into the economic turbulence or the emergence of the danger signals of a deflationary spiral.

3.1.1 Cash Injections for East Asia, but no Stimulation of Demand

In Asia, Japan did not succeed in demonstrating its leadership or in taking on the role of a "locomotive of the upturn" through the opening of its markets and the stimulation of demand. Instead, Japan seemed to fear for its exports to the Asian region.

To be sure, it was at first believed that reduced exports could be taken in stride, as long as only the Southeast Asian countries were affected by the crisis, countries that absorbed about 12% of the Japanese exports (*The Economist*, December 11, 1997, p. 97). But when South Korea, the eleventh largest national economy in the world, whose GDP is as much as those of Thailand, Indonesia and Malaysia combined, was also drawn into the maelstrom, serious setbacks were expected. Thus Japan reduced its imports from the Asian region from $131bn in 1996 to $104bn in 1998 (*The Nikkei Weekly*, August 9, 1999, p. 14). In the same time period, Japan doubled its current account balance to $121bn (*Handelsblatt*, September 22, 1999). Japan thereby differed from the United States, which succeeded in polishing its image as a responsible decision-maker, granting its beleaguered partners additional chances for exports. In any event the foreign trade deficit of the United States rose from $129bn in 1996 to $221bn in 1998. However, observers doubt that the rises in import surpluses were the result of supportive measures from America. The German Bundesbank, e.g., traces their cause to America's headstart in growth and its given import flexibility (*Handelsblatt*, September 22, 1999). To be sure, for the nations in crisis, it was of purely secondary importance whether extra exports to the United States had to do with supportive measures or with import flexibilities in the American economy. The decisive factor was the openness of the American markets, which was all the more highly valued in that among its important partners not only Japan but also the European Union showed only slight willingness to absorb additional imports. In any case, its current account balance surplus sank from ca. $106bn in 1996 only by ca. $5bn by 1998 (*Handelsblatt*, September 22, 1999). On the other hand, Japan showed a strong commitment in financial contributions to provide cash for the destitute national economies. Hence, of the total $124bn in loans granted by the IMF to the countries in crisis, Japan made $19bn available—significantly more than the United States' contribution of $8bn. Japan further offered the countries affected $30bn under the terms of the Miyasawa Initiative, of which $22bn had already been paid out by mid-1999. In addition, Japan guaranteed these countries credit of $17bn (*The Nikkei Weekly*, August 9, 1999, p. 14). It is striking that despite this very considerable financial assistance, Japan was accused of lacking commitment during the Asian crisis. Perhaps Japan's leadership did not know how to present its international contributions in the proper light. And presumably it was in the interest of some of its partners to point to weaknesses in Japan's assumption of world-economic responsibility. There could hardly have been a more drastic expression of Japan's loss of face than when Lawrence Summers commented that Japan could expect no financial help from the Western nations, even though no one in Japan had ever thought of requesting such foreign aid. Mainly, though, the loans and guarantees granted by Japan were seen less as help for its neighbouring countries, but, rightly or wrongly, as a boost for the demand for Japanese products and for the stabilization of Japanese business networks.

3.2 China

Remarkably enough, China emerged from the Asian financial crisis with greater strength, at least at first glance. In the United States, Secretary of the Treasury Rubin praised China as an "island of stability" (*Financial Times*, December 1, 1998). Indeed, China was relatively successful on the broad fronts where Japan came off poorly. Not only did it avoid being sucked into the downward spiral, like some of its neighbours, it was even able to realize relatively high growth rates in its GDP, maintain a stable currency, and increase its currency reserves. Within the Asian region, China acted as a "responsible economic partner" by not devaluing its currency, unlike many neighbouring countries, to gain competitive advantages, but kept it largely at a steady value in terms of the U.S. dollar. By so doing, China even acquired the image of an "anchor" in the Asian region. Contrasted with the "reliability" in monetary policy thus demonstrated was the weakness at the time of the Japanese yen, which Japan was alleged to want to use to gain advantages in exports over its Asian competitors. It is denied that Japan at this time made repeated attempts to strengthen its currency, but received no support in the USA and the EU, or that Japan supplies very demanding export markets, in which the lower-quality products of its Asian neighbour hardly have a chance. Furthermore, China succeeded in advancing into that group of nations which granted assistance to the countries with problems. Its contribution of about $1b was widely respected and sufficed for admission to the exclusive circle of countries that committed themselves to mastering the Asian financial crisis. To this extent, China can be seen as the "winner" and Japan as the "loser" of the crisis, regardless of the economic realities at the time.

3.3 Stabilizing Functions of State Control

Those who just a few years ago regarded China as an economic problem case with serious structural instabilities because of its "half-transformed", "half-opened" and "half-industrialized" economy, must be truly amazed by China's "new" role. True, we must qualify this assertion by noting that it fills this role mainly in the eyes of the Western industrialized nations, not of its Asian neighbours. It is still unarguable that China was able to seal off its national economy from the turbulences of the neighbouring region, and that it showed responsibility in monetary policy, even though the consequence of this was that individual sectors suffered disadvantages over competing exports from the neighbouring countries. Hence, China had to accept drops in exports in the areas of textiles and other simple manufactured products, which competitors in Thailand, South Korea and Indonesia could sell more cheaply on the world market after devaluing their currencies. When we look for reasons for China's stability, a surprising observation emerges: the very elements which a few years earlier were judged to be the causes of intensifying economic problems in China had a stabilizing effect under the conditions of the crisis. The following separate sets of facts were involved:

--It is only rarely that the usual economic criteria of efficiency form the basis for debtor-credit relationships, both those between producing firms and financial institutions and those between producing firms (the so-called triangular debts). In any case, loans are by no means only granted when there is sufficient expectation that the projects they finance will be profitable. They are also granted on the basis of highly specific relationships arising from the still existing system of the planned economy and the resulting personal ties between those in need of cash and those with access to capital. One result of this is that business losses do not lead to a loss of credit status; no one wants to stand accused of making bad decisions when granting the loans. Overall, this mixed regulative system, which is no longer strictly controlled by planning mechanisms but not yet totally guided by market mechanisms, offers a "scope for formative action" which would be inconceivable in a "homogeneous" system. The result is that senseless construction projects and other schemes, found in many eastern regions of China, as well as in the cities bordering on Vietnam, on the island of Hainan, and along the coast from Shandong up into the northeast, did not lead to a collapse, as in Thailand, South Korea, or Indonesia. The personal relationships, which are still intact, acted as a sort of stabilizing glue.

--The opening of China to foreign capital flows is presumably of equal importance. Thus investments in productive real capital are greatly desired and are favoured by a great number of arrangements. By contrast, investments in financial futures are heavily regulated and kept at a low level. In the past, the restrictive posture on foreign financial investments was regarded as a renunciation of dynamic foreign capital and therefore of additional growth effects. But at present this practice is now proving to be a supportive framework, since it is not possible for foreign investors, should they become fearful of critical developments in China, simply to pull the capital they have put into machines, equipment and plants out of the country within a short period of time. However, the volume of Chinese financial futures which foreigners can retain is so small that no very great influences on the domestic economy can arise from their disposal, nor can there be significant devaluation effects on the renminbi from the transfer of the proceeds abroad through exchanges into U.S. dollars or other currencies.

3.4 "Phoney Stability" as a Second-Best Solution

The system of give-and-take based on personal relationships, the dominance of political cadres and the extremely limited acceptance of foreign financial investments are, from a theoretical perspective, probably not even a "second-best" solution. But in practice, they have contributed to the "stabilization" of the country despite all the imbalances. From this fact derives the paradox that China's mixed system of regulatory policies renders a balanced and stable development of the country more difficult, but at the same time prevents it from plunging into a domestic and foreign economic crisis. There is no doubt that this is a phoney stability. A greater liberalization of the economy would likely lead to a disaster comparable to that in the neighbouring countries, unless there were course corrections and supportive measures. To this extent, the events in the neighbouring countries provide a welcome learning experience as to what further liberalization of the economy ought to do, and what it ought to avoid at all costs. On the other hand, the significance of China's stability for the East and Southeast Asian region can hardly be overestimated. An inflation rate of practically 0%, a currency which is stable against those of the major Western nations, and currency reserves sufficient to give China's creditors a sense of security by all the normal criteria, prevent a further aggravation of the Asian financial crisis. Even if China in other respects made only a slight direct contribution to the stabilization and recovery of the countries hit by the crisis, Western countries at least did not view this as an inadequacy. Such contributions were hardly expected from a country that still has the basic structural characteristics of a developing nation and needs to come to terms with complex transforming political processes. What counted was that China, counter to all fears, did not slide down into an economic crisis, and did not take part in the race to devalue.

4 Mergers, Acquisitions and Globalization Processes in Japan and China

Japan and China are considered to be national economies which in the past have resisted the described globalizing tendencies, in different ways and to different degrees. True, as early as the 1950s, Japan's businessmen seized the chance offered by international markets to enter the world markets as global agents. But they also knew how to prevent the strengthening of foreign competitors on Japanese domestic markets. By contrast, China, which had largely sealed itself off from the rest of the world for decades, still has hardly any firms capable of dealing independently with foreign markets. For more than fifteen years, however, China has offered foreign investors a broad spectrum of investment opportunities in order to build joint ventures and authentic subsidiaries, and this has been widely used. Thus there arose within the Chinese economy a sector dominated by foreign capital and foreign managers, alongside the state and cooperative sector. However, it is only weakly tied to businesses from the traditional sectors, and the latter are accordingly not very sensitive to the pressure to conform resulting from globalization processes. In the meantime, we can predict that the hitherto closed off sectors in Japan and China will also begin to feel globalizing pressure as a result of acquisitions and mergers, though in varying intensity and chronological sequences. In this context, the present posture of Western businesspeople is surprising: one would think that Japan would be shunned by foreign investors for all its economic problems. And, on the contrary, it would not be strange if China attracted additional foreign investors due to its high growth rates, maintained even during the crisis. For the present, the facts are different. Western firms are increasingly interested in investing in Japan. In China, on the other hand, projects are being examined and risks calculated anew. This situation finds expression in both countries in the present development of international mergers and acquisitions.

4.1 Japan

Negotiations have taken place between Nissan, Japan's second largest and the world-wide seventh largest automobile producer, and Western automobile manufacturers about the participation of foreign partners. As is known, Renault has by now acquired just about 40% of Nissan's shares. In view of the facts that "Nissan", literally translated, means "made in Japan", and that its president even declared his willingness to change the company name if it merged with Western concerns, this transaction takes on a powerful symbolic meaning. Be that as it may, the amalgamation of Nissan and Renault is only one example of many of mergers and acquisitions of Western firms in Japan, whose scale reached $5.3bn during the first half of 1998. This is of course only a small portion of the like transactions made around the world in the same period, and amounting to $221bn, but it is a dramatic rise compared with the same period the year before, when mergers and acquisitions of Western firms in Japan came to only $0.1bn (*Handelsblatt*, November 3, 1998). According to all the available data, mergers and acquisitions in Japan will continue to increase, because more and more foreign companies are interested in this sort of engagement in Japan, and because mergers and acquisitions are also seen in Japan as a means of strengthening economic power. By September 1999, e.g., such activities are believed to have reached a volume of 7% of the market capitalization of all Japanese joint-stock companies (*Handelsblatt*, September 10/11, 1999). Most of these of course are mergers and acquisitions between Japanese concerns, but it can be assumed that foreign transactions accounted for a significant portion of them. Cross-border mergers and acquisitions, e.g., in the period from January to August 1999, are thought to have made up 12.2% of all such transactions. A rise to 20% is expected in the foreseeable future (*The Nikkei Weekly*, September 20, 1999, p. 1). In this way, numerous recent participations and buyouts have been added to the list of earlier foreign participation in Japanese firms such as Mazda, Suzuki and Isuzu: Bosch has committed itself to the production of car parts, Mannesmann is active in machine construction, the Swiss Banking Corporation and American insurance companies in finance, to take only a few examples. Some typical transactions between Japanese and Western firms can be distinguished: Western firms acquired their shares in their Japanese partners in pre-existing joint ventures, they bought out their Japanese importers and dealers, or they acquired selected production sectors of diversified firms and franchises. The general reasons for the interest in investments in Japan are well known: Western firms are attracted to the world's second largest economic power, with its enormous purchasing power, huge savings and exceptional capacities for research and development.

This present foreign engagement, which is likely to increase in future, was, however, triggered by developments connected with the current crisis. Hence, Western manufacturers can acquire already existing production plants at low prices and in this way directly use technologies, existing research capacities and marketing organisations, along with qualified personnel, for their own interests. There are other stimuli for financial institutions: by acquiring shares in Japanese financial outfits, they can gain a foothold in Japan's financial markets, bring their presumed superiority over the many mediocre banks, investment firms and life insurance companies into play, and break into Japan's enormous savings.

4.1.1 Growing Interest in Foreign Participation

Until recently there was strong resistance to the interest of Western firms in mergers and acquisitions in Japan. But at present Western firms are encountering growing readiness on the part of Japanese firms to change their attitude towards foreign investors and to accept foreign owners and managers. This transformation was forced by a number of economic factors, e.g.:

--Many firms are operating at a loss and are short of cash. But the banks are neither willing nor able to provide them with the necessary financial means, because their leeway in granting loans is restricted by bad loans. When it is difficult to borrow money, companies tend to get capital by selling off parts of themselves, even to foreigners.

--The lack of willingness of the banks to grant loans does not limit just the operational business of the firms. Means are also lacking for research and development, which become ever more important if they are to survive in international competition. The effort to find new partners is intended to open up possibilities of loans.

--In many sectors there exist huge overcapacities. Nissan, e.g., was only utilizing 75% of its production capacities at the end of the 1990s. The general view is that even in cases in which operational capacity rates are raised as a result of public commissions, there cannot be an essential reduction of competitive pressure due to present structural false developments. On the contrary, it is expected that competitive pressure will increase and that numerous firms will go bankrupt. In such a situation, the sale of shares to Western firms is considered as a way of surviving the unavoidable economic culling process.

--Competition is especially strengthened in those branches which enjoyed state protection in the past and are currently regulated. These include the financial sector, whose institutions are increasingly under national and international competitive pressure. Again, in the interests of survival, consideration is given to the sale of shares to foreign banks, because it is believed that benefits will derive from their experience.

--Some highly diversified companies are being forced to rethink their past investment decisions, which were oriented to the expansion of the production programme. The result of the reorientation is often a concentration upon the core business, which usually goes along with the decision to sell off certain production sectors.

--Many of the regionally widespread family firms are confronted with specific problems. Due to falling prices for sites and office space, along with losses in speculation and in business operations, their future as independent companies is in doubt. They can hardly expect help from the banks, which have to trim their volume of loans to their shrinking capital base, and usually do so by cutting off further loans to the customers they perceive as weaker, mainly smaller businesses. The resulting cash-flow problems and the persistent recession force the heirs in the succeeding generations to consider whether it is worth following in the footsteps of their forebears. If they decide to sell out and cannot find a Japanese investor, they are often not unwilling to turn to foreign buyers.

4.1.2 Regulatory Peculiarities Put to the Test

The increasing foreign activities in the context of mergers and acquisitions made

possible by the above developments are going to put many Japanese "peculiarities" in question. Among them are the specific employee-employer relationships, which lead to a practical guarantee of lifelong employment for a certain portion of the employees, and to a dependency of rewards upon not only short-run performance but upon proofs of loyality to the firm. These include cross-participation of firms and resulting long-term relationships in marketing and acquisitions. Finally, the relatively close bonds among large firms, administration and the political structure are important, whereby the last mentioned involves influence exerted on the economy, but the economy for its part can use administration and politics in its own interest. It is possible that some of these elements will be pressured into changing by Western shareholders and managers, mainly those seen in the past,

4.2 China

As described above, Western politicians see China as an "island of stability". However, most Western businesspeople seem to take a different view, at least concerning the future stability of the country. Accordingly, they recognize that China is still turning out relatively high growth rates in its GDP, even though they are a few percentage points below those of the past. But we know that this development is only to a limited degree the result of self-sustaining growth and is instead largely derived from state incentives. These can soften the effect of downswings in the business cycle but at the same time cause problematical imbalances. To be sure, not only the slump in growth rates and questionable interventions in business-cycle policy give foreign investors the jitters. A "normal" recession would probably not have been seen as a large-scale problem. After all, Manhattan was built during a recession and later became the centre of American commercial prosperity.

4.2.1 A New Evaluation of Chinese Risks

Serious concerns, however, were raised by the dissolution of one of the best-known financial institutions, the Guangdong International Trust Investment Corporation. Numerous foreign creditors had established business connections, and they were informed unceremoniously that they could expect neither full reimbursement from the government for their loans which the bankrupt company was unable to service, nor even favoured treatment. In principle, decisions of the government which finally made a clear distinction between private and public debts and debtors should have been welcomed, since the distinction had hitherto hardly been noticeable in the gray area between private and public companies (*Financial Times*, January 12, 1999). As a rule, though, creditors object to decisions, even "correct" ones, that oppose their own interests. But the glimpse into the incompetence and corruption of Chinese state businesses, which was made possible by the crash of the Cantonese financial institutions, was an even greater problem. Western observers were inclined to conclude that many other Chinese businesses, including the ca. 200 regional International Trust and Investment Corporations, were confronted with similar or even worse problems. One feared that the previous data revealed only the tip of the iceberg. Against this background, various forms of behaviour on the part of Western investors towards China can be observed. The wait-and-see attitude is found among those who already have production facilities in China. They do not want to expand their businesses in China until an improvement of the economic situation is detectable. Other firms, who had already begun to carry out their projects before the crisis, have no choice but to press ahead. Examples would include the steel project of Krupp and Baoshan Iron and Steel in Shanghai, and the BASF project in Nanjing. Additional firms, especially those who have already had to deal in the past with problems on site, are considering getting out of China, as regards certain projects, or altogether. Overall, the previous optimism has now been replaced by a rather more skeptical attitude. The statistics also make this clear. China is still the world's biggest recipient of direct foreign investments, but growth rates are no longer recorded. By far the largest portion of foreign capital is invested in newly founded firms, whether equity joint ventures or authentic subsidiaries. The number of mergers and acquisitions, on the other hand, is drastically declining. In the first half of 1998 they only amounted to $2.5bn, whereas in the same period of the previous year they were $6.6bn. Foreign mergers and acquisitions in China's "traditional" sector could contribute even more strongly to the transformation of the country's market economy than other direct foreign investments, which generally lead to new foundations in the sector dominated by foreigners, normally still walled off from the domestic market. The mergers and acquisitions are usually associated with essentially more intensive forward and backward linkages, which is likely one of the reasons why China's "planning faction" opposed them for such a long time. They are a relatively new phenomenon in China, and their reliable versions are very limited. In any case, foreign investors are now permitted not only to bid for firms explicitly offered for sale by the government, but also to buy into non-authorized businesses. Foreign joint ventures and authentic subsidiaries in China seem in this respect to have greater room for manoeuvre than firms not active in China.

4.3 Opening the State Sector to Foreign Investors

Although mergers and acquisitions, compared with other direct foreign investments, are still exceptions and at present seem to be in decline, this could change in the medium term, if foreign businesspeople conclude that their commitment to China's state businesses offers possibilities of profiting from China's growth, and if China wants to seize the chance to modernize its state-owned sector by opening it to foreigners. Mergers and acquisitions of former Chinese state-owned businesses could then provide a further track to connect China with the rest of the world and open it to globalizing processes. To give a hint of what foreign investors can expect if the state-owned sector is opened to a significant degree, we shall present in the following some comments on its basic structures and on the opportunities and hazards of involvement. In the past, China's state-owned sector was the primary growth area of the country. Into it were pumped the greatest portion by far of the savings from the national economy, as well as the most highly qualified personnel and the most important material resources. It is certainly no wonder that it comprehended almost all the larger firms, among them integrated plants with hundreds of thousands of employees, as well as most of the mid-level businesses. In the case of the larger firms, mainly in the sectors of heavy industry and the chemical industry, one is speaking mostly of highly diversified operations, which not only produce a broad spectrum of goods, but also offer their employees numerous social services. In the "old" industrial regions, such as northeastern China, their share of industrial capital is extraordinarily high. Several cities and even larger regions are literally ruled by giant companies. In major structural ways, China's old industrial regions are comparable with the German Ruhr of the 1950s and 60s. The growth and diversification of the state-owned businesses were pushed forward by regional cadres and company directors, who hoped in this way to eliminate the bottlenecks that all too often resulted from inadequate total planning. But they were also the consequence of a conscious development policy with the goal of building firms that would as self-managing as possible, so that they could continue to produce even if military conflicts cut off their supply lines to other parts of the country. From Chinese and Western analyses of the state sector we learn that the technological and organisational inefficiency of the sector is a dangerous constraint on China's future growth and further eats up a large part of China's budget. To be sure, in recent years a few state-owned businesses have progressed in improving their products and raising their productivity (Ishikawa), but the opinion, at the end of the day, is that only by transforming them into some kind of stock company, in which not only the state but also private Chinese and foreign shareholders participate, can one create the prerequisites for an improvement of technical and market-economic efficiency. In order to evolve such business structures, necessary for a market economy, the splitting up of numerous firms, along with consolidations and closures, will be required. The questions as to who should undertake this restructuring, how quickly privatization should occur, who the future owners should be, and others, are still under discussion. Hence, one can encounter the opinion that it is basically a sensible idea to let private owners take decisions about company restructurings. But one is aware that state-owned businesses in their present condition are hardly attractive to private buyers. Apart from that, it is feared that private shareholders will take socially unacceptable decisions, e.g., about firings and the sale of company-owned living quarters. To this extent, the present opinion is predominantly that the bureaucracy still needs to play an important role in the restructuring of the state-owned sector. Most of the reformers are fundamentally in favour of rapid privatization, so that their country can use the positive effects from the transformation of property, which are not only anticipated but considered to be urgently needed, as soon as possible. But even then, if close to the entire population were to acquire shares in the business wealth intended to be privatized, their available savings would enable them to buy only a tiny fraction of the national wealth at prices determined by balanced values. A rapid evolution of privatization would only be possible if, as in the Czech Republic, vouchers for acquiring shares were to be distributed at practically no cost. But the restructuring and modernization of state firms demand extensive "fresh" capital. Free distribution of shares is no option, in the opinion of many reformers. If, however, the shares should be sold at the highest possible prices, then only a privatization process in stages, lasting years or even several decades, is conceivable. Such a cautious procedure would also have the advantage, in the view of its proponents, to allow a constant, clear view of the social, political and other economic risks of the transformation. Future owners are in principle to include workforces, managers, other private Chinese persons, investment companies, pension funds, regional administrative offices, the central state government, and foreigners. The participation of foreign investors is a special cause for debates. Because a "sellout" of the country to foreigners is feared, many people want to limit the maximum possible capital share of foreigners. Despite this, it can be assumed that foreign firms will be offered a broad spectrum of possibilities for participating, because their capital and foreign currencies, as well as their know-how in technology and management are so highly valued.

4.4 Opportunities and Risks for Foreign Investors

For foreigners, sharing in the wealth of former state-owned businesses offers both specific opportunities and risks. Hence there is the possibility of codetermining the new business policies of privatized firms by acquiring a majority of the shares. But even the acquisition of smaller percentages can make sense if it leads to important "connections" and access to information networks. Special opportunities may lie in acquiring shares in China's "core industries," which perform essential preliminary work for the entire national economy. Other possibilities consist in being able to employ experienced personnel. No doubt foreign investors who make commitments to former state businesses will be confronted with the burden of the labour relations and organisational structures left over from the days of the planned economy. But it may well be that workforces from former state businesses are actually more loyal to the new owners than employees from joint ventures, in which, e.g., "jobhopping" has become a normal way of life. The old state businesses, generally backward in their technology, might be attractive to those foreign firms which do not wish to transfer the most modern technologies.

As to the risks, one is that the prices for shares in former state firms could very quickly turn out to be too high, once cooperation begins. The sort of errors in judgement possible in such cases can be seen in the example of the German Trust, which put the value of state-owned enterprises in the former East Germany at ca. DM 600bn when it began its activities, but ended up with losses of ca. DM 180bn. Assets created over decades of socialist planning could, it seemed, all too easily turn into negative figures when market criteria were brought into play. Even if China's state industrial assets do not seem at all likely to lose value so dramatically as those of Germany's East, since China and several of its neighbours provide a huge market for second-class goods, and wages are not being raised so drastically as in the German East, the risk of high losses in value of investments in China's state-owned businesses still seems higher than in other investment projects. Special stresses could arise from the environmental damages caused by the acquired plants. State businesses are often still using equipment with technical standards from the 1940s and 50s and which hardly come up to present environmental requirements. Foreign partners could be held responsible for the resulting environmental harm. If, in addition to this, China's administration tightens the standards for permissible emissions, participation could turn into a heavy burden.

Additional risks face foreign investors in connection with China's transition to a market economy. Investors will have to expect dramatic changes in the business climate, which will require them to be exceptionally flexible. Initially they will likely have to deal mainly with the traditional type of cadre personality, and with contracts, agreements, business relations and personal connections which were made and structured by the bureaucracy. This however will change as a new Chinese managerial type emerges and, presumably, a dynamic, aggressive "middle class", with few scruples, is formed, possibly as in Japan, where in the post-World War II era the Zaibatsu, with their orientation to traditional values, were replaced by a completely new entrepreneurial type, expressly fixated on profit earning (Nakamura). Further changes yet can be expected. We can assume that former state enterprises will be taken over completely or in part by Chinese business-people from Taiwan, Singapore, Hong Kong and Southeast Asia, as well as by Korean and Japanese entrepreneurs. In this case, not only capital and managerial know-how will penetrate China's former state-owned sector from East and Southeast Asia. Businesspeople well acquainted with Asian markets will penetrate existing personal networks and make themselves jumping-off points for the further opening of the Chinese market. Despite these changes, the use of connections to the cadres in the economic administration by the "new" entepreneurs cannot be ruled out. One result could be that former state-owned businesses will behave on the surface like "normal" competitors to achieve their goals, but continue to be able to count on state support. Western investors would very likely find it generally more difficult than their Asian competitors to use the Chinese bureaucracy for their goals, because they rarely have personal, let alone family, connections to the administrative cadres.

4.5 Productivity and Stability: Competing Goals?

Most of these developments would beyond any doubt alter the "atmospheric" conditions and other economic facts formed during the phase of the socialist planned economy decisively, and move them in the direction of a market economy. Business leaders, now confronted with relatively "hard" budgetary restrictions, would have to take account of the laws of the market and could no longer take the support of state banks for granted. On the other hand, state bureaucrats would have good reason to create transparency, establish clear regulations, support market-oriented behaviour and increasingly align their decisions with criteria of economic rationality. In this way, conditions could be improved so that even more foreign investors would involve themselves in China's former state-owned companies, which could one day successfully compete on world markets. Even those sectors of the Chinese national economy hitherto sealed off from the rest of the world would thereby be exposed to globalizing processes.

Of course, an unqualified answer to the question posed at the beginning of these observations, as to whether China will be capable of rising to the challenges posed by globalization processes, cannot yet be given. In the second section, we made the case that during the Asian crisis, China was able to improve its positioning mainly because it had only partly liberalized its domestic economy and its foreign economic relationships, unlike the neighbouring countries in crisis. Despite all imbalances, China was therefore able to preserve its stability, a very fragile stability, to be sure. The reforms envisioned by China's state sector and the increasing acceptance of involvements by foreign capital will surely improve the preconditions for rises in productivity and for the adjustment of supply to demand. But at the same time they will contribute to the elimination of those structural elements upon which China's economic stability rested in the past. Then it will be a matter of China's willingness and ability to create in a timely fashion new institutional and other preconditions, such as the stabilization of modern market economies require. In this respect, the Asian financial crisis offers cause both for pessimism and optimism. Skepticism is called for, because China's neighbours, although, unlike China, they have had had the use of market-economic structures for many decades, ran into extraordinary problems when they were stabilizing their own economies. We can take it as positive that China now is able to learn from the catastrophic experiences of its neighbours.

5 Summary

Summing up we can say that during the Asian crisis China was able to improve its economic positioning by demonstrating, in contrast to Japan, regional economic responsibility. But it would be wrong to conclude from this that Japan's positioning has been permanently weakened. Among other things, the increasing number of foreign mergers and acquisitions in Japan is triggering developments which will improve the preconditions in regulatory policy allowing Japan to face the challenges of globalization with greater success. In China, by contrast, there will initially be a trend toward a worsening of the preconditions for a stabilization of the economy with the aid of "traditional" methods from the planned economy, in connection with the currently insignificant but in future likely growing numbers of mergers and acquisitions, and the numerous other foreign involvements already observable. Only when extensive supportive measures in regulatory policy and other areas have been carried out, will China have a chance to accept the challenges of increasing globalization with success.

List of References

Bergsten, C.F; Henning, C.R.: *Global Economic Leadership and the Group of Seven*. Washington, D.C.: Institute for International Economics, 1996, p. 167.

The Economist, London.

The Financial Times, London.

Handelsblatt, Düsseldorf.

Ishikawa, Shigeru: "China's 'Open Door' and Internal Development in the Perspective of the Twenty-First Century". In: Itoh, Fumio, Ed.: *China in the Twenty-First Century: Politics, Economy and Society*. Tokyo, New York, Paris: United Nations University Press, 1997, pp. 48 – 71.

The Nikkei Weekly, Tokyo.

Rodrik, Dani: *Has Globalization Gone Too Far?* Washington, D.C.: Institute for International Economics, 1997.

Nakamura, Takafusa: *The Postwar Japanese Economy: Its Development and Structure, 1937—1994*. Tokyo: The University of Tokyo Press, 1995.

Effects of Globalization and of Regional and Business Adaptation upon Employment

Shuichi Yatsubayashi

Senshu University

Japan's economy has now begun to a certain extent to rise out of the low point in the business cycle. But its unemployment rate at the beginning of 1999 has already surpassed that of the USA and is still rising. Japan was long famous for its low unemployment rate, and the "Japanese employment system" was often praised in connection with it. If one surveys Japanese unemployment in a longer temporal context, it is easy to see that the unemployment rate, given the modest fluctuations in the business cycle, stayed below 3% through the first half of the 1990s, but in the second half of the 1990s showed a rising trend of from 3% to 4% (see Table 1). Now it has reached its highest point since historically comparable figures for unemployment were first recorded in Japan, in 1953. It can be presumed that along with this rising unemployment rate, significant changes in the employment market or the employment structure will occur in Japan. Let us start with a look at the various aspects of this experience—for us, the first—with high unemployment.

From Tables 2 and 3, which show the long-term changes in basic data relating to the Japanese employment structure, we can tell that both employees and employers decreased in 1998 and 1999. This decrease is a completely new phenomenon in Japan in the post-World War II period. Up until then, an increase rather than a decrease in employees and employers accompanied rises in unemployment. If we focus on the employees and examine their numerical changes in terms of different economic sectors and firm sizes, then employee numbers in the processing industries show a downward trend as early as 1993, and those in the large firms starting in 1995. The growth in trade and in the service sectors was by 1998 and 1999 no longer able to compensate for this decrease, to which was added the downturn in the building industry (see Table 4). From these facts, we can assume that in the second half of the 1990s, in the very heart of the "Japanese employment system,"[1] the large firms of the manufacturing industry, a fundamental change in the employment structure took place. But let us stay for the moment with our analysis of unemployment.

---

1 Despite the highly divergent opinions about the concept of the "Japanese employment system," there is agreement that it is typically found in the large firms of the manufacturing industries.

If we differentiate by age groups, unemployment rose from 1992 to 1998 in all male and female age groups. In 1998, unemployment rates above 7% show men below 24 and in the 60-64 group, as well as women below 19 (see Table 5). But there appear to be different reasons in the younger and older groups for this higher unemployment. Young people probably tend more readily than older people to give up their current jobs in order to find new and better ones. Even so, we must keep in mind that in 1999 there are still 170 000 new graduates of schools and universities without work (*Labour Force Survey*, Statistics Bureau, Management and Coordination Agency). Table 6 makes it clear that in the second half of the 1990s, all the categories of unemployed people indicate an overall rising tendency, but that in 1998 and 1999 only the category "involuntarily separated unemployed persons" shows both an absolute as well as a relative increase. These involuntarily separated unemployed persons are those who lost their jobs, including those retired due to age, or because their firms went bankrupt. There are certainly many involuntarily separated unemployed persons among the unemployed of the age group 60-64, because many Japanese firms set a compulsory retirement age of 60, after which it is very difficult to find a new job. If one compares the employment situation of this age group in Japan with that of the same group in the USA, there are the following notable differences: The employment rate of the Japanese in this age group is 74.8%, far above the rate of 55.4% for the equivalent American group, with the result that the overall rate of employment of the Japanese population is, at 67.3%, much greater than the American, at 53.8%, even though Japanese unemployment, at 10%, outstrips the American rate of 2.9% (*White Paper on Labour*, Ministry of Labour, p. 103). The problem of how to provide enough jobs for people over 60 who want to work is now very serious in Japan.[2]

At the same time it must be noted that the involuntarily separated unemployed persons have also increased in the age group 30-59, although in terms of numbers the increase does not seem very impressive (see Table 7). But the men in this group are usually family providers, whose involuntary unemployment can have serious consequences for the affected families. If we take into account the duration of unemployment, the situation of these unemployed people seems even gloomier, because the rate of unemployment lasting one year or longer among people from a given age group is not only very high among those over 65, but also among the male unemployed between 25 and 64, for whom the level is already about 30% (Table 8).

In this high unemployment rate we see the signs not only of the short-term problems of the Japanese economy due to the business cycle, but also of long-term structural ones. An estimate of the structural frictional unemployment since 1970

---

2 In connection with the criticism of "mandatory retirement," see Seike, Atsushi, *Shougai Genekishakai no Jouken* ("Conditions for a Society of Life-Long Employment"), 1998.

indicates a rising trend in this category, in contrast to the ups and downs of cyclical unemployment, and which has by now already exceeded 3% (Table 9).[3] These structural problems of the Japanese employment structure will be referred to later.

I do not wish at this point to go into the increase in unemployment, but instead to discuss the effects of the increase on the "Japanese employment system." As a general rule, three major elements of this system can be cited:

1. "Lifelong employment," guaranteeing permanent employment until a certain age (in the past, usually 55; at present, 60):
2. The "seniority principle" in determining wages, and
3. the company union system.

This version, to judge by the OECD report "Reviews of Manpower and Social Policies: Manpower Policy in Japan" (1972), has also spread to the Americas and to Europe. My main aim here is to examine how much "lifelong employment," the seniority principle, and other related elements have been altered by increased unemployment.

Let me precede the detailed examination of such changes with a few general remarks.[4] First, not all Japanese businesses adopt the "Japanese employment system," and, vice versa, certain elements of the system can be found in the businesses of other countries, notably in America and Europe. Probably the system is not all that peculiar to Japan.[5] Second, the "Japanese employment system" perhaps has something to do with Japan's long tradition of community, but it has certainly been formed since the period of rapid growth began, first and foremost in the large businesses of the manufacturing industry, later in the small

---

3 These data were acquired by UV analysis (unemployment rate/vacancy rate analysis). Similar conclusions are reached by an evaluation with NAIRU (Non-Accelerating Inflation Rate of Unemployment).

4 The only comprehensive works I can mention on this topic are: Iida, Fumihiko, *Nihonteki Keiei no Ronten* ("Issues of Japanese Management"), 1998, and Inagami, Takeshi/Kawakita, Takashi, eds., *Kouza Shakaigaku*, Vol. 6, *Roudou* ("Sociology in Japan, Vol. 6, Sociology of Work"), 1999.

5 This point is very clearly developed in Koike, Kazuo, *Shigoto no Keizaigaku* ("Economics of Work"), 1991.

and middle-sized businesses and in other sectors of the economy, and has now been adopted as an ideal or norm by employees as well as employers.[6]

First let us examine "lifelong employment." Comparing international data, the average working life of Japanese employees is not particularly long. It is in fact longer than in the USA or England, but it is not very different from that in France or Germany (Table 10). And the Japanese average of 11 years is in any case not long enough. One cannot in fact even work to the age limit, let alone "lifelong." Accordingly, the expression "long-term employment" is now more commonly used. Because the working life of women in Japan is much shorter than that of men, which derives from the "M-curve employee supply" for Japanese women approximately between the ages of 25 and 34 who give up their jobs to raise their children, we shall focus mainly on the employment structure for men.

If we differentiate by economic sectors, working life in the manufacturing industry, in banks, and in the insurance business is longer than in other sectors (Table 11). Furthermore, white-collar working life is longer than blue-collar. The "Japanese employment system" is most widespread in these sectors with longer periods of employment. It is also noteworthy that the average working life is tending to become longer. But if we differentiate by age groups, the picture is somewhat different. As Table 12 shows, the above extension only affects the generations older than high school graduates 50~54 years old and university graduates 55~59 years old, as of 1996 (in bold type in the table). These are precisely the generations who started their working lives during the period of rapid growth. To put it another way, the reason for the extension of average working life is not to be found in the present, but in that period of the past. But one should also note that the opposite tendency, towards a shortening of working life, cannot be clearly observed at present.

"Long-term employment" applies mainly to the regular, core employees under open-ended contract, but not to the part-time or occasional employees, who are on contracts that run for a maximum of one year.[7] Whereas the regular, core employees are usually recruited from the recent graduates and trained in the companies, the part-time and occasional employees are drawn from the external employment market. From 1987 to 1997, the number of part-time or occasional employees in the various economic sectors increased very rapidly by 4.09m

---

6 For an analysis of this norm accepted by the business community, see Inagami/Kawakita, Eds., *loc. cit.*

7 In Japan there are various concepts of part-time, occasional or short-time employees according to the different statistics. But there are no great differences based on the general trend. See Nippon Roudou Kenkyuu Kikou (The Japan Institute of Labour), *Koyo-Chingintou no Jittai wo meikakunisuru Rodo Toukei Deta Shu* ("Data Collection of Labour Statistics to Clarify State of Employment, Wages, etc."), II-4 Patotaimu Rodosha (Part-Time Worker).

(48.2%), and rose in terms of its portion of total employees by 4.6% to 18.8%. In 1999 they already accounted for nearly 40% of employees in trade and restaurants, and in restaurants even exceeded 50%, but in the manufacturing industry, where the "Japanese employment system" seems to be most typical, they have remained by contrast at a stable 11 or 12% (Table 13). As we have seen, the total number of employees first showed a decline in 1998. In contrast, the part-time and occasional employees are continuing to increase. Does this indicate a process of substitution of regular employees by the part-time and occasional ones? The answer is no, for if we observe not the decrease or increase of the two sets of total figures, but take into account those for individual companies, it turns out that there are not many companies in which such a substitution is taking place, and that the regular employees are strongly decreasing in companies in which the part-time and occasional employees are also decreasing (*White Paper on Labour 1999*, Ministry of Labour, p. 175).

Other elements, closely connected with long-term employment, also go to form the "Japanese employment system." In Japan, all pupils and students regularly graduate at the end of March and immediately thereafter go to work in a company. The proportion of these new pupils among newly employed people was relatively stable during the 1990s, at about 20% (Table 14). This means, on the other hand, that every year the number of people who change jobs makes up nearly four-fifths of all new employees, even though these job-changers include those who shift within a firm. In 1996, job-changers within the same firm made up 34.3% of the new employees in firms with over 100 employees, and in firms with over 1000 employees they accounted for 45.9%. If we disregard this particular group, i.e., those who shift within a firm, there are 2.1 times more job-changers in the first case than there are university graduates, and in the second case 1.8 times more than there are university graduates. But in any event, long-term employment never excludes the possibility of changing one's job. Without such frequent changes, the rapid economic growth and the thoroughgoing transformation of Japan's structure of production after World War II would have been impossible. If we differentiate the rate of job-changing according to types of job, the part-time employees show a higher rate than regular employees (Table 15). The general tendency to a rise in the rate of job-changing in the 1990s was essentially increased by the part-time employees. Compared to the USA, this rate in Japan for all age groups is quite low. The conclusion to be drawn is that the external job market in Japan is smaller than that in the USA, and that the Japanese firms accordingly are less dependent on it in hiring their employees.

The younger generations in Japan also have relatively high job-changing rates (Table 16), because they more frequently give up jobs in order to take better ones. It is also notable that among new employees, the number of those who wish to work to the age limit in the same company decreased significantly in the second half of the 1990s compared to the 1970s and 1980s (Table 17), which accords with the general tendency in the younger generations for the job-changing rate to increase.

In hiring new employees, many firms, regardless of their size, continue to target mainly recent school and university graduates (Table 18). Let us examine the hiring policy of Japanese firms a little more closely. To begin with, Table 19 clearly shows that they have tried to get a grip on cyclical fluctuations more with increases or decreases in overtime, or, to a much lesser extent, with changes in wages. By contrast, the number of employees both in the favourable phase of the cycle (from first quarter of 1986 to fourth quarter of 1993) and in the unfavourable phase (from fourth quarter of 1993 to fourth quarter of 1998) remained almost inflexibly linked to the changes in the GDP. As we have already seen, the number of employees in the manufacturing industry has shown a decreasing trend since 1993 (Table 4). Table 20 makes it clear that the attrition rate has remained relatively stable and that even in the second half of the 1990s there is no clear downward trend. Naturally there is at any given time a certain number of job-leavers due to, e.g., the age limit. The entry rate, however, shows some fluctuations and becomes lower in the second half of the 1990s. The necessary conclusion is that the Japanese firms have tried to reduce the overall numbers in their workforces not by letting people go, but rather by reductions in hiring of new employees.

This hiring policy of the Japanese firms corresponds to the fact that most of the newly hired are rated not as specialists but as resources whose capabilities are to be developed within the firms, mainly through "on-the-job training" (OJT). When hiring university graduates, especially as office workers, the firms do not value special knowledge that goes beyond the basics, but emphasize personal qualities such as willpower, mental acuity and social skills. This has hardly changed in 80 years (*White Paper on Labour 1998*, p. 431, supplementary statistics, Table 101). In Japanese firms, relocations of personnel often take place, not only because changes in their departmental organization require increases or decreases in the workforce, but also because skills and abilities of employees can be broadened through experience with different departments, i.e., through OJT (on this point, see in particular Koike, *loc. cit.*).

The so-called seniority principle in setting pay has a great deal to do with OJT. On the basis of Table 21, showing changing differences in pay by age groups, an age-dependent annual wage hike seems to be guaranteed both for white- and blue-collar workers. A slight reduction in wage differences among age groups since 1985 is observable in the case of the white-collar workers, and to that extent there has been a weakening of the seniority principle. Among blue-collar workers the age group receiving the highest pay has shifted from ages 45~49 to 50~54. But the wages referred to here are only the regular earnings. A Japanese employee as a rule receives in addition to his regular earnings some not inconsiderable sums as a bonus, which is much more dependent than regular earnings on achievement and qualifications. Furthermore, the table shows only averages. From Table 22 it is clear that the spread in a given age group increases in direct ratio to age, or, to be precise, to the number of years on the job. It is an expression of the difference in company-specific qualifications, which employees have acquired over their years with the company through OJT. A newly hired job-changer receives as a rule a lower wage than his co-workers who are as old as he, but who started with the firm earlier, precisely because he has substantially fewer company-specific qualifications than they have. Overall, pay is primarily orientated to such qualifications acquired through OJT.[8]

In contrast to the employees with no great difference in spread according to age group, the spread among employees of all age groups is greater and increases with age almost up to the age limit. From comparative case studies of career selection in large Japanese and European firms, one knows that in Japan the selection occurs later, and more frequently (Koike, Kazuo, *loc. cit.*). Accordingly, the "seniority principle" by no means excludes tough competition for higher positions and pay, especially among the white-collar employees of a firm. Japanese white-collar employees are in fact in competition with each other over long periods of time,[9] and this situation has hardly changed in 20 years.

At the end of the careers of most Japanese employees comes the age limit. Along with the shift in the limit to a higher age have come a variety of forms of separation. In 1996 the number of employees who were separated from their firms upon reaching the age limit was under 30%. It is worth noting that there is now an increase not only in employees who work beyond the age limit, but in those who are separated before reaching the limit (Table 23).

The present high unemployment in Japan accompanies a decrease in the number of employees, especially in the manufacturing industry. What changes have been caused in the "Japanese employment system" by this situation? After our survey, the following points can be cited: First, the "Japanese employment system" seems to be very durable. The wage-and-promotion system in Japanese firms appears to show no great change. True, the numbers of part-time and occasional workers recruited from the external job market, and who are therefore basically outside the system, are increasing. They will even continue to increase as the tertiary sector of the Japanese economy continues to grow. But up to now, as we have seen, this growth has by no means meant a replacement of the regular core workforce, since

---

8 Yashiro too stresses the role of acquired qualification in his explanation of the wage hierarchy, but he interprets the "seniority principle" with a certain degree of differentiation as "delayed payment throughout the entire working life." See Yashiro, Naohiro, *Nihonteki Koyokanko no Keizaigaku* ("Economics of Japanese Employment Practice"), 1997, and *Koyokaikaku no Jidai* ("Age of an Employment Reform"), 1999.

9 Takeuchi gives a convincing explanation of why strong competition dominates in Japanese firms, not only among the top white-collar workers, but also among the middle and lower echelons. See Takeuchi, Yoh, *Nippon no meritokurashi* ("Japan's Meritocracy, Structure and Mentality"), 1995.

these employees are trained by the OJT of the individual companies. Furthermore, in future there will probably arise a somewhat larger external job market for certain career categories, such as "scarcity analyst" or "systems engineer," with similarities to the professions. They will have precise qualifications and will be recruited mostly on the external job market. Even so, they will remain a minority among Japanese employees. To the extent that an alternative system of training and qualification to that of OJT does not develop, there will be no large, external job market for regular employees in future, even as there is none at present.[10]

Second, the "Japanese system of employment" is fluctuating in certain respects. The fluctuations are especially conspicuous at the beginning and end of the working life of a Japanese employee. The job-changing rate of young people is relatively high and is trending up. Furthermore, in the present unpromising state of the job market, one has to take into account that among young people, quite a few have no chance of being taken on as core employees. Even among those who have the good fortune to find a job, there will be a number of latent job-changers. It is an open question whether they will become a new, mobile generation that expects no long-term employment. I personally do not think this will happen to any great degree, for on the one hand, Japan has an ageing society, and the number of young people is constantly decreasing, and on the other hand, the present high unemployment is not a permanent phenomenon. For older people, the problem appears more difficult to solve. Taking the long view, one can probably say that in contrast to the period of rapid growth of the 1950s and 1960s, when most firms steadily grew and therefore constantly created more positions for older employees, it will in future be impossible, even without a recession in the business cycle, to provide nearly all the older employees with long periods of employment and fairly high positions and salaries. Older employees, who have acquired their qualifications mainly through OJT in their company, will have trouble finding a new job.

Third, the Japanese economy is now in the midst of a great structural transformation. The rising rate of structural and frictional unemployment is a sign of this. In the period of rapid growth, in which another great structural change took place, employees in shrinking economic areas were able to find new jobs in some expanding industry. But in the present structural change, it is difficult to find such an industry that can take on very many new employees. The "Japanese employment system" is in some respects too rigid to adapt adequately to such a structural change. There will therefore be an overall dual process, namely, the retention of the "Japanese employment system," but with the addition of greater use of the external job market. The two will neither contradict nor replace each other. Of course, these two job markets, external and within the firms, cannot always clearly be distinguished. The border between them shifts a great deal, and

---

10 Miyamoto is of the same opinion: Miyamoto, Mitsuharu, *Nippon no Koyo wo do mamoruka* ("How the Japanese Employment System Should Be Defended"), 1999.

there is an intermediate zone, in which along with OJT, Off-JT and other institutions, such as business schools, will play an increasingly important role.

Table 1: Standardised Unemployment Rate (%)

Year	Japan	U.S.A	U.K.	France	Germany
1975	1.9	8.3	3.9	4.1	3.7
1980	2.0	7.2	6.2	5.8	2.6
1985	2.6	7.2	11.5	10.1	7.2
1990	2.1	5.6	7.1	9.0	4.8
1995	3.1	5.6	8.8	11.7	7.9
1996	3.4	5.4	8.2	12.4	8.9
1997	3.4	4.9	7.0	12.3	9.9
1998	4.1	4.5	6.3	11.7	9.4

Source: OECD, Employment Outlook.

Table 2: Labour Force, Employed, Employees and Unemployment (10thous, %)

Year	Labour Force	Employed	Employees	Unemployed	Unemploy-ment Rate
1975	5,323	5,223	3,646	100	1.9
1980	5,650	5,536	3,971	114	2.0
1985	5,963	5,807	4,313	156	2.6
1990	6,384	6,249	4,835	134	2.1
1995	6,666	6,457	5,263	210	3.2
1996	6,711	6,486	5,322	225	3.4
1997	6,787	6,557	5,391	230	3.4
1998	6,793	6,514	5,368	279	4.1
1999	6,779	6,462	5,331	317	4.7

Source: Statistics Bureau, Management and Coordination Agency, *Labour Force Survey*.

Table 3: Labour Force, Employed and Employees (Changes from previous year, 10thous., %)

Year	Labour Force		Employed		Employees	
	Male	Female	Male	Female	Male	Female
1995	15	7	4	0	13	14
1996	26	18	15	13	23	36
1997	35	41	34	38	26	43
1998	1	7	34	9	21	3
1999	2	12	27	24	28	8

Source: Statistics Bureau, Management and Coordination Agency, *Labour Force Survey*.

Table 4: Trends in Number of Employees by Industry and Company Size (Changes from previous year, 10thous)

Year	All Ind.	Con.	Manu.	Wholes. & retail trades, rest.	Serv.	Others	Non-agricul, Ind. All sizes	1-29	3-499	500-
1992	117	18	25	22	37	15	114	24	31	54
1993	83	26	15	19	41	12	84	24	24	24
1994	34	13	27	5	30	13	33	4	24	4
1995	27	8	32	12	25	14	26	26	16	11
1996	59	7	1	22	34	3	58	30	46	19
1997	69	12	0	12	47	2	71	19	29	9
1998	23	15	49	16	24	1	24	1	32	7
1999	36	4	35	8	2	7	37	13	13	12

Source: Statistics Bureau, Management and Coordination Agency, *Labour Force Survey*

Table 5: Rate of Unemployment by Age Groups (%)

Year	15 19	20 24	25 29	30 34	35 39	40 44	45 49	50 54	55 59	60 64	65
Male											
1992	7.3	3.9	2.3	1.6	1.5	1.1	1.2	1.2	1.9	5.1	1.6
1997	10.3	6.2	3.9	2.7	2.1	2.2	2.1	2.1	2.6	8.3	2.0
1998	12.0	7.3	4.9	3.1	2.8	2.8	2.4	2.7	3.6	10.0	2.6
Female											
1992	6.0	3.7	3.5	3.0	1.9	1.8	1.6	1.4	1.3	1.4	0.6
1997	7.6	6.1	6.3	4.4	2.9	2.1	2.0	2.0	2.0	2.5	0.6
1998	9.1	6.9	6.7	5.6	3.7	2.9	2.4	2.2	2.8	3.1	0.6

Source: Statistics Bureau, Management and Coordination Agency, *Labour Force Survey*

Table 6: Unemployment by Reasons for seeking Job (10thous., (%))

Year	Total	Involuntarily separated unemployed persons	Voluntarily separated unemployed persons	Graduates who have not found employment	Others
1993	166 (100)	41 (25)	69 (42)	7 (4)	39 (23)
1995	210 (100)	55 (26)	83 (40)	11 (5)	50 (24)
1996	225 (100)	59 (26)	87 (39)	13 (6)	55 (24)
1997	230 (100)	54 (23)	95 (41)	12 (5)	59 (26)
1998	279 (100)	85 (30)	101 (36)	15 (5)	68 (24)
1999	317 (100)	102 (32)	109 (34)	17 (5)	77 (24)

Source: Statistics Bureau, Management and Coordination Agency, *Labour Force Survey*

Table 7: Involuntarily separated unemployed Persons by Age Groups (%)

Age Group	1st.Half 1996	1st.Half 1997	1st.Half 1998
Total	1.6	1.7	1.9
29	1.0	1.0	1.2
30 44	0.5	0.7	0.8
45 59	1.1	1.2	1.4
60	11.5	11.6	13.6

Source: Ministry of Labour, *Survey on Employment Trends*.

Table 8: Long-term Unemployment by Age Group and Sex□1998 (10thous., (%))

Age Group	Both Sexes		Male		Female	
	Unem-ployed	Long-term Unemployed	Unem-ployed	Long-term Unemployed	Unem-Ployed	Long-term Unemployed
Total	313	70 (22.4)	189	52 (27.5)	124	18 (14.5)
15 24	70	10 (14.3)	40	6 (15.0)	30	3 (10.0)
25 34	82	18 (22.0)	42	13 (31.0)	39	5 (12.8)
35 44	40	10 (25.0)	22	6 (27.3)	18	3 (16.7)
45 54	51	12 (23.5)	29	9 (31.0)	22	3 (13.6)
55 64	59	16 (27.1)	46	13 (28.3)	13	3 (23.1)
65	11	5 (45.5)	10	4 (40.0)	1	1 (100.0)

Source: Statistics Bureau, Management and Coordination Agency, *Report on the Special Survey of Labour Force Survey*.

Table 9: Estimation of structural and frictional Unemployment Rate (%)

Year	1970	1975	1980	1985	1990	1995
structural and frictional Unemployment Rate	1.68	1.91	2.18	2.73	2.89	3.19
Rate of Unemployment due to deficient demand	0.33	0.39	0.30	0.64	0.12	1.10

Source: Ministry of Labour, *White Paper on Labour 1999*, p.357, supplementary statistics, Table75.

Table 10: Average Tenure (Years)

Year	Japan	U.S.A	U.K	France	Germany	Canada
1985	10.3	7.5	8.3	10.1	9.8	7.4
1990	10.9	7.2	7.8	9.7	10.2	7.2
1995	11.3	7.4	8.3	10.4	10.8	7.9

Source: OECD, Employment Outlook 1997, Table 5.7.

Table 11: Average Tenure by Industry (Years)

Year	All Ind.	Construction		Manufacturing		Wholesale & retail trades, rest.	Bank & Insurance	Services
		Blue Collar	White Collar	Blue Collar	White Collar			
Male								
1991	12.7	10.8	13.2	13.1	15.2	11.8	14.3	10.0
1996	13.1	10.2	12.8	13.9	16.1	12.5	15.0	10.5
1998	13.1	10.4	13.5	13.8.	16.4	12.7	15.5	10.4
Female								
1991	7.4	9.2	7.1	9.0	7.0	6.1	6.9	7.0
1996	8.2	9.8	7.6	10.3	8.5	7.3	8.2	7.3
1998	8.2	9.7	7.8	10.4	8.9	7.5	8.8	7.2

Source: Ministry of Labour, Basic Survey on Wage Structure.

Table 12: Average Tenure by Age Group (Years)

Age Year	All Age Groups	20 24	25 29	30 34	35 39	40 44	45 49	50 54	55 59	60 64
Male, University Graduates										
1981	9.4	1.2	3.9	8.1	12.2	**16.4**	19.2	20.6	16.0	10.0
1986	10.4	1.3	4.0	7.9	12.2	16.4	**20.5**	22.7	19.5	11.4
1991	11.2	1.2	3.9	7.8	11.4	16.0	20.5	**23.7**	22.5	13.6
1996	11.8	1.2	4.1	7.9	11.8	15.4	20.1	23.8	**24.4**	12.8
1998	11.9	1.2	4.0	7.8	11.7	15.3	19.8	23.6	**24.3**	13.5
Male, High School Graduates										
1981	10.7	3.2	6.8	9.9	**13.7**	15.8	17.7	18.5	13.7	9.6
1986	11.9	3.3	6.2	10.1	13.3	**17.1**	19.0	20.0	17.0	10.7
1991	12.6	3.0	6.2	9.3	13.3	16.5	**20.2**	21.6	19.3	10.8
1996	13.3	3.4	6.1	9.3	12.2	16.4	19.5	**22.8**	21.8	12.4
1998	13.4	3.3	6.1	9.1	12.2	15.7	19.6	**22.3**	22.1	12.9

Source: Ministry of Labour, Basic Survey on Wage Structure.

Table 13: Part-time Workers by Industry (%)

Year	All Ind.	Cons.	Manu.	Wholes. & retail trades, Rest.	Services
1991	15.74	3.85	12.24	29.89	14.84
1993	16.75	4.67	11.77	32.22	16.21
1995	16.86	4.06	11.07	32.96	16.72
1996	17.49	4.00	11.35	33.66	17.38
1997	18.11	3.88	11.91	34.81	17.85
1998	18.86	4.41	12.15	36.11	18.71
1999	19.53	4.42	12.61	38.05	18.91

Source: Ministry of Labour, *Monthly Labour Survey*.

Table 14: Ratio of High school and University new Graduates to the total newly hired Employees by Company Size (%)

Year	All sizes	1000	300 999	100 299	30 99	5 29
1980	24.0	37.2	35.6	23.5	16.9	14.5
1985	22.5	34.8	34.5	24.3	15.4	11.3
1990	20.0	32.0	30.8	23.2	13.2	8.7
1993	20.5	35.2	33.5	21.7	15.5	10.3
1994	20.3	29.5	34.0	24.9	15.1	13.7
1995	19.4	27.0	35.1	26.8	15.5	12.9
1996	20.1	26.3	25.6	24.0	17.6	15.8

Source: Ministry of Labour, Survey on Employment Trends.

Table 15: Job Change Rate by Type of Employment (%)

Year	Total Employees	Regular staff	Part-timers
1985	3.3	2.9	6.4
1990	4.1	3.3	8.1
1995	4.7	3.6	10.5
1996	4.8	3.6	10.2
1997	5.2	3.9	11.0

Source: Statistics Bureau, Management and Coordination Agency, *Report on the Special Survey of Labour Force Survey.*

Table 16: Comparison of Job Change Rate by Age Group in Japan and US (%)

Year Country	Total	15 19	20 24	25 34	35 44	45 54	55 64	65
Male								
1987 USA	9.6	29.4	22.2	11.4	7.0	4.7	2.7	1.2
Japan	4.2	12.3		5.3	3.1	2.5	2.8	
1997 Japan	3.8	16.0	10.7	5.7	2.8	2.0	2.8	1.3
Female								
1987 USA	10.4	28.7	21.0	11.8	8.5	4.9	3.2	1.1
Japan	4.8	10.7		6.7	5.1	2.7	1.2	
1997 Japan	5.3	17.4	12.8	7.9	5.8	3.0	1.4	0.5

Source: Ministry of Labour, *White Paper on Labour 1999*, p.250.

Table 17: Attitudes of the newly hired Employees regarding, "how long I work in this company" (%)

Year	to the age limit	Provisionally here	Change owing to the Situation	Don't know
1975	22	20	35	23
1985	23	24	37	16
1990	16	26	43	15
1995	20	26	42	12
1997	18	24	45	13
1998	18	22	47	12
1999	15	23	48	13

Source: Shakai Keizai Seisansei Honbu, Hatarakukoto no Ishikichousa (Opinion Research on Working).

Table 18: Priority of the Companies on the occasion of newly Hiring by Company Size (%)

Company Size	Total	mainly High school and University new Graduates	the same but increasingly the Job changers too	mainly the Job changers
Total	100.0	42.1	56.3	1.6
5,000	100.0	39.7	60.3	0.0
2,000 4,999	100.0	51.6	46.9	1.6
1,000 1,999	100.0	44.4	54.4	1.1
500 999	100.0	37.2	80.5	2.3
499	100.0	39.0	58.4	2.6

Source: Ministry of Labour, *White Paper on Labour 1998*, p.182.

Table 19: The real GDP Elasticities of Wages, Labour Supply, Labour Productivity etc.

	from the 1st Quarter 1986 to the 4th. Quarter 1993	from the 4th Quarter 1993 to the 4th. Quarter 1998
Labour Productivity	0.399	0.647
Labour Supply	0.585	0.348
Number of Employees	0.187	0.188
Actual Hours Worked	0.392	0.160
Overtimes	3.206	1.866
Real Wages	0.400	0.308

Source: Ministry of Labour, *White Paper on Labour 1999*, p.140.

Table 20: Accession Rate and Separation Rate in Manufacturing Industry (%)

Year	Accession Rate	Separation Rate
1975	1.3	1.7
1980	1.4	1.4
1985	1.4	1.4
1990	1.51	1.35
1995	1.14	1.35
1997	1.28	1.34
1998	1.12	1.32
1999	1.16	1.40

Establishments with 30 or more employees. Source: Ministry of Labour, *Monthly Labour Survey*.

Table: 21 Trend in Wage Difference (20 24 100)

Age Group Year	18 19	20 24	25 29	30 34	35 39	40 44	45 49	50 54	55 59	60 64	65
White Collar											
1980	80.9	100.0	125.8	159.7	193.5	220.4	238.2	242.1	214.1	172.5	148.9
1985	82.3	100.0	123.8	157.3	189.8	223.6	248.8	256.7	229.6	181.7	151.1
1990	81.1	100.0	122.1	151.0	181.5	212.4	240.5	256.4	236.7	176.6	162.9
1995	83.1	100.0	121.1	149.3	178.2	205.9	231.9	252.9	241.7	190.5	144.0
Blue Collar											
1980	84.1	100.0	123.5	144.3	159.3	164.8	162.2	161.9	142.7	116.5	105.4
1985	86.4	100.0	122.2	144.5	161.2	174.4	175.1	170.6	156.3	125.1	111.8
1990	86.7	100.0	118.7	137.8	155.0	168.9	177.8	174.4	158.0	124.0	109.4
1995	87.4	100.0	118.9	136.2	150.6	163.9	174.4	178.4	168.5	131.3	112.9

Source: Ministry of Labour, Basic Survey on Wage Structure.

Table 22: Decile Dispersion Coefficient of Wages

Year	White Collar						Blue Collar					
	30 34	35 39	40 44	45 49	50 54	55 59	30 34	35 39	40 44	45 49	50 54	55 59
1980	0.22	0.26	0.33	0.39	0.45	0.55	0.20	0.20	0.20	0.22	0.25	0.30
1985	0.22	0.25	0.30	0.35	0.42	0.53	0.21	0.20	0.22	0.22	0.23	0.26
1990	0.23	0.27	0.31	0.35	0.38	0.49	0.22	0.21	0.22	0.21	0.21	0.26
1993	0.22	0.28	0.31	0.33	0.37	0.47	0.21	0.21	0.20	0.21	0.21	0.24
1994	0.23	0.28	0.30	0.32	0.36	0.45	0.20	0.21	0.20	0.22	0.22	0.24
1995	0.23	0.27	0.31	0.33	0.35	0.43	0.21	0.21	0.21	0.22	0.21	0.23
1996	0.24	0.29	0.31	0.32	0.35	0.41	0.21	0.21	0.20	0.21	0.22	0.23

Decile Dispersion Coefficient 9th Decile 1st Decile 2×Median

Source: Ministry of Labour, *Basic Survey on Wage Structure*.

Table 23: The over 50 Years old separated Persons by Type of Separation (%)

Year	before the mandatory retirement		by the manda. Retire.	after the additional employment			the mandatory retirement not applied	no mandatory retirement
		before manda. Retire. with compen..			after the prolongation of the employment	after the reem-ployment		
1988	30.1	8.0	37.8	15.3	7.9	7.4	8.9	7.8
1996	33.5	9.3	29.4	17.6	10.2	7.4	9.3	10.3

Source: Ministry of Labour, *White Paper on Labour 1998*, p.211.

Effects of Globalization on Employment and Wealth

Christian Watrin

Universität zu Köln

"This division of labour from which so many advantages are derived, is not originally the effect of any human wisdom, which foresees and intends that general opulence to which it gives occasion. It is the necessary, though very slow and gradual consequence of a certain propensity in human nature which has in view no such extensive utility; the propensity to truck, barter, and exchange one thing for another." Adam Smith (1776) p. 25

1 Globalization: The New Form of International Division of Labor

In the May 1997 issue of the "World Economic Outlook" from the International Monetary Fund, the phenomenon of globalization is accurately described as an increasingly international integration of markets for goods, services and capital. The globalization processes are presented as a reoccurrence of developments in the world economy, which have been observed for more than the past hundred years.

More recent history of international trade and commerce can be divided into *three phases*. The *first phase* spans from the beginning of the nineteenth century to 1914. Back then, international trade grew rapidly as a result of new developments in transportation technologies. At the same time expansive settlement in the Americas and Australia coincided with the fact that traditional fields of production (especially agricultural goods) shifted from continental Europe to foreign countries in the wake of sinking transportation costs. In contrast to today (following the collapse of Eastern Europe and the opening of China to the forces of the market economy), a period in which practically all nations participate in the international division of labor, in this first phase of the developing global economy the various regions of the world were not involved in worldwide integration processes to the same extent. The center of economic activity lie more in the Western[1] states.

During the 19th century a high level of economic prosperity blossomed in regions where international trade was free to develop. The terms, employment and full-employment, were still unknown at the time. However, the hidden unemployment in agriculture and private households was reduced despite a high simultaneous population growth and increasing incomes per capita. More people left the less-productive home economy and achieved a higher income by entering the job market.

The *second phase* of international economic relations encompassed both world wars, the years in-between and the first few years following 1945. The outbreak of World War I in 1914 led to a sudden collapse of the international division of labor. The two central institutions of the world economy at that time, the gold standard and multilateral free trade based on most-favored-nation status, tumbled down[2]. During the period between World War I and II, especially the years of the world depression following 1929, new forms of protectionism, foreign exchange control, bilateralism, barter trade and attempts to practice autarky gained ground in Germany as a result of massive unemployment and widespread social disruptions. As a result a dramatic decline in international trade, costly national production of goods and services, which could have been imported for more advantageous conditions from other countries, and serious distortions in the national productive capital stock followed. The decline in the standard of living was considerable.

---

1 The "West" includes not only Europe, but also the oversee European settlements, e.g the Americas, Australia, New Zealand and other regions.

2 The gold standard was initially a purely national currency system. Its most significant feature was the "golden brake on the money machine" (Schumpeter), i.e. the close ties between the national currency level and the available gold supply. Based on the so-called gold parity, an international currency order developed without the establishment of international contracts and world economic organizations. The exchange rates between the various currencies (e.g. German mark of the Third Empire, French franc, English pound, etc.) corresponded to the relative amount of gold supporting the national currency. Barring a few exceptions a silent agreement existed between the partner nations that the rules of the gold mechanism should support an economic policy aimed at exchange rate stability. Thus, the gold-based currency and its international counterpart were the product of spontaneous order and not international planning (Watrin, 1998). The international trade order behaved in a similar manner. It developed from the willingness of the world trading nations to incorporate the most-favored-nation trading status into their bilateral trading contracts. In essence the partners of an international trading contract agreed reciprocally on the same conditions that they offered to a third nation. The possibility of discrimination of a contract partner was, thereby, banned. When generally applied, the most-favored-nation trading status led to free trade (for details read Haberler, 1936, pp. 372+).

In many countries the concept of re-nationalization was combined with an aggressive military ideology according to which industrial economies should be able to be self-sufficient also in the production of agricultural products. In those cases where the agricultural basis was to small, the proponents of the so-called "Großraumwirtschaftsideologie" did not shy away from applying military force. In the German case the Ukraine should become the Reichs granary. In the thirties massive unemployment resulted from the world depression, which began in 1929 in the USA and in Europe. This development was fought off in Germany with an expansive credit policy and the simultaneous introduction of exchange rate controls and foreign trade quotas, in other words by pulling out of the international division of labor. This self-sufficiency approach was initially successful in promoting employment and, thus, admired by foreign countries. However, in 1936 the German employment wonder entered a phase of inflation, which the national-socialist government attempted to control with a general price stop and with steering the economy on the basis of "Four-years-plans" (Vierjahrespläne). World War II beginning in 1939 led to a war economy with extensive rationing and compulsory work duty for everyone not serving in the military.

Several years after the war, the *third phase* began gradually to reestablish the international division of labor based on the resolutions from the Bretton Wood Conference in 1944. Certainly, in this period leading up to modern-day globalization, which began around the early eighties, no country considered submitting their currency to the old rules of the gold standard and the most-favored-nation status was not reintroduced in its old form. Rather, many nations deemed it necessary to substitute the silent consensus of the past with concrete rules for a world economic order in the realm of international organizations. They were entrusted with the monitoring of international agreements on the exchange rate policies and foreign trade policies of member states. The rules established back then were often changed. The changes are most apparent in the international monetary order, where the principle of fixed exchange rates was superseded in 1973 by flexible exchange rates. Today, a compulsory exchange rate regime does not exist worldwide; each member country of the International Monetary Fund is free to choose the system it prefers. The corresponding arrangements are rather diverse. Everything exists from a free float, to currency boards and even regional exchange rate unions in Europe which will be followed by a single money, the Euro at the End of 2001.

The GATT, which was responsible for the dismantling of tariffs and quantitative trade restrictions (i.e. quotas), was superseded by the World Trade Organization (WTO) in 1994. It focuses its attention on removing numerous non-tariff trade restrictions. In the course of deregulation and the international networking of the financial markets, world trade has experienced average growth rates twice as high as the increase in the 'gross world product'. At the same time the number of multinational corporations has climbed dramatically. It is currently estimated that more than 40,000 of these businesses exist.

Globalization can be classified in this institutional framework. It can partially be viewed as a continuation of the development before World War I, however, containing qualitatively new elements, e.g.: the rapidly falling costs of information and communication, low-costs in transportation, the speedy transfer of technical knowledge, the transformation of developing nations into newly industrialized economies (NICs), new methods for organizing production worldwide and operating businesses on a supranational level and the creation of large international financial markets.

The last quarter of the 20th century in most continental European countries was characterized by a stubborn growth in unemployment despite numerous state-run employment programs. Since the mid-seventies a process can be observed in Germany, by which in economic periods of growth unemployment is only partially reduced. This phenomenon differs from earlier decades and results in a high base unemployment, which remains even in the growth phase of the business cycle. In the course of several business cycles this base expands from cycle to cycle. In Western Germany, for example, 1 million people were registered as unemployed in the mid-seventies. In the nineties this number grew to over 3 million people. In the near future even an expected growth rate GNP of more than 2 percent is not expected to noticeably reduce the level of unemployment.

The general public appears to link the repeated decline in the level of employment to globalization processes. Currently, an explosion of new technologies is changing the face of the earth and the international economic relationships, similar to the effects in the middle of the 18th century, when the industrial revolution first took hold in Great Britain[3]. Some authors claim that globalization will permit market forces to reign over the economy and politics, will lead to a commercializing of life's earnings and will trigger a global race toward higher efficiency and lower earnings (Noé, 1996; Martin and Schumann, 1997, pp. 25). Higher income countries like Germany would be especially hard hit by such changes.

On the other hand one could argue that globalization offers chances for all economies and leads to an increase of wealth throughout the entire world (Deutsches Institut für Wirtschaftsforschung, 1997, p. 419; International Monetary Fund, 1997, p. 3; Watrin, 1999, pp. 47). The International Monetary Fund stresses that: „There is no doubt that globalization is contributing enormously to global prosperity". The increase in wealth worldwide could also become the motor for developing peaceful democratic relations between nations.[4] Thus, globalization

---

3 W. W. Henning shows that the typical description of the "industrial revolution" as a technical revolution does not correspond to the facts. It was less a revolution and more a process evolving in a series of stages.

4 This is the main thesis of the book from F. Fukuyama (1992), if you separate it from its Hegelian details.

should lead to a significant reduction in world wide unemployment. – What can we make of all these claims?

2 Globalization and the Theory of International Division of Labor

The theory of 'comparative cost advantages' is relevant to this discussion. Its main concern is an explanation of the division of labor via markets as opposed to the division of labor via businesses. The "Wealth of Nations" (A. Smith) bases its arguments on the extent and depth of the societal division of labor in and between states, whereby 'states' represent economic entities in this definition and not political units. Within their borders free trade and uninhibited mobility of factors of production exist. However, between them factors of production are immobile or barriers to trade hinder economic exchange.

This idea is modeled in economic theory. Every economic participant specializes in the production of those goods and services, for which he or she possesses a comparative advantage. By selling the goods and services produced, the participants can obtain other products and services from other producers, thus, being better of than in a situation of autarky. Economic exchange in markets is, thereby, indirect production. The greater the division of labor is in a society, the more specialization opportunities can arise for every economic participant and the higher the profit for everybody from specialization will be. Therefore, trade can be interpreted as a win-win game for every participant.

The possibility of mutual beneficial exchanges is not – even seen on a historical basis[5] - restricted to small regions. It stretches from region to region and land to land. Thus, globalization today can be seen as an additional stage in the long process of the cross-border division of labor. If we abstract from all the restrictions to a further international development of the division of labor (for the case of argument), we could conclude that the available potential of wealth worldwide can only be exhausted, when a free exchange of goods and services exists across the globe. Then, the production of goods and services would take place at the location with the greatest cost advantage.

---

5 The view of the German Historical School that the process of societal division of labor can be observed as progressing from the village, to the city, to the nation and finally to a global economy is historically inaccurate. It is only helpful as a didactic method for explaining complicated processes.

This utopian view should not be confused with an end-state, which the human race is supposedly attempting to reach.[6] A worldwide space of free trade is not identical to a stationary condition of the economy. Rather, in an "open society"[7] one can assume that technical progress and cross-border migration continue to change economic data. In this sense globalization involves an ever open and not an end goal-oriented process.

Has a period existed in economic history, in which the process of the division of labor developed a clear tendency toward cross-border liberalization? How did wealth develop in such periods and what effect did this have on employment? The last 150 years are rather informative in this respect. Historical studies show that especially in the period from 1850 to 1914 the countries using the gold standard pursued widespread free trade, free capital mobility and considerable inner-European and worldwide labor mobility[8]. Similar to today world trade grew faster than world production, and the additional indicators point toward a phase of high economic prosperity. At the same time the period before World War I displayed an alignment of the living conditions in the countries participating in the emerging world trade order. Considerable stocks of capital flowed into the periphery. The USA and Canada imported capital over several decades, since they were considered to be nations promising high potential growth. The Western world (in the broadest sense) underwent a period of prosperity, in which the endemic unemployment and poverty of earlier centuries drastically decreased. However, the problem of business cycles and the unemployment resulting from them were left unsolved[9]. The modern social state attempted to create a net of support to counteract these trends.

Not only the period before World War I confirms the thesis that the "Wealth of Nations" is decisively influenced by the international division of labor. This thesis has also applied in the phase of worldwide reintegration since World War II. Nations like Japan and Germany, which opened their borders relatively early to

---

6 This is the error that the historical philosophers Comte, Marx and Fukuyama recently made.

7 This term from Karl R. Poppers can be applied to open economies.

8 The German empire led by Bismarck left the group of free-trade nations for political reasons in 1878 and introduced "moderate" tariffs on agricultural goods and iron and steel despite the protest of various circles. They were "moderate" compared to the trade restrictions in place during the phase of worldwide disintegration (1914-1950) (see Röpke, 1942), and "moderate" in view of the non-tariff trade restrictions practiced today.

9 The development of wealth in the 19th century belongs to the group of controversial topics in economic history, which Friedrich Engels condemned in his writings about the position of the working classes in England. Today, it can be maintained that the theory of the impoverishment of the proletariat developed by K. Marx (and repeated many times since) was not fitting for the growing number of "advanced economies". Poverty is certainly one of the most serious problems in the history of the human race. However, its causes can not be found in the exploitation theory of the Marxist school.

the world market, achieved top-level per capita incomes surprisingly quickly despite significant disadvantages due to extreme destruction from the war and its corresponding burden. In contrast countries with relatively protectionist policies in the initial years following the Second world war, like Spain and Portugal, remained at a disadvantage for decades. Despite their introduction of the rules of an open economy in the Eighteenth, they still have not closed the gap between themselves and other nations in the European Union. Nations like Albania, Cuba and North Korea, which have pursued a self-sufficiency policy for years belong to the poorest of the poor. On the other hand the most convincing example of the advantages from the integration into the international division of labor can be seen by the four 'Asian tigers' (Hong Kong, Singapore, South Korea und Taiwan). For many years they followed a policy of substituting imports with their own production. However, in the last two decades they have changed to an export-oriented and liberal-minded policy. Their successful integration into the worldwide division of labor spurred GNP growth rates and improvements in employment, which would have been considered impossible in the preceding decades. In view of their high standard of economic development today, these countries (and Israel) belong to the "advanced economies" and no longer to the developing nations[10]. Although the Asian crisis of 1997 and 1998 meant a major setback for these countries and others in the region, significant signs of improvement can be measured at present.

At long last even the former command economies (China, the former Soviet Union, the nations seceding it and its satellites as wells as numerous socialist-oriented developing countries) have abolished their protectionism. They are attempting to successfully integrate themselves into the worldwide division of labor with quite different levels of success. The fact that this necessary structural change leads to the dismissal of numerous members of the workforce is rather apparent. For a complete evaluation it is important to measure, whether the process of re-employment in those countries is faster than that of dismissal. via the process of "creative destruction" as J. A. Schumpeter said.

3 The Interpretation of Globalization as a Process of Destruction

Any extension of the international division of labor and, thereby, further globalization implies from an economic perspective that an improved worldwide

---

10 For an explanation of this reclassification of countries read the report from the International Monetary Fund May 1997, p. 4. The upgrade is more than a simple change of a statistical category. It implicitly raises the question of the downgrading of less successful nations.

allocation of productive resources (compared to the previous situation, where protection from foreign production reigned) raises the wealth of the world economy through additional work and an increased supply of goods. This does not mean that the situation of every participant or participating country is improved. Winners and losers can exist in this game, the same as anywhere else. The well-founded supposition applies that the positive effects of the extended division of labor not only outweigh its negative effects. On the contrary the process as a whole can lead to a mutually advantageous cooperation (i.e. a win-win situation), when the participants show a sufficient willingness to adapt themselves to the new situation.

Where do the gains and losses arise as a result of globalization? Here, it is advantageous to mention the theory of creative destruction from J. A. Schumpeter (1912/1926, pp. 99)[11]. Globalization advocates and opponents emphasize (even if with differing valuation) the role the dynamic entrepreneur plays in the global economy. The fundamental innovation of the globalization process is not a product; its more of an innovative process, namely the re-organization of production far beyond the borders of original national production locations by involving the world as a whole. Countries, that only produced a modest amount or absolutely no industrial goods or services earlier, have entered the markets for components of sophisticated goods like airplanes, ships or automobiles. They have achieved this status through technology transfers and often through improved education for their population. Whenever they possess a comparative advantage, they obtain the deal. Production sites migrate to other regions, new competitors enter expanding markets and inefficient suppliers are driven out of the capitalist production process, no matter if they are, entrepreneurs or workers. The participants affected by this process find new employment, when their prices (or wages) have adjusted to new circumstances, so that such employment pays – a necessary result of capitalist growth, which was admired not only by Schumpeter, but even by Marx[12].

Thus, two effects stem from globalization as a new force of growth and employment. First, it can improve the relative economic position of a country and its populace or worsen it, if insufficient adaptability exists, thereby also, reducing the political influence of the corresponding nation. On the other hand individual businesses or entire branches can experience major losses due to dynamic and radical change; they may even be destroyed – in Schumpeter's sense of the word – at their old production sites. This infers that productive factors, which are no longer profitably utilized are released. They could be employed in new uses or have to seek them out.

---

11 For an application of Schumpeter's theory in regard to the American economy see Hughes (2. Ed. 1983, p. 327).

12 See, e.g., The Communist Manifesto with its praise of the achievements of capitalism (p. 821).

3.1 Changes in the Relative Position of Wealth of a Country Through International Trade and Globalization

A common subject of international comparisons of wealth is the rise and fall of nations. In Woodall's opinion (1994, p. 10) China was technically the leading nation on the Eurasian continent up to the 16th century. Sometime thereafter Europe developed economically, technically, politically and militarily into a leading continent[13] - a process, which led to a worldwide dominant position up to the middle of the 20th century, when it began to reach its political zenith as a result of de-colonization. Of particular interest is the economic and political position that Great Britain achieved in the world around 1750, when it captured a powerful colonial empire. This leading economic position and the "pax Britannica" stemming from it were lost at the verge of World War I. The United States of America overtook the role of the British thereafter.

The shift of this leading position from Great Britain to the USA raises the question, whether the USA will be superseded by another nation in the near future. In an OECD prognosis the view is presented that from the 'big five' (China, India, Indonesia, Brazil and Russia), which are all considered to have a high potential of growth, China is expected to have the best prospects. The Chinese GNP could quadruple by 2020 (Die Welt, June 28, 1997, p. 14; Woodall, 1994, p. 10), thereby, climbing above that of the USA. With increased economic power China could play an entirely new role in world politics and militarily. Independent of this role in twenty years the 'big five' would produce almost two-thirds of world production (instead of the current two-fifths) and the share of all twenty-four OECD nations (currently producing three-fifths of world production) would fall to approximately one-third in the next two decades.

Long-term prognoses are rather risky and often incorrect, which could be claimed with respect to the OECD's estimation of Russia and Indonesia. This assessment does not rule out the possibility that changes in the relative economic position of nations could develop into a more common phenomenon than in the past. For example, the literature covering the 'rise and fall' of nations emphasizes this point. Nevertheless, diminishing shares of world production should not immediately be seen as a reason for doubt, if the per capita income does not fall at the same time. This situation can be observed in the USA. Their share of world production amounted in 1950 to around fifty percent. Since then, their share has fallen to twenty-five percent as a result of growing production in other industrial nations. At the same the USA profited substantially from the growing wealth of

13 For the driving forces of the "European Wonder" (Jones), which developed based on the diversity of the European nation states and not the political unity, see studies from Weede u.a.

their trade partners. The rapid expansion of Europe and Japan particularly in the fifties and sixties led to the highest growth in per capita income in the history of the USA according to Woodall (1994, p. 10). A similar situation could develop in the old industrial nations of Europe as a result of globalization. Such a process would serve as a verification of the ideal that the developing nations profit from the wealth of their rich neighbors. On the other hand poor neighbors are not attractive customers.

In recent years a intensive discussion has emerged dealing with whether the world economic growth process can influence the position of individual countries in the world scale of wealth on the whole. A distinction is made between convergence and divergence. It is rather apparent that relative shifts in the national positions of wealth follow as a result of dynamic processes. Such processes also arise with respect to growth on the national level between branches and businesses. Surely some individuals are hit hard from these changes. If the per capita income is taken as a measuring stick, then little reason exists to believe the well-known thesis of increasing divergences, according to which: there must be countries destined to decline as a result of the rise of other countries. International trade is not a zero-sum-game. The metapher of a flood is more fitting, where small and large ships are both raised.

3.2 A Relapse Into Mercantilism and the "Pure Capitalism" Argument

A series of arguments can be cited criticizing the deregulation of markets and the resulting intensification of economic integration and stiffer competition. Most arguments are well-known from older debates about international trade. Particularly interesting is the shift in positions as a result of public discussion. In the seventies and eighties developing nations were still considered to be in a position requiring assistance. However, a critical wave has emerged claiming that the traditional industrial nations now are being damaged by the growing economic strength of numerous developing nations. Some claim that in the day and age of borderless production a new unbridled or 'pure capitalism' threatens the first world, i.e. the old industrial nations. International exchange (or indirect production through trade) is no longer viewed as an economic relationship, from which both partners benefit. On the contrary the transportation and production of goods on a cross-border basis is modeled as a game, in which the advantages of one party lead to disadvantages for the other.

In this model the refuted teachings of the Mercantilist School are reintroduced, whereby, the wealth which one land or its populace obtains is the consequence of another countries sacrifices[14]. Certainly, one unaired secret of the mercantilist position remains: namely, why in such a world exchange takes place at all on a voluntary basis between people, businesses and organizations of every type.

The argument about 'pure capitalism' is closely related to the one above. It builds upon the school of thought that (in the civil society of today) it became finally possible to combine market economy and democracy, wealth and social compensation, self-fulfillment and solidarity, freedom and equal opportunity in the framework of an enlightened and social market economy. It also was possible to defend modern democratic societies against communist totalitarianism and its worldwide ambitions. As long as the communist threat existed, it had the unintentional effect that the capitalists and bankers living in the framework of a democracy had to show consideration for workers in order to insure that a socialist regime was not voted into power. With the implosion of socialism the most significant reason for such political consideration deteriorated. The "naked power of markets" (according to Noé, 1996) could, thus, enfold.

As an objection to this view, "globalization" is a not very well fitting expression for a long-term process stretching back into the early 19th century, an even longer period than the one in which the communist dictatorship appeared unchangeable. In the entire "period of globalization" i. e. since two hundred years world trade in the Western world has continually developed in a positive direction. However, with the supposed begin of the "naked power of the markets" a noticeable caesura should have occurred: something like an extraordinary jump in world trade. Nonetheless, this cannot be statistically shown. In addition, we should have observed plutocratic parties (representing the interests of the capitalists and the financiers) coming to power by winning elections. A course in politics which definitely did not happen.

On the contrary the older Western democracies give the impression that their political systems were not affected in the least by the collapse of socialism. Exactly the same parties with their aged welfare-state programs rule as before the failure of socialism. Even the structure of coalitions and interest groups seeking to influence the redistribution of wealth in today's democratic societies has not been altered in a sustainable manner. And in the few cases where welfare services were

---

14 Oncken recites (1922, p. 152) a popular quote from Voltaire, who formulated this situation with the following words: „Il es clair qu'un pays ne peut gagner sans qu'un autre perdre". As Oncken emphasizes the two most important recommendations of the mercantilists were the activation of the political and the trade balance. The balance of power was to be shaped principally by military measures and at the same time the success of the trade balance should stem from a tactful foreign policy in economic matters (see the previous entry p. 153). The concept that in such a world conflict and not cooperation has to reign can be derived from the simple observation that not all countries can enjoy a positive balance of trade (in this case the same as balance of payments) simultaneously.

successfully reformed (e.g. in the Netherlands and New Zealand), social democratic parties were decisively involved.

3.3 Do Exports of Developing Nations Damage Wealthy Countries?

Globalization possesses a variety of aspects and facets, which are difficult to grasp. In wealthy countries it is judged from a national perspective and not, first and foremost, from a world economic perspective. The question is whether globalization actually (or only supposedly) improves or harms national wealth and employment. Among the standard arguments of critics the claim can be found that growing pressure from the exports of developing nations destroy jobs in advanced economies, thus, exacerbating joblessness. In an effort to fight such a trend, an explicit or implicit demand is made for securing and maintaining jobs through trade restrictions.

This argument includes many aspects. First of all, it is true that imports endanger domestic competitors and can even force them out of the market, which means an initial loss of jobs. Should we, therefore, follow the recommendation of introducing a luxury tax of thirty percent on "the purchase of real estate, which goes beyond personal use at one's place of residence, and the purchase of limousines, high-sea yachts, private jets, valuable jewelry, cosmetic surgery and other things"? (Martin and Schumann, 1997, p. 334). Such an action would be not only an "attack"[15] on Germany's wealth, but also on that of the corresponding exporting nation. For the export nation the price increase due to the tax on these items would lead to a reduction in jobs and income. Advocates for such a tax could argue that this effect is not particularly interesting to the domestic economy, since here possibility exists of substituting the imported goods with domestic production, thus, increasing income and employment at home.

From an economic perspective this does not represent the whole truth. When low-priced foreign goods are substituted by domestic production, the advantages of the international division of labor are sacrificed. Domestically, factors of production must be reallocated from the manufacture of export goods to that of goods substituting imports. As a result, factors of production are switched to less favorable uses and the relevant domestic production becomes more expensive. Also the repercussions of a luxury tax on the foreign country cannot be viewed with indifference. Ignoring the "veil of money", trade implies an exchange of goods for other goods. If domestic policy disturbs the export markets of foreign countries by introducing trade restrictions, the purchasing power abroad is

---

15 See the subtitle of the book from Martin and Schumann.

affected, which may have been allotted for purchasing the exports from the country introducing the tax. Seen as a practical mirror image, income and employment are impacted, yet again. In sum, both trading partners can be seen as losers due to one-sided taxes or trade restrictions.

This is not only true for this static example. The same process in a dynamic economy would be similarly affected. What is a sensible economic solution in this case? The actual problem is the adjustment to continually changing demand and supply structures of a dynamic economy. In order to tackle this situation, a market economy offers the best solution in comparison to other known allocation systems. By employing flexible prices, which show the changing plans of all economic actors and signalize where profitable or loss-making developments arise, the market economy is definitely the best way to solve such problems.

If the signals from the market are followed, which requires adjustments (and flexibility) from all parties involved, prosperity will result. In the event various participants are not willing to adapt, their market exit becomes an unavoidable result. However, when producers (in the sense of workers and employers) adapt to changes, international trade does not lead to negative effects on total employment in the long run. A gradual shift from non-competitive domestic industries substituting imports to competitive export industries results. This is the real economic problem to be solved.

And how important is the import problem, when applying trade statistics as an interpretation? For the industrial nations as a whole, the imports from developing nations amount to a few percentage points of total imports. Many people come to the conclusion based on this statistic information that a serious threat from globalization does not exist. Even if this argument is not accepted or foreign exports are concentrated in specific sectors or dramatically increase in the future, the problem of flexibility and adjustment still remains as the focal point. Rising imports place pressure on the industries they compete with. Wages and prices are affected by this in the sense that the entire economy experiences greater efficiency. In the event production is suppressed in the sense of Schumpeter's "creative destruction", it is important to see how "creative" the people are in starting something new. Therefore, the point should be studied, whether the incentive structures in a country promote innovation, the development of new products and the substitution of traditional practices with improved ones.

3.4 The Migration of Industries to Low-Wage Countries

The possibilities of international capital mobility have expanded in the last two decades probably much further than in the days of the gold standard. Fears are tied to high capital mobility and they should certainly be viewed with concern, if they prove to be true. Opponents of globalization describe a situation, in which competition for the lowest wages and the highest efficiency has begun. The ease of transferring modern technology into all regions of the world enables businesses to relocate in regions with the lowest wages – in other words combining the best methods of production with the lowest costs in order to achieve the highest profits. In view of the economic distress of many developing countries, capitalists would be able to dictate their conditions for settling there to the respective governments, thus, reducing the costs of production yet again and increasing profits.

This often held view is an extremely misleading. An abrupt and long-lasting transfer of numerous manufacturing sites into developing nations would naturally cause major problems in the industrial nations, if it would happen. The available productive capital stock would not be renewed and, thus, decay. In the event domestic workers followed the emigrating capital, they would have to reckon with rejection from the populace in the foreign country, since these people would view them as unwelcome competitors in the job market. However, if they decided against migration, higher unemployment and lower incomes would result in their own country. In either case conflicts and social disruptions could develop.

Such a scenario ignores the present situation and the feedback mechanisms of markets. The countries receiving capital will enjoy an improvement in their economic condition and higher levels of employment, whereby, in the long term typically demands for higher wages will arise. The cost situation of the capital-importing countries worsens and the capital export nations are presented with a new chance of reaching their former position, if their wages and prices show more flexibility than those abroad. The less friction there is in the economic process, the lower the swings in either direction.

And how do things behave in reality? In Germany the imbalance in direct investments as a result of capital shifts to other countries has been the source of a lively debate. For quite some time high German investments abroad can be compared to rather moderate inflows to Germany. Some critics interpret this as an acute location disadvantage for Germany. However, more detailed analysis of the real capital movements show that this superficial assessment is unsatisfactory and that the quality of data is quite weak in many respects (Jost 1997, pp. 60). German investments abroad occur for a variety of reasons, especially as a tool for securing foreign markets. When establishing sites abroad, businesses often pursue the goal of securing domestic jobs tied to exports and not of relocating them. Even if direct investment abroad primarily results from high wages, high taxes and diminishing competitiveness at home, the utilization of the exit-option (Hirschman) should not be seen as an argument for politically impeding capital mobility, which has often been demanded (Huffschmid, 1997, p. 251). On the one hand the mere announcement of such a policy would lead to an increase in capital mobility or even force a serious withdrawal. On the other hand the goal of a sound economic policy would continue to be neglected, namely, the employment of a policy to improve the working of markets.

Apart from specific problems in Germany, the worldwide growth in capital mobility due to globalization implies that the chances for increasing wealth and reducing poverty have improved tremendously. Capital is no longer bound by national borders or regional alliances; it can migrate to the locations bringing the greatest return. This is rather good news for those people hoping to for the world economy as a whole to fight poverty worldwide.

4 Globalization and the International Economic Order

Globalization in the sense described here can also be understood as an extension of market freedom. National sovereignty in the sense of power over citizens declines or disappears as a by-product of the more intensive division of labor. Individuals are allowed to operate as entrepreneurs, workers or investors in their own country or choose other countries as well. In this situation one must consider the fact that human migration encounters barriers unknown in other centuries. The American 'green card', a permanent work and residency permit for the USA, has practically achieved a proverbial sense. Nowadays, it can be obtained through a state-run lottery or for the less fortunate it can be secured through a marriage of convenience. Restrictions to personal mobility do not paralyze all forms of substitutes. Trade outside of national borders is one form, since the units of work employed to manufacture a product travel with it.

The intensification of the division of labor between societies beyond national borders and the international trends in production (i.e. the processes behind the term 'globalization') require a simultaneous widening and deepening of the international legal system. The international division of labor can only develop, when reliable rules exist. For example, if delivery contracts would not be performed in the way, as it was the case in the former Eastern bloc economies, than production would falter and a process of impoverishment would begin like the one leading to the downfall of socialism. Therefore, an international, reliable and functional legal system possesses significant societal value[16].

Modern legal systems are territorially bound, which underlies the statement that the extent of the division of labor depends upon the size of the legal space[17]. Thus, the integration of worldwide manufacturing activities can only achieve success to the extent that property rights (in an economic sense) are preserved. The

16 Adam Smith made such claims 1776/1976, p. 910: „Commerce and manufactures can seldom flourish long in any state which does not enjoy a regular administration of justice, in which the people do not feel themselves secure in the possession of their property and in which the faith of contracts is not supported by law".

17 Schmidtchen und his students developed this aspect further.

establishment of contracts, in which one can sue for recovery, also plays a role. However, in today's world of nation states both conditions are rarely fulfilled continuously[18]. This has wide-reaching consequences for globalization. The differing qualities of legal systems raise not only the costs of global production (as well as so-called transaction costs), they also decrease the degree of integration that can be achieved. The opinion is often expressed that "everything can be produced and bought anywhere in the world" (Thurow, 1996, p. 22). Nonetheless, this view does not fit with reality. Two things are apparent: the image of modern information and communication technology making anything possible is as incorrect as the claim that the world is caught up in a capitalist tornado, which levels everything.

To speak of a 'future capitalism' with a single world market, a single legal system and possibly a world state is inappropriate. It would even be problematic from an economic perspective to push for a development in this direction[19].

Law can be organized in a state under the rule of law; it can spontaneously arise as well. A good example of the latter is 'ius commune' – a combination of Roman law with Christian law from the Middle Ages[20]. Such an evolution of law would have little chance today. Over time a legislative standardization of legal systems occurs as found in international economic organizations. Even though one can assume that the evolution of law in private agreements (private ordering) leads to an efficient arrangement of international relationships, this fails to apply to the legal development in international organizations. The danger implicitly exists that law will be used as an instrument to follow obvious or hidden political goals. This can be clearly seen in debates on the further development of the world trade order. Here the wealthier Western nations wish to combine the opening of their markets with the demand for minimum worldwide standards for employment and environmental protection, which is directed at the developing nations.

Minimum employment standards are often founded on the argument that the situation of workers in poorer countries should be improved. At the same time it is made clear that unjust wage advantages exist in these countries. Minimum standards for social conditions in these developing nations are also demanded. Examples for working conditions similar to those described by Dickens (an English author from the 19th century) are quite numerous and shocking. They span from child labor in India to accidents at the work place – with exorbitantly high

---

18 In several transformation economies the "wonder of the market" cannot properly unfold, since so-called "bandit capitalism" rules, where the rights of the stronger apply.

19 Refer to Watrin 1997, where an attempt is made to show that a polycentric world with varying legal systems has its advantages from a dynamic perspective compared to the propagated trends toward centralization and harmonization.

20 Paradoxically, ius commune was destroyed by the national standardization of law in 19th-century Europe.

numbers in comparison to Western nations. Nevertheless, representatives of many developing nations raise the objection that a forced adjustment in an effort to meet Western standards would eliminate their sole cost advantage, namely, lower costs of employment. The social motive of the West camouflages a new form of protectionism. This raises the question, whether trade sanctions from wealthier nations are suitable for improving working conditions and for realizing bans on child labor, especially in view of numerous loopholes in states with a rather rudimentary (if any) rule of law.

The same problem arises with respect to environmental standards. According to the intention of influential political movements, such standards should become part of future trade agreements. But such trade sanctions would result in a slowing down of the growth process in developing nations instead of its acceleration. Since environmental protection is a good, which is only demanded with increased wealth, trade restrictions would not further the goal of improving environmental quality, they would delay or annul it. The higher the level of poverty is the lower the financing capacity for environmental protection.

The view that 'unrestricted competition' (in the form described in the agreements of the European Community) or 'fair competition' is a objective measure for shaping the world economic order, involves a type of hidden protectionism similar to that of the minimum social standards presented above. It fails to consider the fact that nations – seen as political communities – possess varying opinions about what is just and useful. In addition, the two hundred or more nations in the world community enjoy differing resource bases, which can be altered through political or individual action.

The countries obtaining the status of wealthy nations in the last one hundred and fifty years have shown that the process of increasing wealth not only (not even primarily) implies the satisfaction of mere material needs. "Open societies" prove to be creative, ingenious and innovative in various fields.

List of References

Deutsches Institut für Wirtschaftsforschung (1997), Berlin, Wochenbericht 23/97 vom 5.Juni 1997, Globalisierung: Falle oder Wohlstandsquelle, pp. 413-419.

Fukuyama, Francis (1992), The End of History and the Lost Men, Avon Books, New York (German title: "Das Ende der Geschichte", München, 1992).

Haberler, Gottfried (1936), International Trade

Huffschmid, Jörg (1997), Globalisierung - das Ende der Wirtschaftspolitik? In: *Wege zu einem anderen Europa*. Hrsg. Beirat für gesellschafts-, wirtschafts- und umweltpolitische Alternativen, Köln.

Hughes, Jonathan (1987), American Economic History (2. ed.) Glenview, Illinois and London, England.

International Monetary Fund, World Economic Outlook, Globalization. Opportunities and Challenges. May 1997, Washington D.C.

Jones, Eric L (1981), The European Miracle. (German titel: Das Wunder Europa, Tübingen (1991)).

Jost, Thomas, Direktinvestitionen und Standort Deutschland. Diskussionspapier 2/97. Volkswirtschaftliche Forschungsgruppe der Deutschen Bundesbank.

Martin, Hans-Peter und Schumann, Harald (1997), Die Globalisierungsfalle. Der Angriff auf Demokratie und Wohlstand, Hamburg.

Marx, Karl und Engels, Friedrich (1948/1971), Manifest der kommunistischen Partei. In: *Karl Marx, Werke*, edited by H. J. Lieber and P. Fürth. Wissenschaftliche Buchgesellschaft, Darmstadt.

Noé, Claus (1996), *Die Zeit*, No. 47, 1996, p. 4.

ohne Verfasser, China wird größte Wirtschaftsmacht. In: *Die* Welt, from June 28, 1997, p. 14.

Oncken, A. (1922), Geschichte der Nationalökonomie, Leipzig.

Röpke, Wilhelm (1942), International Economic Disintegration, London.

Schmidtchen, D. (1993), Neue Institutionenökonomik internationaler Transaktionen. In: Schließer, U. und Schmidtchen, D.; Makro, *Geld & Institutionen*, Tübingen.

Schmidt-Trenz, H.-J. (1989), Außenhandel und Territorialität des Rechts. Baden-Baden.

Schumpeter, Joseph A (1912/1926), Theorie der wirtschaftlichen Entwicklung (5. ed.), Berlin.

Smith, Adam (1776/1979), An Enquiry into the Nature and Causes of the Wealth of Nations (Glasgow Edition).

Thurow, Lester C. (1996), Die Zukunft des Kapitalismus, Düsseldorf-München.

Watrin, Christian (1997), Integration durch Recht, erscheint demnächst in Buar, Jürgen und Watrin, Christian, (Editors) In: *Recht und Wirtschaft der Europäischen Gemeinschaft auf dem Prüfstand*, Köln.

Watrin, Christian (1997), Währung und Währungspolitik (appearing soon by Fritz-Knapp-Verlag, Frankfurt, Handbuch des Geld,- Banken und Börsenwesens, Hrsg. Friedrich Thießen.

Woodall, P. (1994), A Survey of the Global Economy; in: *The Economist*, 1. October 1994 (supplement).

Some Features of Japanese Direct Investment after the Second World War from the Perspective of East Asia

Johzen Takeuchi

University of Nagoya

1 Preface

During the last few decades, Japan has often been called one of the "economic great powers." This was a source of much satisfaction to many Japanese. However, they were usually indifferent to the implications of the term. It would be too snobbish to take satisfaction in an epithet like "great power" if it were based only a country's fulfilment of some limited criteria of modern economics. Nowadays, the basic framework of modern business and employment is drastically expanding beyond the confines of national borders, but the basic concepts of modern economics have been established within the boundaries of the national economy. These days, an economy which is unable to take such matters into consideration could not be called a driving force within the world economy. If Japan had not prepared adequate human resources and multinational systems, as required for its multinational activities in the process of its economic growth, it would merely have deserved to be called a pseudo-great power.

This paper will undertake a short investigation into Japanese multinational business activities, and ask whether multinational corporations have succeeded in establishing any international frameworks. However, it will neither go into the dimension of human resource development, which is one of the most urgent subjects for their global strategies, nor into certain matters like multinational project management and contingency response, which have often been criticized with regard to Japanese reparation payments and regional development programmes, even though these will be the determining factors in the growing sophistication of Japanese international activities.

Compared with the traditional behaviour patterns of European or American companies, Japanese companies have been criticized for their closed attitude and exaggerated obedience to their parent companies or to political authorities during the period of their expansion abroad. In spite of these criticisms and aspersions, they have managed to expand their activities and not a few of them have succeeded in intensifying their own activities and being more appreciated in the last few decades. Among these experiences, we can present some positive and impressive examples which contradict the usual perception of Japanese foreign activities. Moreover, it is not difficult to show that some of these firms are going to develop new strategies and systems which are not familiar either to Japanese or foreigners, and this short paper will identify the socio-economic backgrounds of such strategies and systems pertaining to the economic activities of Japanese enterprises in East Asia, especially in the Asian NIEs and ASEAN countries.

When investigating East Asian matters, it would be misleading to suggest that Singapore belongs both to the NIEs and ASEAN, and to aid better understanding, it is necessary to set out some terminology for this paper:

1. In this paper, "ASEAN4" means Thailand, Malaysia, the Philippines and Indonesia, excluding Singapore. This is because these 4 countries are in similar stages of economic development and Singapore is the country of outstanding economic development among ASEAN, in terms of some basic economic indexes like per capita income, social overhead, etc. This paper will mainly analyze Singapore as one of the Asian NIEs.

2. Here, "ASEAN5" means both Singapore and the above-mentioned ASEAN4, excluding a small but very rich country, Brunei, and when this paper refers to the "ASEAN region", it means ten countries, since an additional four countries, i. e., Laos, Cambodia, Vietnam and Myanmar, were recently admitted to membership in this regional organization.

3. When this paper mentions "East Asia," it includes Asian NIEs, ASEAN, China and Japan. Furthermore, "Far East Asian Regions" means China, Japan and Asian NIEs, excluding Singapore. An analysis of North Korea and the Russian Far East is not a subject of this paper.

2 International Economic Indexes and Japanese Overseas Investment

It was first in the 1970s that Japanese business activity and economic performance attracted any international attention. Japanese global economic activity was neither active nor stable before that. Table 1 shows that its balance of trade suffered a sequential deficit until 1957, and it was still severely fluctuating before 1964. Foreign currency reserves were not sufficient, and they were less than $1bn until 1958, as is shown in Table 2.

It was the import aid program of the Allied Army that saved Japan from a crisis of international payments in the latter half of the 1940s. It was equivalent to 77% of the total amount of Japanese imports in 1947, and it amounted to the greater part of the receipts of the unpaid balance, shown in Table 1. This aid was reduced to 8% of the balance in 1951. It was American military expenditures that substituted for the decline of the occupation aid. The relative importance of this scheme was reduced at the end of the 1950s, but even so, the military demand was as much as $404m in 1958 and the deficit of international trade in the same year was $370m (The Bank of Japan 1963, p.2). Due to this special demand, many industrial sectors like automobiles and parts, military goods, coal, foods, textiles, etc., had an opportunity and ready markets for their revival after the fatal decline of the war. Military demand by America still exists today, and although its annual amount has not declined, its relative importance has become very small because the scale of the national economy has expanded so rapidly.

After the relative reduction of military expenditure by America, international organizations took its place, and supplied sufficient foreign currency in terms of official loans. In particular, the loans from the World Bank were intensively utilized for the building of social infrastructures like the Shinkansen (bullet train) and the highway network of Japan in the first half of the 1960s. After the construction of these infrastructures and sufficient managerial development of Japanese firms, it became popular for the American and European private sector to invest directly in Japan, starting from the latter half of the 1960s. It is possible to identify this movement from the trend of long-term capital, shown in Table 1.

Generally speaking, the Japanese postwar economy was not tough enough to sustain itself without any assistance from abroad, but it had already started to have its own business activity and foreign investment in the 1950s. Firstly, it concentrated on constructing public organizations and official facilities, but it started to reconstruct the trade network for supplying Japanese commodities outside Japan after 1952, when Japan recovered its diplomatic independence, and into which Japanese companies poured as much as $60m on average annually from 1952 to 1958. The major target was the US, but they also concentrated on building up their business network in the countries of Asia and the Pacific Basin, where they tried to obtain sufficient materials like coal, iron ore and cotton. In 1955, the Japanese government started its reparation payments and tried to utilize domestic commodities and production facilities for its payments. This offered a chance for the private sector, such as general trading companies and some leading manufacturers to expand their businesses into these countries. Of course, such newly established offices and branches were fully utilized to obtain any natural resources and materials for the Japanese manufacturing sector.

It was in the latter half of the 1960s that Japanese foreign direct investment started to expand drastically, and it surpassed $1bn in 1968. It should be noted that at this point Japan was able to promote this positive rush of foreign direct investment without suffering a deficit in its international balance, partly because it succeeded in improving dramatically its balance of trade in the 1960s. The annual surplus in international trade exceeded $1bn in 1965, and it did not drop below this figure even at the time of the first and second oil shocks. Furthermore, it increased up to $50bn in 1985, and against intensified foreign direct investment. Japanese long-term capital investment surpassed $10bn in 1978 and this level was successfully maintained in 1980, just after the second oil shock. It expanded to $23bn in 1981, $32bn in 1983, $59bn in 1984, and almost reached $82bn in 1985. Due to this sky-rocketing increase, setting up some kind of institutional arrangement was unavoidable, and this was the Plaza Accord, which caused a drastic change in the business strategy of Japanese companies.

3 Japanese Foreign Investment and Its Features

Developmental economists have laid stress on the fact that Japanese activities in foreign direct investment (FDI) concentrated mostly on North America and Europe, and then began to shift to the Asian region in the latter half of the 1980s, because of the high appreciation of the Japanese currency (Yamashita 1991; Hirakawa 1992). They believed that Japanese companies were going to relocate their production bases to Asian countries in order to maintain the market share that they had achieved in the industrialized countries. Moreover, many of them emphasized that Japanese FDI had shifted to NIEs and then to ASEAN, and further to China and Vietnam, as if it followed the hypothesis of the "pattern of flying geese" (Akamatsu 1935; Watanabe 1985). In the case of some limited industries like garments and their related sectors, this was surely a defensible hypothesis. However, if we take a look at the long-term statistics of FDI, it should be noted that:

1. In the commercial and service sectors, Japanese FDI was dispersed over almost the entire world. In the early stages of foreign investment, it was concentrated in the industrialized countries, but in accordance with the development of Japan, target zones were quickly expanded.

2. In the manufacturing sectors, Japanese companies intensified their investment mainly in Asia at an early stage of their expansion abroad, and especially in ASEAN countries, instead of NIEs, where they encountered strong anti-Japanese feelings, which were common among numerous national populations after the Second World War.

Table 3 is not sufficient to show this trend, but it reveals that North America occupied the major part of Japanese FDI in the manufacturing sectors just before the Plaza Accord, which caused the drastically high appreciation of the Japanese currency, and caused Japanese investment to increase more rapidly in the latter half of the 1980s. At the same time, East Asia succeeded in gaining more Japanese investment, but its relative share decreased dramatically. It was after 1994 that the region again increased its share. FDI to East Asia rose to $5.2bn in 1994, and it expanded to $80bn in the following year. Target zones were enlarged from NIEs, ASEAN and the coastal area of China, to the inland area of China and Vietnam, and further to India. There were plenty of reasons why Asian development economists became enthusiastic about adopting the hypothesis of the pattern of flying geese (World Bank 1993). However, Japanese manufacturers were going to increase their investment in North America and Europe during these years. It should be noted that Asian investment is now one of the decisive dimensions of Japanese business activities, but it should not be evaluated only by certain quantitative aspects.

As this paper has stressed, Japanese FDI in Asia did not shift from advanced areas to less advanced areas. It would be possible to say that it shifted from NIEs to ASEAN only if we depend upon the data taken since the middle of the 1980s, but if we take it after the 1960s, as shown in Table 4, we would be unable to say this. Particularly in the middle of the 1970s, investment in ASEAN5 was larger than that in North America. When Japanese manufacturers were going to expand their target zones of investment from ASEAN to Asian NIEs, they were also obliged to shift to highly industrialized countries to compensate for the imbalance of trade with them.

Japanese FDI in Asia expanded very quickly in the middle of the 1990s, but this was related to the abrupt increase of investment in China, where Japanese companies were reluctant to invest for a long time. Excluding that in China, it is possible to say that North America has occupied the lion's share of Japanese FDI since the 1980s. Europe's share has constantly been about 10-15%, except for the days just before the EU was organized, when Japanese companies were nervous about whether they would be locked out of this high-potential market, and they hurried to increase their investment (Takeuchi, 1997). At this time the share became more than 20%. At this point, we need to investigate briefly the sectoral features of Japanese FDI. Table 5 will give a rough sketch of them:

1. From the amount of investment classified by industrial sector, it is obvious that the commercial, service, and financial sectors were the main stream of Japanese FDI.

2. The share of the manufacturing sectors became steadily larger only in the 1990s.

3. Among the manufacturing sectors, the biggest shares were occupied by electrical machines and appliances, along with transportation machine sectors, and these are still expanding in the 1990s.

In addition to these points, it is possible to point out that the shares of the chemical industry and mining are expanding. It is difficult to identify from this table, but it should be noted that Japanese investment concentrates mainly on intermediate processing and manufacturing, and finished goods manufacturing, but not always on direct development of natural resources. In other words, Japanese companies are good at setting up sufficient competitiveness in the middle and downstream areas, especially in the sectors which heavily depend upon intermediate process manufacturing, and at organizing the assembling and parts manufacturing sectors for the manufacturing of mass production final goods.

Compared with Japanese industrial structure, British and other European societies' competitiveness is prominent, especially in the financing and insurance sectors and information sectors. They are also good at natural resource development and some limited, but important manufacturing sectors like natural resource processing, and system and scale oriented processing, including the processing of uranium and plutonium. They still maintain superb competitiveness in manufacturing numerous luxury goods. Recently, some Japanese manufacturers have succeeded in getting top-graded primary goods like cotton, wool, coffee, etc., and have been able to gain a limited share of the world markets for high-quality goods. However, it is hardly necessary to point out that American and some European companies still maintain the major shares for the highest quality primary goods for manufacturing luxury consumption goods, including tea, coffee, cacao, leaf tobacco, wool, precious metals and stones, etc. Manufacturing sectors relating to these materials are under their firm control.

It is noteworthy that sectoral features of the international division of labour can also be seen at the level of regional or national analyses. Table 6 shows Japanese FDI in Europe, classified by industrial sectors. It does not go into detailed subsectors, and it might give the impression that the Japanese are good at system and scale oriented chemical sectors. However, they mainly concentrate on intermediate or final goods. In other words, they have tried to expand their line of businesses, not in the scale-oriented upstream sectors, but in the mid- and down-stream sectors. In the textile industry, weaving sectors were also concentrated on, not primary processing of raw materials. This paper does not supply the data classified by the amount of investment, but Japanese manufacturers promoted their big investments mostly in machine, electrical and electronic parts and appliances, and transportation machine sectors. It should be noted that they maintained similar patterns of investment in Europe as indicated by their global FDI (Takeuchi, op. cit.).

We can find this pattern in a more typical form in the case of Pakistan. Table 7 contains simple data which the author classified in terms of investment and industrial sectors. Utilizing the data from the government of Pakistan, we can clearly see the "division of capital" in this country. Investors from English-speaking countries occupy the major part of the agro-based sectors, metals and petrochemicals. Japanese companies are concentrated mostly in the machine and appliance sectors. It is difficult to identify whether this relation is a kind of multinational symbiosis, or whether it merely symbolizes the traditional relation that latecomers have to collect together in niche sectors, or the areas where technology is not easily transferred through the ordinary operational manual system. This author could only establish that Japanese staff revealed no particular traits, but tried instead to develop the industrial sectors which forerunners had already given up. However, there is an exceptional region where Japanese investors were able to adopt a different kind of strategy. This is East Asia, at which this paper will take a short glance in the following section.

4 Japanese FDI in East Asia

One of the most prominent features of Japanese investment in East Asia is that it covers almost all manufacturing sectors. Petrochemicals and other synthetic-material related sectors are obviously occupied by Americans or Europeans in many regions of the world, but in East Asia they seem to have been indifferent to maintaining their own supremacy.

Table 8 does not contain new data, but it shows the situation of Japanese FDI before 1985. After this year, not only Japanese leading companies but also small and medium-scale firms (SMFs) in numerous sectors started to shift their production bases to other countries. However, this table shows the typical features of Japanese FDI to East Asia. Excluding the countries where local governments preferred to establish their own local manufacturers, Japanese manufacturers occupied the biggest market share in this region. In automobile and electrical appliances especially, Japanese brand names were popular and some journalists criticized their over-representation in the region. Nevertheless, in terms of the total amount of investment, these new sectors were not as large as common industrial sectors such as textiles, chemical goods, and metal processing, which are shown in the table. In addition, the Japanese succeeded in developing some industrial sectors such as petrochemicals in which they could not have gained sufficient competitive advantage in the West, where they had to concentrate on certain limited sectors in which they could maintain some comparative advantage.

Briefly put, Japanese manufacturers had to conform to a "multinational corporations' division of labour" accommodating North America and Western Europe, but they seem to have decided that they were going to organize a "fully ranged industrial division of labour" and also a "regional division of labour" in East Asia. As they were so nervous about maintaining their market share in industrialized countries, they tried to keep pace with other competitors of Japan, and for this simple reason, almost all leading companies in certain industrial sectors tended to have similar investments in the same regions of the West. However, in East Asia, where they could neither have enough of the domestic market nor utilize sufficient infrastructure, each company had to set up its own strategy at its own risk. This is the reason why Japanese investment in East Asia differs in each country, as is shown in Table 8. Moreover, it should be noted that investment also differs in each company.

Japanese investment in the textile industry was greatest in Indonesia, followed by Thailand. The investment in Thailand was bigger than that in Korea, whose share was the biggest among Asian NIEs. Petrochemicals were mostly concentrated in Singapore, partly because of the convenience of delivery from oil-producing countries and for Japanese joint ventures in neighbouring countries. Korea also promoted Japanese investment in petrochemicals because of the importance of increasing the supply of intermediate materials for the local textile industry. Singapore collected the biggest investment for the industrial machine industry, and Indonesia had the biggest share of the metal industry. NIEs excluding Hong Kong attracted the major part of electrical appliances and electronic parts wares. ASEAN4 gained a bigger share than that of Asian NIEs for the automobile industry.

These "international divisions of capital" could be one of the positive factors for promoting the industrialization of each country and interregional trade in this region, especially of ASEAN4, and this became one of the major factors for the Japanese rush to investment after 1985. In particular, the Japanese concentrated on automobiles and parts, and electrical and electronic goods and parts, and it is well known that the investment by SMFs became popular at this time.

Another trend should be noted here. As the wage level of Asian NIEs swelled, Korean and Taiwanese companies intensified their own supplies of substitutive commodities for Japanese goods, and this trend was more intensive in Korea than in Taiwan. Regarding their strategy, some economists emphasized that they had historical anti-Japanese feelings, and others put stress on the effectiveness of the hypothesis of the pattern of flying geese. A far more important factor was that East Asia was bound to have a big market without paying attention to the importance of international division of labour in the region. After the short business decline at the beginning of the 1980s, ASEAN4 countries succeeded in expanding their own markets, and they were destined to have their own wave of motorization in the middle of the 1980s. This wave coincided with the high appreciation of the Japanese currency. Moreover, there was another reason for the

Japanese rush to ASEAN4. Japanese leading manufacturers of some major industrial sectors mentioned above were heavily dependent on SMFs. They had to ask small manufacturers to shift overseas by cajoling and threatening. In accordance with the economic development of ASEAN4, it was difficult for big Japanese manufacturers to expand their production capacity without sufficient assistance of SMFs.

In the latter half of the 1980s, there emerged a large and global production base in East Asia. Japan Auto-Parts Manufacturers Association (JAMA) reported that the US share of Japanese auto-parts manufacturers' FDI was 26% (Fig. 1), but that of ASEAN was as much as 30%, and China and "other Asia" took 11% and 17% respectively (JAMA 1997, p. 2). This trend of an East Asian shift was further intensified in the 1990s. The report also shows that the Japanese established 456 new factories in the 1990s and 67% of them were located in Asia (Fig. 2). It is obvious that they promoted their shift to ASEAN, and in the case of automobiles in particular it was to ASEAN4 (Fig. 3). This trend can be confirmed through the empirical survey of the research group of Nagoya University and the materials supplied by the Toyota corporation (Fig. 4; Fig. 5; Fig. 6). Some auto-parts manufacturers concentrated their overseas activities in the US, but many of them were shifting their production bases to ASEAN.

In spite of the severe financial crisis in the latter of the 1990s, business relations between Japan and East Asia seem to have become tighter, as far as manufacturing sectors are concerned. Table 9 shows that Japanese investment to ASEAN was maintained even in the midst of the Asian financial crisis. The total amount was reduced, but not as drastically as that of the NIEs or China. This means that the presence of ASEAN has become more important for Japanese business activities in the last couple of decades, and the region has also developed business relations with Japan in terms of the transfer of technology combined with capital relations, as is shown in Table 10. According to the data, there were 153 companies which arranged technology contracts with Japanese companies in ASEAN5. The number is smaller than that of the US where there were 173 companies, but bigger than that of the whole of Europe. Further, in terms of equity ties, Japanese companies arranged contracts with 100 counterparts in ASEAN5, which is bigger than that of the US where they succeeded in getting 52 contracts. This technological assistance, combined with capital relations, means that Japan will transfer its latest technology, mainly because its companies are obliged to join the global competition.

An increase of overseas production and the increased level of transferred technology created some new conditions for Japanese manufacturers, and this paper will discuss the case of the automobile industry. The Japan Automobile Manufacturers Association declared that the year 1994 was epoch-making, because the number of cars produced overseas by Japanese-related car makers exceeded that of the exports from Japan. This is not as advanced as the overseas production of some electrical appliances, whose import has already surpassed the amount of domestic production in the latter half of the 1980s, but undoubtedly that year became the precise turning point for the managerial decision-making of many automobile manufacturers in Japan.

It is well known in the history of business that certain private companies or capital groups have promoted the international division of labour, and that it has intensified a monocultural economy of developing countries and a unilateral relation of colonialism. On the opposing side, some multinational companies will establish new relationships among developing countries, and intensify the industrialization and sophistication of industrial structures in those countries. As relates to some Japanese multinational manufacturers, this trend became typical at the end of the 1980s in certain ASEAN countries. When they took the initiative in supplying electrical appliances to industrialized countries like the US, they were obliged to establish effective systems for the supply of various parts, because the number of items they needed for their production had already expanded to the level of more than several tens of thousands at this time. They started to install a "value added information network" among ASEAN countries, and this system turned out to be one of the leading factors for some countries, like Malaysia, to develop as major supplier countries of modern commodities, like colour TVs, video recorders, etc. Nowadays, many Japanese companies have R&D sections and design centres in ASEAN5. It is possible to find many local enterprises that utilized those business relations and developed quickly, and not a few of them actually started as tiny subcontractors of Japanese joint ventures (Takeuchi 1991). Provided that new local enterprises and human resources increase rapidly from now on, this trend could be a new element to which Dr Krugman has not referred.

5 Concluding Remarks

This paper has tried to present some limited aspects of Japanese FDI, utilizing well-known official statistics and prominent leading surveys of Asian development studies. There are numerous matters which this paper has neglected, but its focus has been on the analysis of the manufacturing sector. Of course, we need to investigate the function of the finance sector, commercial sector, information sector, etc., in order to identify more realistically the features of Japanese FDI and its impact on Asian society. This paper did not attempt to go into details of such matters. Although the survey is not sufficient to identify the basic characteristics of modern international business activities, it is possible to make some concluding remarks here:

1. Japanese FDI managed to achieve a favourable regional balance among North America, Western Europe, and East Asia only in the 1980s.

2. When Japanese companies set out to invest directly in North America and Western Europe, they did not always have sufficient information or an adequate information network. However, their sense of competition against their domestic competitors intensified their activities, and overflowed to the outside world.

3. In the case of Asian investment, the companies' activities differed, depending on the situations of related countries. They had to collect their own information and set up their basic strategy planning for their development. However, in the case of numerous subcontractors, the decision-making was completely different.

4. International division of labour among Asian NIEs and Japan has been extremely unsatisfactory, but they will coordinate on this matter.

5. Historically, Japanese FDI has been concentrated on the ASEAN region, and in some aspects, this was closely related to reparation payments.

6. ASEAN5 is now the major target for Japanese SMFs, partly because Japanese business activities have had a long historical background and it is easier for them to arrange a sufficient human resource network.

7. Japanese FDI in China expanded quickly at the beginning of the 1990s, but recently it has been stagnating and shrinking.

8. The international division of labour between the ASEAN region and Japan is now smoothly expanding. This is the result of the intensive managerial strategies of numerous companies. However, we can not predict the long- term results of this international relationship.

This paper could not go into details about some new trends which have become conspicuous in the past couple of years. Historically, the Korean government has preferred for its people to maintain strong anti-Japanese feelings. However, particularly after the recent financial crisis, its attitude has been changing, because some of the government staff and private sectors have appreciated the difference in attitudes toward the recent crisis of the US and Japan. They started to open their market for Japanese goods and deregulated cultural exchange in 1999. Taiwanese, especially those who migrated from the mainland after the war, were reluctant to have active contacts with the Japanese, but their attitudes are also changing after the long-term activities of business and cultural exchanges, and further, after Japanese assistance in the matter of earthquake damage protection. However, this paper is not concerned with the details of these matters.

Table 1: Balance of International Payments

(Unit: million US$)

Year	Current Balance	Current Trade	Services	Un-Requited Balance	Long-term Capital	Basic Balance	Short-term Capital	Errors & Omissions	Overall Balance	Balance of Monetary Movements	
1946	-78	-238	-35	195	22	-56	----	-3	-58	----	----
1950	476	34	12	429	-93	384	1	49	434	----	----
1955	227	-54	259	22	-24	202	102	-19	285	30	----
1960	143	268	-100	-25	-55	88	-16	33	105	502	-397
1965	931	1.901	-884	-86	-414	517	-62	-51	404	108	296
1970	1970	3.963	-1.785	-208	-1.591	379	724	271	1.374	903	593
1975	-682	5.028	-5.354	-356	-272	-954	-1.138	-584	-2.676	-703	-1.973
1980	-10.746	2.125	-11.343	-1.528	2.324	-8.422	3.141	-3.115	-8.396	4.905	-13.301
1985	49.169	55.986	-5.165	-1.652	-64.542	-15.373	-936	3.991	-12.318	197	-12.515

Source: Bank of Japan "Balance of Monthly Payments"

Table 2: Gold and Foreign Exchange Reserves

(in millons of U.S. dollars)

Year	Gold and Foreign Exchange Reserves	Gold	Foreign currency	Year	Gold and Foreign Echange Reserves	Gold	Foreign currency
1952	930			1971	15235	738	13783
1953	913			1972	18365	801	16483
1954	637			1973	12246	891	10203
1955	738			1974	13518	905	11347
				1975	12815	865	10627
1956	941						
1957	524	23	501	1976	16604	859	13883
1958	861	54	807	1977	22848	920	20126
1959	1322	244	1077	1978	33019	1093	28896
1960	1824	247	1577	1979	20327	1117	16357
				1980	25232	1081	21567
1961	1486	287	1199				
1962	1841	289	1552	1981	28403	987	24669
1963	1878	289	1589	1982	23262	935	19075
1964	1999	304	1495	1983	24496	888	20249
1965	2107	328	1569	1984	26313	835	22113
				1985	26510	931	21916
1966	2074	329	1469				
1967	2005	338	1453				
1968	2891	356	2261				
1969	3496	413	2614				
1970	4399	532	3188				

Source: Bank of Japan "Economic Statistics of Japan" and "Economic Statistics Annual"

1) Represents the official holdings of gold and foreign exchange (including foreign currency, bank deposit abroad, foreign securities) of government and the Bank of Japan, exvluding the IMF gold tranche position until 1063. Beginning 1964, includes gold, foreign currency, SDR, and the IMF reserve tranche position.
2) From 1952 through 1955, as of the end of March.

Table 3: Trends in Japan's FDI by Manufacturing Sectors, 1968-1997

(Unit: million US$, %)

Year	Total $M	Total of Manfg. $M	Share of Manfg %	Share by Asian region	Value $M	North America	Europe
1968	557	67	12.0	50.7	34.0	20.9	4.5
1969	665	133	20.0	50.4	67.0	3.0	0.8
1970	904	236	26.1	40.7	96.1	33.5	8.9
1971	858	290	33.8	42.8	124.1	11.4	7.2
1972	2338	525	22.5	52.8	277.2	10.0	1.1
1973	3494	1496	42.8	32.5	486.2	18.0	6.0
1974	2359	874	37.0	41.0	358.3	11.7	6.6
1975	3280	924	28.2	39.7	366.8	15.2	4.3
1976	3462	1025	29.6	27.8	285.0	21.8	4.8
1977	2806	1074	38.3	31.1	334.0	20.2	5.4
1978	4598	2038	44.3	42.1	858.0	16.1	7.9
1979	4995	1693	33.9	25.8	436.8	26.4	9.6
1980	4693	1706	36.4	42.4	723.3	23.3	9.4
1981	8932	2305	25.8	29.8	686.9	43.6	8.6
1982	7703	2076	27.0	26.2	543.9	39.4	6.7
1983	8145	2588	31.8	28.5	737.6	38.3	9.5
1984	10155	2505	24.7	20.6	516.0	49.6	13.5
1985	12217	2352	19.3	19.6	461.0	52.0	13.7
1986	22320	3806	17.1	21.1	803.1	57.8	9.7
1987	33364	7832	23.5	21.4	1676.0	61.9	10.9
1988	47022	13805	29.4	17.2	2374.5	66.6	11.2
1989	67540	16284	24.1	19.8	3224.2	58.9	19.0
1990	56911	15486	27.2	19.8	3066.2	43.9	29.7
1991	41584	12311	29.6	23.8	2930.0	47.7	21.9
1992	34138	10057	29.5	30.9	3107.6	41.5	20.9
1993	36025	11132	30.9	32.9	3662.4	37.2	18.3
1994	41051	13784	33.6	37.6	5182.8	34.6	13.5
1995	50694	18623	36.7	43.3	8063.8	39.3	10.7
1996	49172	20829	42.4	32.6	6790.3	43.5	14.2
1997	53972	19339	35.8	37.8	7310.1	42.5	12.7

Note: 1. Data based on notification to MoF
Source: Teshiba M. [1998] and JETRO [1999]

Table 4: Trends in Japan's Foreign Direct Investment, 1968-1997

Unit: $million, %

Year	Total $M	Total Growth Rate	Asia	NIES	ASEAN	China	USA
1968	557	102.6	14.0	3.1	10.6	0.0	26.0
1969	665	19.4	29.6	6.0	10.7	0.0	17.9
1970	904	35.9	18.5	6.6	11.6	0.0	10.3
1971	858	-5.1	27.6	11.2	16.1	0.0	25.2
1972	2338	172.5	17.2	9.7	7.4	0.0	15.2
1973	3494	49.4	28.6	12.9	15.6	0.0	22.9
1974	2359	-32.5	30.5	8.9	21.4	0.0	20.8
1975	3280	39.0	33.5	8.5	24.4	0.0	25.8
1976	3462	5.5	36.0	6.5	29.4	0.0	19.2
1977	2806	-18.9	30.8	10.3	20.3	0.0	24.5
1978	4598	63.9	29.1	12.9	16.2	0.0	27.9
1979	4995	8.6	19.5	12.3	6.8	0.3	26.9
1980	4693	-6.0	25.3	8.1	16.8	0.3	31.6
1981	8932	90.3	37.4	8.1	28.8	0.3	26.4
1982	7703	-13.8	18.0	9.6	8.1	0.2	35.5
1983	8145	5.7	22.7	13.7	8.0	0.0	31.5
1984	10155	24.7	16.0	8.0	6.7	1.1	33.1
1985	12217	20.3	11.8	5.9	4.9	0.8	44.2
1986	22320	82.7	10.4	6.9	2.5	1.0	45.5
1987	33364	49.5	14.6	7.7	3.1	3.7	44.1
1988	47022	40.9	11.8	6.9	4.2	0.6	46.2
1989	67540	43.6	12.2	7.3	4.1	0.6	48.2
1990	56911	-15.7	12.4	5.9	5.7	0.6	45.9
1991	41584	-26.9	14.3	5.3	7.4	1.4	43.4
1992	34138	-17.9	18.8	5.6	9.4	3.1	40.5
1993	36025	5.5	18.4	6.7	6.7	4.7	40.9
1994	41051	14.0	23.6	7.0	9.5	6.2	42.2
1995	50694	23.5	24.2	6.3	8.1	8.8	43.8
1996	49172	-3.0	24.2	7.4	10.3	5.3	45.8
1997	53972	9.8	22.6	6.3	10.6	3.7	38.4

Note: 1. Data based on notification to MoF

Source: Teshiba M. [1998] and JETRO [1999]

Table 5: Japanese Foreign Direct Investment by Industry Sector

(Unit: US$100m,%)

	1995			1996			Total 51-96	
	Amount	Share	Compare to prev. years	Amount	Share	Compare to prev. years	Amount	Share
Total	50694	100	23.5	48019	100	Δ5.3	562320	100
Manufacturing industry Sub Total	18623	36.7	35.1	20258	42.2	8.8	167777	29.8
Food	844	1.7	Δ33.0	729	1.5	Δ13.6	8956	1.6
Fiber	1043	2.1	62.7	606	1.3	Δ41.9	7831	1.4
Lumber, Pulp	357	0.7	154.6	619	1.3	73.6	5173	0.9
Chemical	2114	4.2	Δ18.7	2059	4.3	Δ2.6	23074	4.1
Iron, Nonferrous	1555	3.1	49.8	2446	5.1	57.3	17833	3.2
Machinery	1870	3.7	15.3	1438	3	Δ23.1	16421	2.9
Electric	5288	10.4	100.8	6513	13.6	23.2	41670	7.4
Transport machinery	1989	3.9	Δ1.6	3873	8.1	94.7	22890	4.1
Others	3564	7	95.1	1974	4.1	Δ44.6	23929	4.3
Non-Manufacturing industry Sub Total	31121	61.4	15.8	26741	55.7	Δ14.1	385032	68.5
Agriculture, Forestry	139	0.3	Δ10.9	139	0.3	Δ0.1	2280	0.4
Fisheries	56	0.1	Δ73.8	98	0.2	75.8	1322	0.2
Mining	1046	2.1	120.1	1570	3.3	50.1	22850	4.1
Construction	397	0.8	11.4	321	0.7	Δ19.2	4702	0.8
Commerce	5299	10.5	20.7	4782	10	Δ9.8	59836	10.6
Finance, Insurance	5471	10.8	Δ15.8	7776	16.2	42.1	101017	18
Service	10496	20.7	48.6	4046	8.4	Δ61.4	71755	12.8
Transportation	2271	4.5	Δ12.8	1799	3.7	Δ20.8	30482	5.4
Real estate	5947	11.7	16.1	6210	12.9	4.4	83245	14.8
Others	-	-	-	-	-	-	7543	1.3
Expanding Branches	950	1.9	143.3	1020	2.1	7.3	8916	1.6

Note: prev.=previous
Source: JETRO 1985, p.529

Table 6 : Japanese Direct Investment in Europe, Classified by Nation and Sector

Sector / Nation	1	2	3	4	5	6	7	8	9	10	11	12	13	14	15	16	17	18	19	Total	DC R&D
United Kingdom	4	4	4	2	-	33	-	2	3	-	4	11	18	37	30	4	19	12	19	206	83
France	21	2	3	2	-	17	3	4	3	-	4	3	11	22	8	2	6	6	4	121	34
Germany	3	1	1	-	1	11	5	2	3	1	1	6	20	18	17	-	3	10	3	106	53
Netherlands	3	-	-	1	-	13	1	1	1	1	-	2	6	2	5	1	3	3	2	45	16
Belgium	1	-	-	-	-	14	1	1	5	-	-	1	2	7	2	1	2	1	2	40	16
Luxembourg	-	-	-	-	-	1	-	-	-	-	-	-	-	1	-	-	-	1	-	3	
Ireland	-	2	-	-	-	4	3	-	2	-	2	1	2	4	9	-	-	1	1	31	7
Spain	1	1	1	1	1	13	4	1	2	1		4	6	8	4	5	8	1	2	64	26
Italy	-	3	9	-	-	7	1	1	1	-	1	3	10	6	1	3	3	-	3	52	14
Finland	-	-	-	-	2	-	-	1	-	-	-	-	-	-	-	-		1	1	5	
Norway	-	-	-	-	-	-	-	-	-	-	-	-	-	-	-	1		-	-	1	1
Sweden	-	-	-	-	-	2	-	-	-	-	-	-	3	-	1	-	2	1	1	10	5
Denmark	-	-	-	-	-	1	-	-	-	-	-	-	1	-	-	-		-	1	3	1
Austria	-	1	-	-	-	2	-	-	-	-	-	4	2	1	-	-	1	1	5	17	3
Portugal	-	2	-	-	1	2	-	-	-	-	1	-	-	-	-	1	3	-	2	12	
Switzerland	-	-	-	-	-	3	-	-	-	-	-	-	2	-	-	-	1	1	1	8	4
Greece	-	-	-	-	-	1	-	-	-	1	-	-	-	-	-	-		-	1	3	
Icelands	-	-	-	-	-	-	-	-	-	-	1	-	-	-	-	-		-	-	1	1
Total	33	16	18	6	5	124	18	13	20	4	14	35	83	106	77	18	51	39	48	728	264

Source: JETRO 1985, p.6

Note : 1. Food products and beverages, 2. Textiles, 3. Apparel, 4. Furniture, 5. Pulp & Paper, 6. Chemicals, 7. Medical products, 8. Rubber products, 9. Cement & Ceramics, 10. Steel products, 11. Non-.ferrous metal, 12. Metal goods, 13. Machinery, 14. Electrical & Electronic Machinery & Apparatur, 15. Electronic parts, 16. Transportation machinery, 17. Transportation machine parts, 18. Precision Machinery, 19. Others

DC = Design Centre; R&D = Research and Development Centres.

Table 7: Fopreign Direct Investment in Pakistan

Nation	Term	(1) Food Tabacco	(2) Textiles	(3) Chemicals Cement Ceramics	(4) Cosmetics Pharmacy products	(5) Petroleum Gas	(6) Metal Ores	(7) Machines& Apparatus	(8) Machinery	(9) Other Manufacturing	(10) Service	Total
United Kingdom	I	9	2	8	10	5	5	5	-	2	-	46
	II	6	3	8	4	1	2	1	-	3	1	29
	Total	15	5	16	14	6	7	6	0	5	1	75
United States	I	8	1	7	9	-	1	1	1	1	6	35
	II	5	1	8	4	1	2	7	-	5	4	37
	Total	13	2	15	13	1	3	8	1	6	10	72
JAPAN	I	-	1	1	1	-	-	-	4	-	-	7
	II	-	1	1	-	-	-	3	3	-	1	9
	Total	-	2	2	1	-	-	3	7	-	1	16

Source:Gouvernment of Pakistan, Ministry of Industries; Repatriable Foreign Private Investment (1947 to 1977), 1988; Repatriable Foreign Investment Approved by I.P. Bureau (July 1977 to February 1988), 1988;

Note: (2) includes synthetic fibres, (3) includes glass & rubber, (5) coal & gas, (6) wire & cable; Hotels, engineering and others are included in "Service".

Table 8: Structure of Japan's Manufacturing FDI in the Asian NIEs and ASEAN Countries by Industry (Cumulative Total as of the End of march 1985)

Industry / Host Country	Tex-tiles	Chemi-cals	Iron & Steel/ Nonferrous Metals	Mach-inery	Electric/ Electro-nics	Transport ation Equip-ment	Total	
Asian NIEs	29.8	66.2	10.9	81.2	76.4	37.3	43.4	
Hong Kong	10.0	0.5	0.3	3.6	3.1	0.0	3.3	
S. Korea	14.4	22.0	5.1	11.1	23.4	8.1	12.9	
Taiwan	4.0	5.7	2.6	15.1	23.7	8.1	8.1	
Singapore	1.4	38.1	2.9	51.4	26.2	21.1	19.2	
ASEAN	69.6	32.6	87.6	18.3	22.2	58.0	54.5	
Indonesia	41.0	9.8	72.3	4.8	5.4	18.9	32.2	
Malaysia	11.7	14.4	8.3	2.2	12.0	16.5	10.8	
Philippines	1.8	5.3	4.9	1.0	1.4	15.3	4.4	
Thailand	15.1	3.2	2.1	10.3	3.3	7.4	7.2	
Asia Total	100.0	100.0	100.0	100.0	100.0	100.0	100.0	
S.M.	1173	1253	1661	504	781	541	7057	
Asian NIEs	11.4	27.1	5.9	13.3	19.5	6.6	100.0	3065
Hong Kong	50.2	2.6	2.1	7.7	10.3	0.0	100.0	233
S. Korea	18.6	30.4	9.4	6.2	20.2	4.8	100.0	908
Taiwan	8.22	12.4	7.5	13.3	32.3	7.7	100.0	572
Singapore	1.3	35.3	3.6	19.2	15.2	8.4	100.0	1352
ASEAN	21.2	10.6	37.8	2.4	4.5	8.2	100.0	3847
Indonesia	21.2	5.4	52.9	1.1	1.9	4.5	100.0	2270
Malaysia	18.1	23.7	18.2	1.4	12.4	11.7	100.0	759
Philippines	6.8	21.2	26.0	1.6	3.5	26.7	100.0	311
Thailand	34.9	7.9	6.9	10.3	5.1	7.9	100.0	507
Asia Total	16.6	17.8	23.5	7.1	11.1	7.7	100.0	7057

Note: The cumulative manufacturing FDI total in Asia as of end of March 1970 was \$320m. Therefore, the total as of end of March 1985 had increased about 22 times in 15 years.

Source: Calculated from MOF 1985.

Table 9: Japan's FDI in East Asia

(Data based on notification to MoF)

	FY 1996	FY 1997		First Half 1998	
World Total	48019	53972	(12.4)	16782	(-28.6)
East-Asia	10997	11094	(0.9)	2871	(-52.7)
Asian NIEs	3538	3411	(-3.6)	681	(-54.6)
S. Korea	416	442	(6.4)	175	(35.7)
Taiwan	521	450	(-13.7)	112	(-59.4)
Hong Kong	1487	695	(-53.2)	122	(-69.1)
Singapore	1115	1824	(63.5)	272	(-61.1)
ASEAN 4	4949	5696	(15.1)	1754	(-48.5)
Malaysia	572	791	(38.4)	274	(-10.6)
Thailand	1403	1867	(33.1)	709	(-37.4)
Indonesia	2414	2514	(4.1)	635	(-62.1)
Philippines	559	524	(-6.3)	136	(-53.5)
China	2510	1897	(-20.8)	435	(-62.4)

Source: JETRO 1999, p. 4.

Note : Figures in brackets indicate change from previous year or from same period of previous year.

Table 10: Japan's Technology Export Contracts, 1996 Survey

Import Country	No.	Technology Contracts by Industry					Equity Ties		
		Electric/ Elec-tronic	Mach-inery	Chemi-cals	Metals	Others	None	< 50	>= 50
Asia:	489	133	116	111	70	59	271	101	117
S. Korea	127	32	41	28	11	15	102	18	7
Taiwan	67	25	13	19	6	4	43	10	14
Hong Kong	6	1	3	0	1	1	5	0	1
Singapore	18	3	0	11	1	3	3	2	13
Indonesia	36	8	3	9	7	9	16	4	16
Philippines	24	9	3	3	7	2	6	9	9
Malaysia	21	5	0	4	9	3	8	7	6
Thailand	54	11	11	11	14	7	20	22	12
China	93	31	27	14	10	11	40	18	35
USA	173	68	44	25	10	26	121	10	42
Europe	120	32	21	29	10	20	95	6	19
World Total	842	243	190	171	127	111	522	133	187
									%
Asia:	58.1	27.2	23.7	22.7	14.3	12.1	55.4	20.7	23.9
S. Korea	15.1	25.2	32.3	22.0	8.7	11.8	80.3	14.2	5.5
Taiwan	8.0	37.3	19.4	28.4	9.0	6.0	64.2	14.9	20.9
Hong Kong	0.7	16.7	50.0	0.0	16.7	16.7	83.3	0.0	16.7
Singapore	2.1	16.7	0.0	61.1	5.6	16.7	16.7	11.1	72.2
Indonesia	4.3	22.2	8.3	25.0	19.4	25.0	44.4	11.1	44.4
Philippines	2.9	37.5	12.5	12.5	29.2	8.3	25.0	37.5	37.5
Malaysia	2.5	23.8	0.0	19.0	42.9	14.3	38.1	33.3	28.6
Thailand	6.4	20.4	20.4	20.4	25.9	13.0	37.0	40.7	22.2
China	11.0	33.3	29.0	15.1	10.8	11.8	43.0	19.4	37.6
USA	20.5	39.3	25.4	14.5	5.8	15.0	69.9	5.8	24.3
Europe	14.3	26.7	17.5	24.2	15.0	16.7	79.2	5.0	15.8
World Total	100.0	28.9	22.6	20.3	15.1	13.2	62.0	15.8	22.2

Source: STA 1998, p. 142.

Fig. 1: Location of Overseas Car Parts Manufacturing

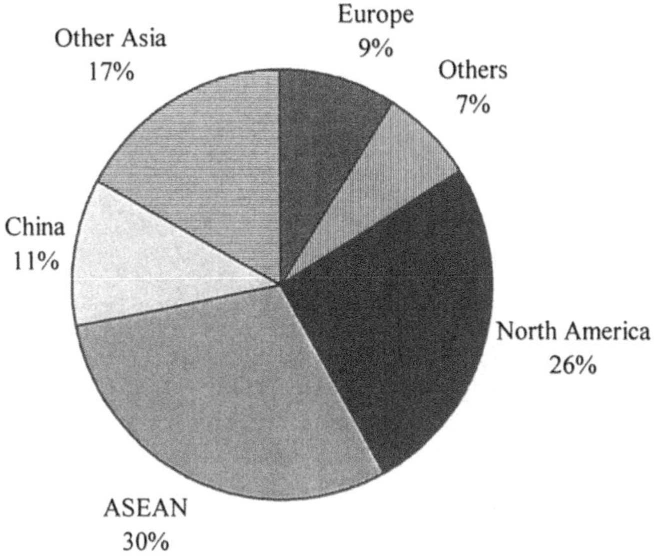

Source: JAMA 1997, p.2.
Note : Data from 918 factories

Fig. 2: Location of Newly Established Factories, 1990-1996

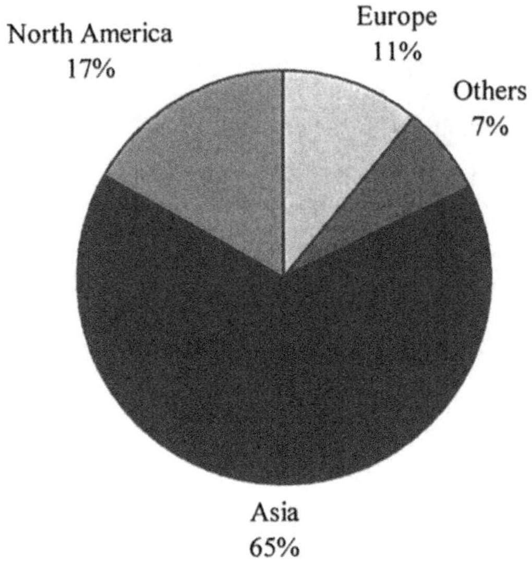

Source: JAMA, op. cit.
Note : Data from 456 factories established from 1990 to 1996

Fig. 3: Japanese Investment in Auto Parts Manufacturing in Some Major Countries, 1996 & 1997

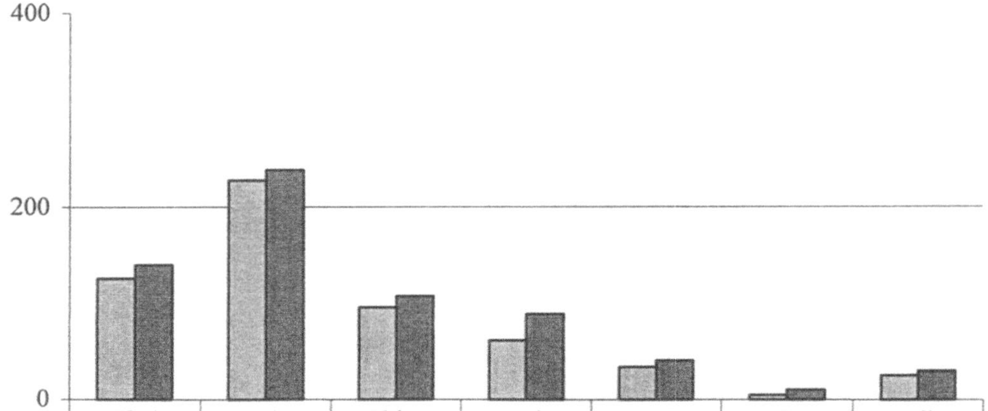

	Thai	US	China	In'sia	UK	VN	India
1996	126	227	96	62	34	5	25
1997	140	238	108	89	41	10	30

Source: JAMA 1997, p. 198..
Notes : Thai= Thailand, In'sia= Indonesia, VN= Vietnam

Fig. 4: Location of Parts Manufacturers of Toyota-Related Companies before 1990

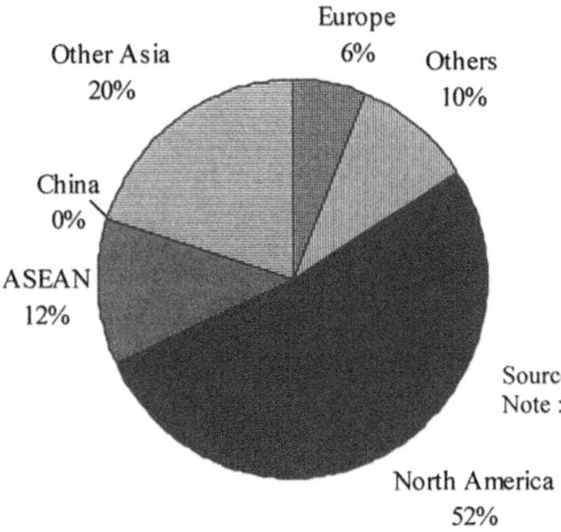

Source: Shi 1999, p.
Note : Data from 51 factories

Fig. 5: Location of Parts Manufacturers of Toyota-Related Companies after 1990

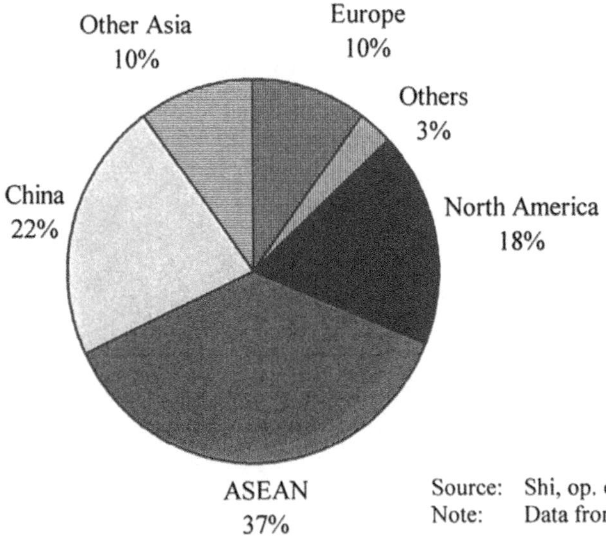

Source: Shi, op. cit.
Note: Data from 40 factories.

Fig. 6: Japanese Car Manufacturers' Production and Exports

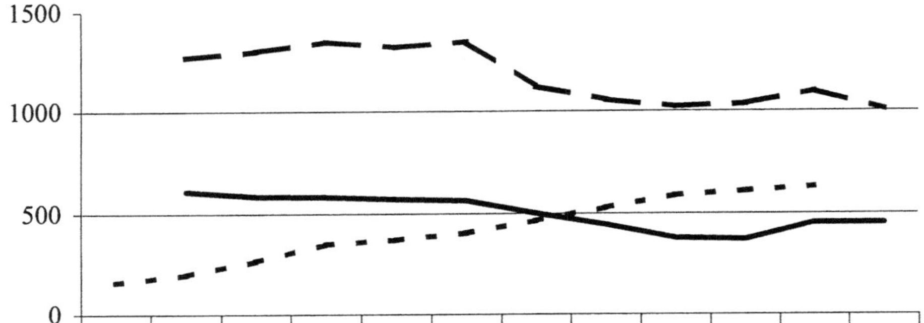

	87	88	89	90	91	92	93	94	95	96	97	98
Dm Mfg.		1270	1302	1349	1324	1350	1122	1055	1020	1034	1097	1005
Export		610	588	583	575	567	502	446	379	371	455	453
Os Mfg.	158	198	267	351	370	405	467	529	589	611	632	

Source: Toyota Corporation 1998, pp. 81, 93, 101.
Notes : Dm Mfg= Domestic Manufacturing.
Os Mfg= Overseas Manufacturing.
Data for domestic manufacturing exclude light vehicles.
Data for oversears manufacturing exclude CFM and KD.

Fig. 7: ASEAN Complementary Schemes by Toyota Group

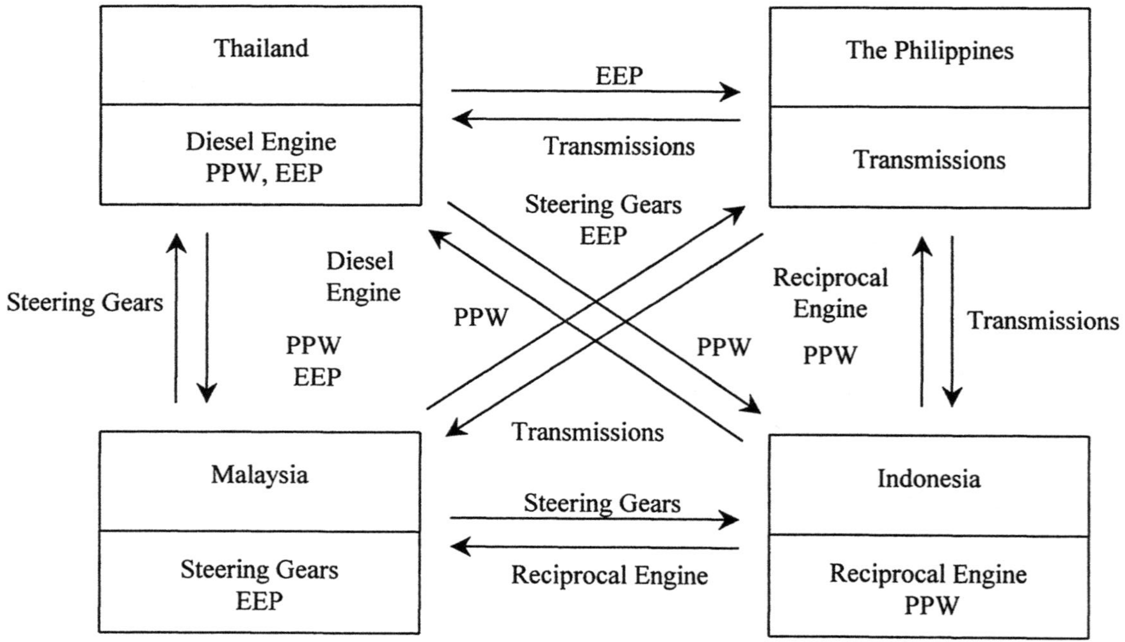

Source: Sato 1997, p. 179.
Notes: PPW=Pressed Parts Wares.
EEP=Electrical & Electronic Parts

List of References

Abegglen, J.C., Sea Change: Pacific Asia as the New World Industrial Center, NewYork: The Free Press, 1994.

Akamatsu, Kaname, "Wagakuni Yomokogyohin no Boekisusei" (Trend of Trade of Japanese Woolen Wares) Nagoya Higher Commercial School, Shogyokeiei Ronshu (Journal of Commerce and Economics) Vol. 13, 1935.

ASEAN Center, ASEAN Japan-Statistical Pocket Book, Tokyo: ASEAN Center, 1999.

The Bank of Japan (BJ), Balance of Payments of Japan –1958-, Tokyo: BJ, 1963. Economic Planning Agency, Japan Ajia Keizai (Asian Economy 1999), Tokyo: Okurasho Insatsukyoku, 1999.

The Export-Import Bank of Japan, Wagakuni Kaigaitoshi no Genkyo To Tenkaihoko Daiyonkai Kaigaitoshi Anketochosa Hokoku (Situation and Prospect of Japanese Overseas Investment: A Report of the 4th Questionnaire Survey of Japanese Private Investment Abroad), Tokyo: The Export-Import Bank, 1974.

Fukagawa, Yukiko, Kankoku Sensiukoku Keizairon (Korea: On Industrialized Economy) Tokyo: Nihonkeizaishinbunsha, 1997.

Hirakawa, Hitoshi, NIES: Sekaikeizai Shisutemu to Kaihatsu (NIEs: World System and Development), Tokyo: Dobunkan, 1992.

Japan Auto-Parts Manufacturers Association (JAMA), Kaigaijigyo Gaiyochosa Hokokusho (A Report on Overseas Business), Tokyo: JAMA, 1997.

Japan External Trade Organization (JETRO), Zaio Mikkeikigyo no Keieijittai: Daijyukkai Jittaichosa Hokoku (Business Performance of Japanese Manufacturing Firms in Europe: the 10th Questionnaire Survey), Tokyo: JETRO, 1994.

---,Seizogyokigyo no Kaigaijigyo Katsudojittai Chosa (Survey on Overseas Business Activities of Manufacturing Firms), Tokyo: JETRO, 1998.

---,JETRO Kaigaitoshi Hakusho 1999 (JETRO's White Paper on Overseas Investment), Tokyo: 1999.

Japan Finance Corporation for Small Business, ASEAN niokeru Jidoshasangyo no Doko to Wagakuni Chusho Buhin Meka heno Eikyo nitsute (A Prospect of Automobile Industry in ASEAN and Japanese SMFs of Parts Ware Manufacturing), Tokyo: JFCSB, 1998.

Kim, Yongho, Higashi Ajia Kogyoka to Sekaishihonshugi (East Asian Industrialization and World Capitalism), Tokyo: Toyokeizai, 1991.

Ministry of International Trade and Industry, Japan (MITI), Dainiyurokkai Wagakuni Kigyo no Kaigai Jigyokatsudo (The 26th Survey on Overseas Business Activities of Japanese Firms), Tokyo: Okurasho Insatsukyoku, 1996.

---,Tsusho Hakusho Heisei 11 nenban (White Paper on International Trade 1999), Tokyo: Okurasho Insatsukyoku, 1999.

Phongpaichit, Pasuk, The New Wave of Japanese Investment in ASEAN, Singapore: Institute of Southeast Asian Studies, 1990.

Sato, Ichiro, "ASEAN no Jidoshasangyo to Nikkeikigyo ni shinsenryaku" (ASEAN Automobile Industry and New Strategies of Japanese Joint Ventures), in Kitamura, K. ed.) Higashi Ajia no Sangyokozo Kodoka to Nihonsangyo (East Asian Industrial Structure and Japanese Manufacturing), Tokyo: DIE, 1997.

---, Adachi, Fumihiko, Nihongata Keiei to Jidoshasangyo no Genba Karano Kosatsu (Japanese Style Management and Technology Transfer: A View from Thai Automobile Industry), Nagoya: ERC, University of Nagoya, 1998.

Science and Technology Agency, Japan Nihon no Gijutsu Yushutsu no Jittai (Technology Export of Japan), Tokyo: STA, 1998.

Sekiya, Hiroyuki, Wagakuni Minseiyo Denshikikisangyo no Takokusekika Senryaku (Multinationalization Strategy of Consumer Electronics Equipment of Japan), Tokyo: STA, 1998.

Shi, Shimin, Jidosha Buhinsangyo no Gurubaruka (Globalization of Automobile Parts Manufacturing), Nagoya: ERC, University of Nagoya, 1999.

Statistics Bureau, Management and Coordination Agency (SB), Nihon Choki Tokei Saran Dai 3kan (Historical Statistics of Japan Vol. 3), Tokyo: Japan Statistical Association, 1988.

Takeuchi, Johzen "'Technology Transfer' and Japan-Thai Relations" in (Yamashita ed. 1991)

---,"Eikoku niokeru Nikkeikigyo no Keieidoko" (Business Activities of Japanese Joint Venture in UK), Hiroshima Daigaku Keizaikenkyusho (Hiroshima University Economic Research) Vol. 11, Hiroshima, 1997.

---, "Japanese Business Activity in Thailand: Presence and Performance" Economic and Political Weekly, Vol. XXXIV, No. 22, 1999.

---, "Historical Features of Japanese Small and Medium Enterprises: A Comparative Economic Approach" in K. Odaka & M. Sawai eds., Small Firms, Large Concerns: The Development of Small Business in Comparative Perspective, Oxford: OUP, 1999.

Toyota Corporation, Toyota no Gaikyo (Prospectus of Toyota), Nagoya: Toyota Corporation, 1998.

Watanabe, Toshio, *Seicho no Ajia Teikai no Ajia* (Developing Asia and Stagnating Asia), Tokyo: Toyokeizaishinposha, 1985

---, H. Kajiwara, and K. Takanaka, *Ajia Sogoizon no Jidai* (Asian Mutual Dependency Era), Tokyo: Yuhikaku, 1991.

World Bank, *The East Asian Miracle: Economic Growth and Public Policy, A World Bank Policy Research Paper*, Oxford: OUP, 1993

Yamashita, Shoichi, ed. *Transfer of Japanese Technology and Management to the ASEAN Countries*, Tokyo: University of Tokyo Press, 1991.

Financing Industrialization in Emerging Economies by Capital Inflows: A Matter of Regulation or Deregulation? Experiences from Asian Countries

Günter Heiduk, Nicole Pohl

Universität Duisburg

1 Introduction

Most publications on the Asian financial crisis have considered this period as an isolated event without acknowledging that it is embedded in a wider set of developments that can be summarised under the terms of globalization, technological and economic development and restructuring of institutions.

...Globalization has become a widely used slogan and has been subject to much misuse. However, there are still some important aspects in the ideas behind globalization. One of these is that economic developments can no longer be understood merely by observing what national political and economic agents do. Globalization is frequently measured by the growth of international flows of goods, services, FDI and portfolio capital, information and technology transfer. Globalization is fostered by new possibilities of organizing activities on a broad spatial scale, by growing competition (which might also be a consequence of globalization) and by government policies that support liberalization, integration and openness. The developments that have been introduced by globalization have led to a new relationship between the intellectual community and the business community. It implies the idea of managing economic transactions globally.

It seems important to note that globalization also implies increasing dynamics in world capital markets. This is due to the increasing internationalization of the banking sector, which leads to increasing international interbank transactions, a number of new possibilities of exchanging and gathering information, the structural changes of long-term capital flows to short-term engagements, the development of new financial tools and derivatives that imply higher risks and volatility. Finally, we have to take into account that the small national financial markets of the emerging economies have been dependent on large OECD markets.

Clearly, the developments in Asian emerging economies (ASEMECs) cannot be considered without recognizing that these tendencies have had an important impact on all of these countries. Moreover, we have to understand that these new developments not only bring new opportunities of growth for countries that open up, but also bring new requirements for a number of economic sectors as well as for political decision-makers. In order to understand the dynamics of growth, crisis and recovery in Asia, we will have to gain an understanding of the speed with which catching-up processes occur. We may suggest that growth as we observed it in the emerging economies is first of all a process of industrialization (except perhaps in the case of Singapore as a trading and financial centre). Other sectors, especially services, banking, etc., lack this ability of rapid adjustment to the requirements of a fast growing open economy. It is obvious that it has been much easier to introduce new measures to support industrialization than to change traditional rules, regulations, networks in the financial sector of Asian emerging economies. This has lead to a two-tier catching-up process. When the financial sector lags behind the catching-up of the industrial sector, small, unexpected changes in key variables (e.g. interest rates) have been able to destabilise the economies of the countries. The main question is whether this interrupts the industrialization and the integration process only temporarily or whether an emerging economy will be doomed to a long-term set-back. This question goes to the nature of this kind of „crisis“. The recent recovery of many countries has shown that they may come back on track, if fundamentals are strong and remain so and consolidation of the lagging sectors is successful. It is even possible that a crisis gives them a chance for an „early restructuring“ of the industrial sector. Compared to some old industrial countries, the emerging economies may have gained new momentum for global competitiveness. Moreover, the fast growth seems merely to have revealed previously existing vulnerabilities in the economic and political systems of the countries.

The good recovery we observe in most of the emerging economies leads us to the conclusion that crises can be a logical consequence, but also only an interlude and an opportunity in the catching-up process. They are part of a dynamic process in a global and changing world economy. For this and other reasons we are forced to rethink the current debate about regulation versus deregulation.

The literature on the Asian crisis has been extensive and sometimes also redundant. However, a review of the existing literature is not the aim of this article. Rather it focusses on giving a structured overview of what happened and on emphasizing that multilevel dynamics with different speeds have to be taken into account in order to understand the history and future of Asian emerging economies.

2 Economic Growth in Asian Emerging Economies

From 1960 to the middle of the nineties the Asian emerging economies were able to realise a high-speed industrial growth (Table 1) that can only be understood against the background of a globalizing world economy.

Table 1: GDP growth: East and South East Asian Emerging Economies, 1970-1996, average annual % growth)

	1970-1979	1980-1989	1990-1996
Hong Kong	9.2	7.5	5.0
Singapore	9.4	7.2	8.3
Taiwan	10.2	8.1	6.3
South Korea	9.3	8.0	7.7
Malaysia	8.0	5.7	8.8
Thailand	7.3	7.2	8.6
Indonesia	7.8	5.7	7.2
China	7.5	9.3	10.1

Source: Michie/ Smith 1999, p. 12

Even though we can observe a high cultural, economic and political diversity among these countries, there are certain similarities as to their economic system:

Basically, they can be described as „developmental state economies„„ which implies close relationships between the government and business, administrative guidance, and managed competition.

Their development was led by export orientation (except during some „experimental“ periods) and a strategic industrial policy.

Their monetary system was characterized by pegged exchange rates.

Their markets are relatively small.

„Western“ organizations, e.g., the World Bank, criticised the growth-oriented economic policy of these countries, especially the wide range of interventions. Many of the industrialization programs were focused on guaranteeing financial support, meaning, financial advantages, to target industries. Despite this fact the World Bank stated that „market forces and competitive pressures guided resources into activities that were consistent with comparative advantage" (World Bank 1993). This view changed rapidly after the crisis had set in in 1997. The IMF changed its opinion from characterizing the features of the Asian emerging economies as a „miracle" to an opposing point of view: The co-operative model was regarded as the source of crony capitalism, as a possibility for the nation-state to guarantee support for private business activities in crisis and in extreme cases as a replacement of the market economy by corrupt and ineffective nepotism. The crisis quickly changed the evaluation of the Asian economies from „miracles" to failures.

Table 2 gives an idea of some key indicators of Asian countries before and after the crisis.

Table 2: Key indicators for Asian emerging economies: Malaysia, Indonesia, Thailand and Korea (% of GDP unless otherwise noted)

	1975-1982 (average)	1983-1989 (average)	1990-1996 (average)	1995	1996	1997 [a]
Malaysia						
real GDP growth[b]	7.1	5.4	8.8	9.5	8.6	7.0
inflation[c]	5.3	2.0	3.5	3.4	3.5	3.7
domestic saving	21.6	29.4	32.1	33.5	36.7	37.0
fixed capital formation	29.4	28.5	38.3	43.0	42.2	42.7
current account	-2.0	-0.7	-6.0	-10.0	-4.9	-5.8
fiscal balance	-6.3	-4.0	0.0	3.8	4.2	1.6
external debt service	3.8	9.0	6.0	6.6	5.4	8.4
Indonesia						
real GDP growth[b]	6.2	5.5	8.0	8.2	8.0	5.0
inflation[c]	15.0	8.1	8.6	9.4	7.9	8.3
domestic saving	19.3	23.2	28.9	29.0	28.8	27.3
fixed capital formation	19.8	24.3	27.4	28.4	28.1	26.5
current account	-1.2	-3.5	-2.6	-3.3	-3.3	-2.9
fiscal balance	-2.6	-1.3	0.3[d]	0.8	1.4	2.0
external debt service	3.5	6.8	8.6	8.5	9.0	10.5
Thailand						
real GDP growth[b]	7.0	8.1	8.6	8.7	6.4	0.6
inflation[c]	9.0	3.1	5.1	5.8	5.9	6.0
domestic saving	19.6	25.4	34.2	34.3	33.1	31.8
fixed capital						

formation	23.6	27.7	40.4	41.8	40.8	35.8
current account	-5.6	-3.2	-6.9	-8.0	-7.9	-3.9
fiscal balance	-5.8	-3.0	2.8	2.6	1.6	-0.4
external debt service	3.8	5.8	4.5	5.0	5.4	7.1
Korea						
real GDP growth[b]	7.0	9.6	7.7	8.9	7.1	6.0
inflation[c]	17.6	3.8	6.4	4.5	4.9	4.3
domestic saving	25.7	32.7	35.0	35.1	33.3	32.9
fixed capital formation	29.4	29.4	36.7	36.6	36.8	36.6
current account	-4.6	2.5	-1.9	-2.0	-4.9	-2.9
fiscal balance	-2.7	-0.3	-1.0	0.0	0.0	0.0
import cover[g]	n.a.	1.4[e]	2.2[f]	n.a.	n.a..	n.a.

Source: Michie, J./ Smith, J. G. (1999), p. 13
a IMF estimate
b percentage per annum
c average annual % change of consumer price index
d 1991 and 1994 data available
e 1980-1990
f 1995 figure
g gross international reserves in months of import cover

In contrast to regions in Latin America and Africa the fast growth in Asia was accompanied by a declining inequality in income distribution (UNCTAD 1997). Stiglitz's recommendation that the US and Western countries could well learn from the East Asian experience in this respect seems surprizing (Stiglitz 1998). Most of the key macro-economic indicators of the countries were positive before the crisis. Especially the extremely high fixed capital formation (around 35 % of GDP) created positive perspectives for continuing growth. Small shadows in this picture were cast by the growing external debt service. Despite the high domestic saving rates, this reflects the increasing importance of external sources to finance the high growth (Table 2).

3 The Role of Capital Inflows in Financing Industrialization

Industrialization in Asian emerging economies was altogether different from the experience of „industrialized countries“ in the 19th century. This was due to the size and location of some of the countries (e.g., in the case of city states like Hong Kong and Singapore), to the different structure of firms and interfirm-relationships (e.g., chaebols in Korea) and to the type of competitive advantages these countries had. These countries are trying to catch up in the industrialization process as latecomers. In the beginning they were imitating the economic „history" of the developed countries, e. g., as regards the industries they were starting their industrialization with. However, in later periods their development took a different path and was above all much faster than in the „industrialized countries".

All the ASEMEC have two features in common: On the one hand the decrease of the share of the agricultural sector in industrial output, while the service sector contributed an increasing share to GDP (OECD 1999). In some countries the industry's value added increased and in some it decreased. On the other hand, in the middle of the 90s the contribution of the external sector to growth decreased. Growth in domestic demand was the result of increasing investment and to a smaller degree also consumption.

Rapid industrialization in ASEMECs had to be accompanied by a rapid-build up of a modern infrastructure and a modern educational system. Technology transfers from abroad and the establishment of foreign firms played an important role. The high need for capital that was necessary for such a fast industrialization could not be provided by domestic sources. In order to increase capital inflows, the ASEMEC changed their policy towards a high degree of openness. This turnaround was not only induced by IMF-liberalization requirements, but was also a consequence of „world politics": „...the momentum of liberalization accelerated once security concerns for countries like the United States could no longer override long-standing domestic and international interests that demanded government help in forcing the world open for trade and investment...." (Winters 1999, p. 80).

To manage these huge capital inflows efficiently on a micro- and macroeconomic level, new expertise and an „appropriate" framework had to be developed. Experiences from other countries that had a similar development process and a similar transition of their economic policies show that financing industrialization by high capital inflows can be both beneficial and risky. Even if theory tells us that in globally integrated capital markets the differences in interest rates will determine the allocation of capital, in reality some other factors have to be added to make the market work „perfectly". In the case of ASEMEC, these countries profited from the favourable climate of the world economy in the 80s and early 90s. Some authors argue that up to the end of the 80s „the region's geopolitical significance during the Cold War...gave it access to much foreign aid..." (Grabel 1999, p. 43).

Net long-term capital inflows to Indonesia, Malaysia, Philippines and Thailand increased from 2.0 % of GDP in 1985-88 to 6.9 % of GDP in 1993-96. During the same period short-term private flows increased from 0.1 % to 2.3 % (table 3 and A1). These capital inflows led to a dramatic increase in the external debt (Winters 1999, p. 82). Despite the fact that this may be considered a „normal" development within the starting phase of a catching-up process, the risk potential of this process can be evaluated by having surveying the development of the structure of the external debt: The share of short-term debts and the private non-guaranteed debt increased considerably. The changes in the structure of external debt were also reflected in its currency composition. In most ASEMECs the share of foreign debt in Yen grew dramatically. Even this does not necessarily lead to such severe problems. But one has to take into account two other factors that were independent of this:

The exchange rate systems (Alba 1999, p. 13)

The behaviour of the currency arbitrageurs (Winter 1999, p. 82, 83)

Table 3: Magnitude and composition of capital inflows, 1985-1996 (per cent of GDP)

	ASEAN 4 (Indonesia, Malaysia, Philippines and Thailand)		
	1985-88	1989-92	1993-96
net long-term capital flows	2.0	4.8	6.9
- net official flows	1.2	1.3	0.4
- net private flows	0.8	3.5	6.6
bank/ trade lending	-0.3	0.9	0.8
portfolio bond	0.2	-0.1	1.4
FDI	0.9	2.3	2.4
portfolio equity	-0.1	0.4	2.0
IMF credit	0.1	-0.1	0.0
other private flows	0.3	2.0	-0.1
of which: short-term debt	0.1	2.0	2.3

Source: Alba 1999, p. 11

Easy access to foreign capital led to a tendency of over-investment and to a discrepancy between capital inflow and technological capabilities in these countries. The industrial structure was unbalanced because of an expansion of large enterprises and unfavourable conditions for small and medium enterprises. A considerable part of the short-term capital inflow was not directly related to financing the catching-up process. Foreign speculators sought to capitalize on the high returns available in these booming economies. „Rampant real estate speculation throughout the region resulted in property value inflation, and hence induced a general inflation in the value of loan collateral. In the context of rising collateral values, domestic and international lenders were eager to make low-cost loans available to the private sector.“ (Grabel 1999, p. 44).

Especially some targeted sectors and firms got government support, which enabled domestic banks to extend their credit in these cases. The booming Asian economies experienced higher interest rates than the Western countries. This set incentives - especially for US and Japanese banks – to lend loans in US-Dollar and Yen directly to domestic firms.

A further proof that the increase in short-term capital inflows was more or less a result of the booming economies is the development of FDI in these countries. FDI lost its dominant role gradually in the 90s as measured in % of total capital inflows.

It seems to be a paradox that despite the increase in investment, national savings and the current account deficit, the increase in capital inflows led to a 100 % increase in currency reserves in four Southeast-Asian countries (Table 4).

Table 4: Investment, savings and capital flows, 1985-1996 (per cent of GDP)

	ASEAN 4 (Indonesia, Malaysia, Philippines And Thailand)		
	1985-1988	1989-1992	1991-1996
Investment	25.7	32.6	35.0
national savings			
- private	23.9	28.6	30.3
- public	13.2	20.0	20.4
current account deficit	1.1	3.8	4.6
total capital inflows	2.2	6.7	6.8
reserve accumulation	1.0	2.9	2.2

Source: Alba 1999, p. 12

The confidence of foreign investors was not only based on the high growth, but also on the sound macroeconomic policies: The overall public sector budget in the region moved steadily from deficit to surplus. Throughout the region the public sector debt/GDP ratios fell. It has also been observed that the exchange rate policy avoided currency overvaluation from the mid 80s to the mid 90s, thus discouraging speculation. In addition to this, instruments of monetary policy were used to stabilize the effects of balance of payments fluctuations on the domestic macroeconomic variables.

4 The Crisis: a Result of Building-up Vulnerability

The causes and effects of the „Asian Crisis" are still top themes of economists in the scientific community as well as in organizations like the IMF and the World Bank. The discussion is focused on the following topics:

explaining the crisis by an empirical analysis of the conditions, framework and development of the East Asian economies from 1996 to 1998. Some authors have stressed political and sociological aspects besides the economic ones;

a) building-up models of financial crisis;

b) challenges to economic policy, especially to the reform of the international financial architecture.

As to a), it seems to common sense that the starting-point of the „Asian crisis" was a slowly growing process of „shadow vulnerability". Despite policy measures to stabilize capital inflows, the liquidity in these countries increased. This enabled banks and other financial institutions to lend more money to private firms. The result was an investment boom. Because of a relative slow reaction of the production potential, the asset prices increased, leading to a consumption boom. The countervailing, restrictive monetary policy which increased interest rates also created new incentives for capital inflows.

Another reason for the growing „shadow vulnerability" can be found in the fact that obviously credits from banks and other financial intermediaries played a more important role to finance investment than money (Table 5). If this credit channel is not under a similar market- and/or policy-based control like equity or bond markets, the restrictive monetary policy might not realise the expected effects. As long as the economic development creates positive expectations, the growth will reinforce itself.

Table 5: The credit channel in East Asia: correlation between output and money, and output and credit

	MONEY (M1)		CREDIT (banks and non-banks)	
	contemporaneous	lagged one quarter	contemporaneous	lagged one quarter
Canada	-0.075	0.222	0.359	0.248
Germany	-0.012	0.360	0.159	0.333
USA	-0.036	0.0205	-0.107	0.206
Indonesia	0.156	0.054	0.400	0.168
Korea	-0.117	0.143	0.12	0.088
Malaysia	-0.039	-0.130	0.277	0.011
Thailand	0.112	0.356	0.374	0.455

Source: Alba, P., in: Agenor, p. 19

a industrial production, except in Indonesia: GDP and in Thailand: electricity consumption

The potential vulnerability of the emerging economies was also due to the fact that the adaptation of the institutional system did not keep pace with the process of opening up. In the monetary sector a number of weaknesses had not been discovered:

I. undercapitalization of banks,

II. insufficient bank supervision,

III. weak position of the central bank.

Moreover, government-to-business-to-banks networks were destabilized because of the strong external influence („growing instability because of pressure to change the old way of doing business"). There are a number of reasons for the assumption that the IMF policies have also been a destabilizing element for the economic and social balance in emerging economies

The existence of „shadow vulnerability" implies that the growth process would not be disturbed, if there were no exogenous shocks. The external driving forces of the ASEMEC were strong enough to hide their internal weaknesses. In Asian emerging economies it could be measured by the following facts: The real growth of bank credit and credits from other financial institutions was much higher than real GDP-growth during the period from 1993 to 1996. This led to rising profits in the banking sector on the one hand and on the other to an assessment of risks posed by the borrower or his projects that has not always been careful enough. These, however, cannot be shown by any of the data commonly used. In general, this means that the „hidden risks" - measured by the decreasing capacity to overcome sudden exogenous shocks – were growing. In addition to this, real estate prices were rising in the booming Asian economies so that real-estate lending increased. This increased exposure also led to a higher burden of risks.

It goes without saying that this risk exposure of banks and other financial institutions is mirrored by the increased vulnerability in the corporate sector. This can be measured by the growing imbalances in the liability structure, e.g., relatively high debt/equity ratios, relatively high short-term-to-long-term ratios. Moreover, in connection with the declining performance of firms the debt determined their ability to cover interest rates payments (Table 6).

Table 6: Increasing Corporate Vulnerability in East Asia 1991-1996

		1991-1993	1994	1995	1996
Îndonesia	growth in fixed assets (%)	22	37	36	35
	debt/equity ratio	1.8	1.8	1.8	1.8
	short-term/ total debt (%)	56	58	58	57
	interest coverage	n.a.	2.2	3.1	2.4
Korea	growth in fixed assets (%)	11	15	24	-
	debt/equity ratio	3.2	3.3	3.4	3.2
	short-term/ total debt (%)	54	59	60	59
	interest coverage	1.4	1.9	1.8	1.1
Malaysia	growth in fixed assets (%)	15	21	18	26
	debt/equity ratio	0.6	0.7	0.8	0.9
	short-term/ total debt (%)	73	73	72	70
	interest coverage	9.4	11.7	9.6	6.7
Thailand	growth in fixed assets (%)	25	47	27	17
	debt/equity ratio	1.5	1.6	1.7	1.9
	short-term/ total debt (%)	71	72	67	67
	interest coverage	4.4	3.8	2.5	1.9

Source: Alba, p. 28

As regards the macroeconomic external „shadow vulnerability" the best indicator of the growing risk is the increasing ratio of short-term external debt to external reserves (e.g. for Korea in June 1997 this ratio was higher than 200 %).

Last but not least, „shadow vulnerability" resulted also from a parallel development of the domestic business cycles and the inflow of private capital. This – in part – was caused by the mix of macroeconomic policies during the borrowing phase. In case of growing demand pressure (1994-1996) the interest rates were increased, thus widening the international interest rate differential. The exchange rate policy (convertibility, pegged rates, interventions to prevent real exchange-rate appreciation) made nominal exchange-rate movements predictable. This decreased the incentives to hedge short-term capital flows. The reduced exchange rate risk for investors seemed to decrease the vulnerability of the countries. This was a wrong strategy as far as it encouraged the accumulation of unhedged foreign obligations. The expectation that the government would support banks in case of a crisis led to a situation of moral hazard.

The regulatory framework of the countries showed the following weaknesses:

I. insurance on liabilities by the government,

II. insufficient capital adequacy ratios,

III. inadequate legal lending limits on single borrowers,

IV. inadequate asset classification systems,

V. insufficient transparency of bank operations.

A strong argument for the fact that the phase before the crisis can indeed be characterized by „shadow vulnerability“ is that the credit ratings of commercial banks in the Asian emerging economies did not get worse between June 1996 and December 1997. Furthermore, it has to be mentioned that the „old“ regulatory framework was not changed after the domestic and capital account liberalization. In order to avoid increasing „shadow vulnerability“ liberalization would have had to be accompanied by tightened regulatory conditions in the financial sector.

In addition to this, the corporate sector was characterized by weak corporate governance: Competition policy was weak, tolerance against many types of relationships between banks and firms restricted the working of the market mechanism and there was weak control of accounting practices.

Last but not least economic policies did not stress the importance of supporting the integration of domestic financial markets in accordance with their integration into world financial markets.

5 From Crisis to Collapse

As mentioned before a great number of economists have offered explanations for the Asian crisis: Krugman, Corsetti, Perenti and Roubini stressed that overinvestment (fundamentals) and panic (non-fundamentals) played an important role (Krugman 1998, Corsetti/ Perenti/ Roubini 1999). Others (e.g. Radelet/ Sachs 1998) focused their analysis on the financial sector, arguing that moral hazard and a „disorderly work-out“ were at the forefront of the crisis. More and more economists agreed that various aspects were intertwined without giving a clear picture of this process. It seems that an analysis which focuses on the financial system, the exchange rate system and the policy response can provide an understanding of the complex processes, if it acknowledges that „shadow vulnerability“ played an important role.

„Shadow vulnerability“ turned into the „Asian crisis“ when these economies were hit by negative shocks. Economists mostly deal with the macroeconomic „mechanisms“ of the crisis. Behaviour is only included in these analyses in a rudimentary way. Shortly before the Asian crisis the growth of positive expectations seemed to continue with decreasing marginal rates when approaching the breaking point. In the literature this is related to „speculative attacks“ as an example of negative shocks. These external and internal shocks forced the governments to depreciate exchange rates. This however caused a massive outflow of capital. As a result the financial sector collapsed. The fear of a solvency crisis of the sovereign turned a currency crisis into a collapse of the exchange-rate systems.

Obviously, the response of economic policies was not adequate to mitigate the effects of this situation.

However, the key question which has not been answered in the broad literature about the crisis is what exactly caused the initial massive reversal of capital flows within a few days. This point seems to be crucial as it started a process of actions and reactions of agents that led not only the monetary sector from crisis to collapse, but also influenced also the production and consumption sectors. Contagion was the driving force which spread this process to most of the ASEMECs.

Very few economic activities were spared at least some of the effects of the crisis. One of them was direct foreign investment.

6 Recovery – the Program

The upturn of most of the emerging economies to fast recovery as early as 1999 was relatively unexpected by many observers. This recovery has last but not least been induced by restructuring measures the countries were forced to take because of the crisis. The upturn is not the result of new regulation. Rather, national political decision-makers have

I. realised adaptations of fixed prices that should have been made before, e. g., exchange rates;

II. decided in favour of measures to stabilise the economic system (banking supervision, anti-corruption, etc.).

The first step in stopping or to reversing the situation of economic crisis is to find a solution for dealing with the foreign creditors of national state as well as with the creditors of the domestic sector. In cases in which the national state made it credible that foreign creditors would be fully repaid (e.g., in the case of Korea and Thailand), this was accomplished with the support of the IMF which organized a „lender-of-last-resort liquidity program".

If the confidence of the foreign borrowers in the ASEMEC returned, it could be expected that their currencies would stabilize and stock markets would recover. But besides these „outside" preconditions for recovery, a domestic reform package had to be started. In this respect, the following tasks had to be fulfilled:

I. restructuring the financial and corporate sector:

- decisions about which firms and banks should be closed down,
- decisions on which banks and firms are to be rescued and recapitalized by bail-outs,

II. reorganization of the financial and corporate sector, especially in countries with strong conglomerates (some authors point out that destroying traditional structures and relationships in developmental state economies may cause a number of new problems),

III. establishing a legal framework (especially in the financial sector) that guarantees standards of rules as regards

- transparency in the financial system,
- effective risk control systems,
- adequate capital requirements,
- prudential regulation (bank licencing, governance of banks, quantitative supervisory tools),
- redefining monetary, fiscal and exchange rate policy by learning from experiences in boom and crisis phases,

IV. redefining the role of the IMF (Meltzer report, Kumar/ Masson/ Miller 2000)

There is an intensive debate in the literature on the concrete implementation of the recovery programs. It focuses on country-specific recovery packages, on sequences of steps in the recovery program, on concrete measures of the implementation of the learning process and on the trade-off and adequacy between destroying traditional („Asian") structures and customs and introducing „Western" standards. An important point is to restore confidence that an insolvency of the national state is not to be feared. It goes far beyond the aim of this paper to summarize and evaluate this broad discussion. There is only one question which is of basic importance for the future role of the ASEMECs in the world economy and which shall be discussed in chapter VIII: the controversy as to whether regulation or deregulation should be the appropriate strategy.

7 Recovery – the Process

As far as statistical data and empirical studies are available, these show that the ASEMEC recovered at a speed and to an extent which was significantly underestimated by most forecasts (BIS 2000, p. 34). The growth rates of the real GDP were positive in 1999 in all Asian emerging economies. They ranged from

10.7 % in Korea to 0.2 % in Indonesia. Despite the fact that net capital flows were still negative in 1999, the net outflow decreased from – US$43b to –US$27b. The stabilising role of a steady and high inflow of FDI seemed to be very important. This was partly due to the trend towards more global production structures, but partly also to the further liberalization of FDI inflows as well as to attractive investment opportunities in domestic (e.g. privatised) companies. As the BIS states, the sizeable current account surpluses in Asia permitted repayment of banking debts without hurting the recovery. The foreign exchange reserves increased in 1998 by US$114b and in 1999 by US$96b. One of the most obvious signs of the recovery was the continuing decline of cross-border bank lending. The five „crisis“ countries (Indonesia, Korea, Malaysia, Philippines, Thailand) have reduced their outstanding debt to international banks from US$329b in June 1997 to US$190b in December 1999 (Table 7).

Table 7: Growth, inflation and current account

	real GDP (change compared to previous year %)			consumer prices (change compared to previous year %)			current account (% of GDP)		
	1992-97	1998	1999	1992-97	1998	1999	1992-97	1998	1999
China	11.5	7.8	7.1	13.3	-0.9	-1.4	1.0	3.0	1.5
Hong Kong	5.2	-5.1	2.9	7.8	2.8	-4.0	0.1	0.5	4.4
Korea	6.8	-6.7	10.7	5.2	7.5	0.8	-1.8	12.6	6.0
Singapore	9.1	0.4	5.4	2.1	-0.3	0.5	14.7	25.4	25.3
Taiwan	6.6	4.6	5.7	3.2	1.7	0.2	3.1	1.3	2.0
Indonesia	6.9	-13.7	0.2	8.2	58.4	20.5	-2.4	4.4	3.8
Malaysia	9.2	-7.5	5.4	3.6	5.3	2.7	-5.7	13.7	16.9
Philippines	3.8	-0.5	3.2	7.8	9.7	6.7	-4.2	2.0	9.2
Thailand	6.5	-10.2	4.1	5.0	8.1	0.3	-5.9	12.5	8.9

Source: BIS 2000, p. 36

If the general view of Asia is differentiated country by country, remarkable differences can be observed as regards the recovery from the output losses in 1997/98 (BIS 2000, p. 40). Korea and Singapore turned back to the pre-crisis growth trend of their industrial production; Malaysia is narrowing the gap; Thailand and Philippines reached the pre-crisis level. In Indonesia the recovery process is progressing very slowly.

The „dark“ side of the recovery is the growing government debt, especially in Korea, Indonesia and Thailand. One of the causes is the costs of the anti-crisis government programs. But one also has to bear in mind that the increasing debt/GDP ratios are also influenced by the shrinking GDP and not only by increasing debts.

The recovery can also be observed in the monetary sector. First of all the Asian currencies had partly recovered their losses by early 1999; some are fairly steady against the dollar on a 60 % level of the pre-crisis level (e.g. Thailand, Malaysia), some appreciated gradually during the year (Korea, Philippines) (BIS 2000, p. 44). Except for Malaysia, Hong Kong and China the central banks adopted floating exchange rate regimes.

On the microeconomic level the corporate and financial restructuring started in some ASEMEC without great enthusiasm. E. g., in Korea the institutional framework was strengthened, prudential regulations forced banks to tighten their lending practices and risk assessment, and a specialised bankruptcy court was established. Many of the top 30 chaebols downsized and improved their production structure by focusing on their core strengths (BIS 2000, p. 47).

As regards the recovery on the microeconomic level, an empirical study of the Korean steel industry (Park/Tscha 2000) shows that the crisis seems to be only a short interruption within the maturing stage which started in the mid-1990s. In 1997 the apparent consumption grew less than 2 %. The negative economic growth in 1998 led to a dramatic decrease of domestic steel consumption (-34.8 %). This reflects in part the bankruptcies of some steel consuming chaebol. The decline in steel production (1998: -6.2 %) was relatively moderate. The main reason was the extremely high growth of the Korean steel exports (1998: +57.7 %). It seems that the devaluation of the Won increased the Korean steel industry's competitive advantages on the world market. The recovery in 1998 brought the production back to a level which was 6 % higher than in 1996. In contrast to 1998 the domestic demand increased sharply while exports declined by more than 20 %. The restructuring of the Korean industry and also the Korean steel industry has not yet been completed. The crisis seemed to be an interlude which sharpened minds to concentrate on long-term challenges.

In other ASEMECs the progress in corporate restructuring has been more limited. Indonesia especially is still lagging behind because of the sheer scale of the problem, but also because of the slow pace of change of the institutional framework.

The strategies regarding the refinancing and restructuring of the bank systems differ. The Korean and Malaysian government forced banks to sell non-performing loans at large discounts to „Asset Management Companies“ which are owned by governments. Those banks considered weak, but capable of „surviving“ were supported by government capital. Other countries (e. g. Thailand) put more trust in market forces. In all ASEMECs bank deposits were protected in case of bankruptcy. In addition, supervisory oversight was strengthened and a bundle of prudential measures was introduced. [1]

Forecasts of different institutions are at present optimistic about the growth of the Asian economies in 2000 (Table 8).

Table 8: Asian countries' real GDP growth

	HK	China	Taiwan	S. Korea	Thai.	Malay.	Sing.	Indo.	Phil.
1999	2.9[a] -1.3[b] -0.5[c] 1.5[d] 1.2[e]	7.1[a] 7.0[f] 6.8[c]	5.7[a] 5.07[g] 5.5[c]	10.7[a] 4.8[b] 8.0[c] 5.0[d]	4.1[a] 2.0[b] 3.0[c] 2.0[h]	5.4[a] 1.8[b] 2.0[c] 2.0[h]	5.4[a] 3.2[b] 5.0[c] 3.0[h]	0.2[a] -1.3[b] 2.0[c] -2.0[h]	3.2[a] 2.7[b] 3.0[c] 2.5[h]
2000	0.2[b] 1.5[c] 3.6[e]	8.2[b] 6.0[c]	5.7[g] 6.3[c]	4.9[b] 6.0[c]	3.5[b] 5.0[c] 4.0[h]	3.8[b] 3.9[c] 4.0[h]	4.9[b] 6.0[c] 5.0[h]	5.8[b] 4.0[c] 2.5	4.0[b] 4.5[c] 3.5[h]

Sources: Wong 1999, BIS 2000
a Bank of International Settlements, 70th Annual Report, Basle 2000, preliminary estimation
b Hong Kong Economic Journal, 25 Aug. 1999 (from Morgan Stanley)
c Hong Kong Economic Journal, 15 Sept. 1999 (from Asian Development Bank)
d N.E Asian Quarterly, Standard Chartered, Hong Kong, June 1999
e Hong Kong Economic Times, 24 Sep. 1999 (from International Monetary Fund)
f Chinese Economic Trends, Whurr Publishers, London, 1999.1
g Directorate-General Budget, Accounting & Statistics, Executive Yuan, Taiwan, Republic of China
h S. E. Asian Quarterly, Standard Chartered, Hong Kong, July 1999.

8 Regulation versus Deregulation: Rethinking an Old Discussion

The debate on whether regulation or deregulation is the right strategy, especially for developing/emerging countries, is an old one. In the case of the Asian emerging economies one of the most discussed aspects of regulation has been whether the inflow and outflow of capital in these economies should be limited. Deregulation on the other hand was considered the basic reason why the countries had been able to attract domestic investment and thus foster growth in the initial stage of their development. The discussion as to which of the strategies should be preferred is a complex one, and there are arguments for both sides, some

1 For a more detailed description of the measures to restructure the financial system see BIS 2000, pp. 47-50.

favouring regulation and some favouring deregulation (Wong 1999). In order to evaluate the applicability of models dealing with the effects of international capital flows, we have to take into account that in contrast to the assumptions of many models, capital mobility is in reality imperfect. This is due to transaction costs, information asymmetry, heterogeneity between domestic and foreign assets and administrative requirements. Because of these frictions, policies may cause reverse results compared to the arguments derived by theory. Moreover, current theoretical work on currency crises focusses on the importance of self-fulfilling prophecies, which have not been part of traditional models (e.g. Mundell-Fleming). Finally, in the case of ASEMECs it seems to be difficult to isolate currency crises from bank crises, which also forces us to take into account the regulatory system of the banking sector.

Many of the arguments in favour of regulation are due to the aim to limit volatile short-term capital flows and their effects on the balance of payments and the exchange rate. This was why Tobin proposed a tax to „throw sand into the wheels“ of short-run capital flows, while affecting long-term flows only marginally (Tobin 1978). Dornbusch proposed a dual exchange-rate system which would offer a similar protection for the real sector, while limiting short-term capital flows (Dornbusch 1986). Thus, much attention has been paid to the distinction between (harmful and volatile) speculation and (growth-inducing) long-term capital flows and their effects on the real economy. Opponents of these arguments argued, however, that speculative attacks would have their reason in a misalignment of interest rates and exchange rate with fundamentals. Moreover, it was underlined that restrictions would not only curb outflows, but also discourage inflows.

Thus, the opinions on regulation versus deregulation were diverse. The decision as to which of the two might be more favourable depends on a number of specific conditions of the situation and assumptions about the behaviour of agents. However, even this view is short-sighted because it does not take into account that regulation and deregulation are not two alternative decisions. Rather, the regulatory framework of a country is made up of a complex set of decisions. Few authors acknowledge that deregulation of capital markets might even have created new regulatory needs (Griffith-Jones/Papageorgiou 1993). This means that it is not a return to old rules that is needed. Instead, these countries need frameworks that are appropriate to their individual economic systems. However, the Asian „emerging“ economies are one of the best examples of the fact that an economic system is an evolving structure, and the same should be true of the regulatory framework accompanying this structure. Still, this is a simplified picture, as markets – if flows are relatively free – have the possibility of changing and evolving on their own through the interplay of economic agents. This has been reflected in the growth of Asian emerging economies and also in their temporary decline. On the other hand, the regulatory system is a matter of political decision-making. Political decision-making is based on discrete choice and is subject to rigidities. Established systems are likely to persist until pressure on them is big enough to sacrifice old traditions by new and hopefully more rules that are hopefully more adequate for the economic system. Thus, the political system is naturally a system that is characterized by lagged responses that may often only occur after a certain critical threshold has been passed. Regulatory dynamics can often be expected only after significant negative effects in the economic sector have been felt. These ideas are reflected in Figure 1.

Fig. 1: Lagged adaptation of "regulatory" and economic dynamics

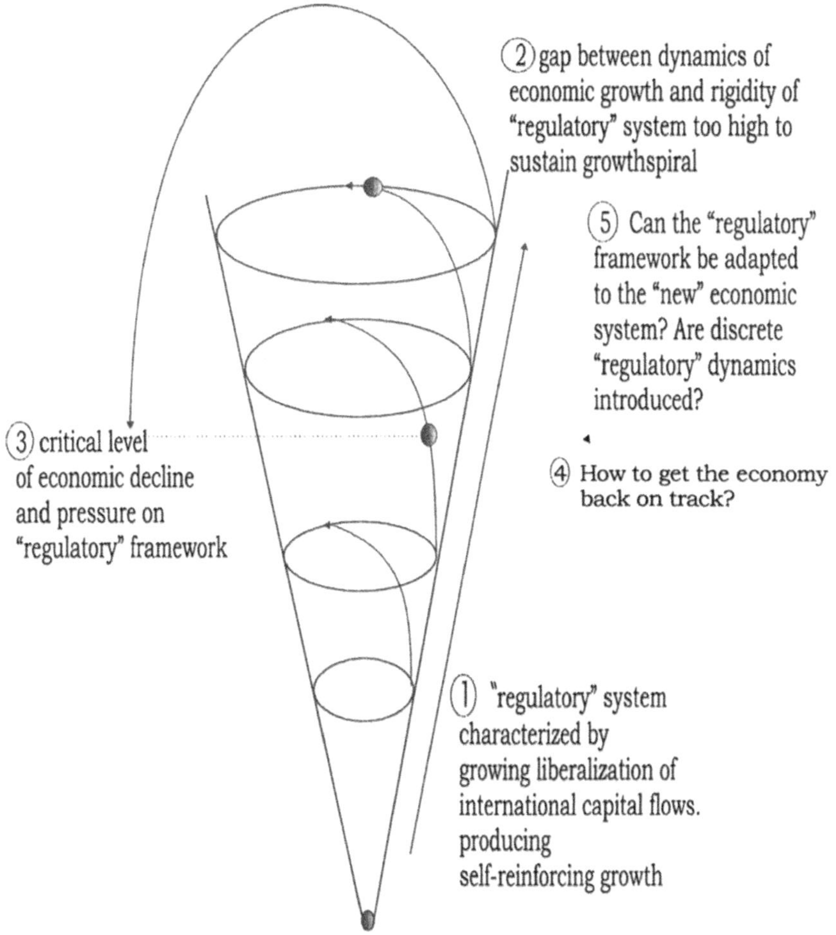

The debate about regulation versus deregulation in many ways seems to be a question of either/or. Today a number of these aspects are often subsumed under the heading of the „new financial architecture". This underlines the systemic and complex view of a stable regulatory framework much better. The discussion also shows that there is no agreement on the structure of „regulatory" bodies, the methods of regulation or deregulation, its objectives and the legal approach. However, it has the disadvantage that it is a badly defined concept that has been filled with a diversity of contents. Another point is that the term „financial architecture" implicitly hints at the fact that a number of national, international and supranational agents are involved in building such pillars of the financial system. However, it might also render responsibilities in this system less clear. The discussion about the new international financial architecture was very animated immediately after the Asian crisis. During this time, there were a number of proposals for a rebuilding of the international financial system. In 2000 political decision-makers seem to be less susceptible to such fundamental proposals. This shows, yet again, that willingness to change is much greater when there is acute systemic risk, whereas it loses dynamism when markets calm down (Frenkel/ Menkhoff 2000).

9 Conclusion

The preceding comments were intended to show that the development and the aftermath as well as the crisis itself have to be understood from a broader perspective that takes into account the fact that different sectors of the ASEMECs have evolved with a different speed; change in the industrial sector has surpassed change in the regulatory, political sector. Taking into account that the successful working of the economy relies on the interdependence of these sectors, it is obvious that crisis will be triggered whenever one of the sectors is significantly lagging behind the other.

The distinction between 'fast' and 'slow' variables is, explicitly or implicitly, at the base of much theorizing and debate in economics.... What is important to observe in general is that the evolution over time of a system where both fast and slow variables are present, is mainly determined by the slow variables. (Gandolfo 1997, p.533)

Moreover, we have to accept that not only the patterns of industrialization and growth change in time, but also those of crises. This is due to a number of aspects that are frequently also summarised under the terms of globalization.

Starting from financial liberalization and following the way up to the present recovery, Fig. 2 tries to give an idea of the development in the ASEMECs.

Fig. 2: Development in the ASEMECs

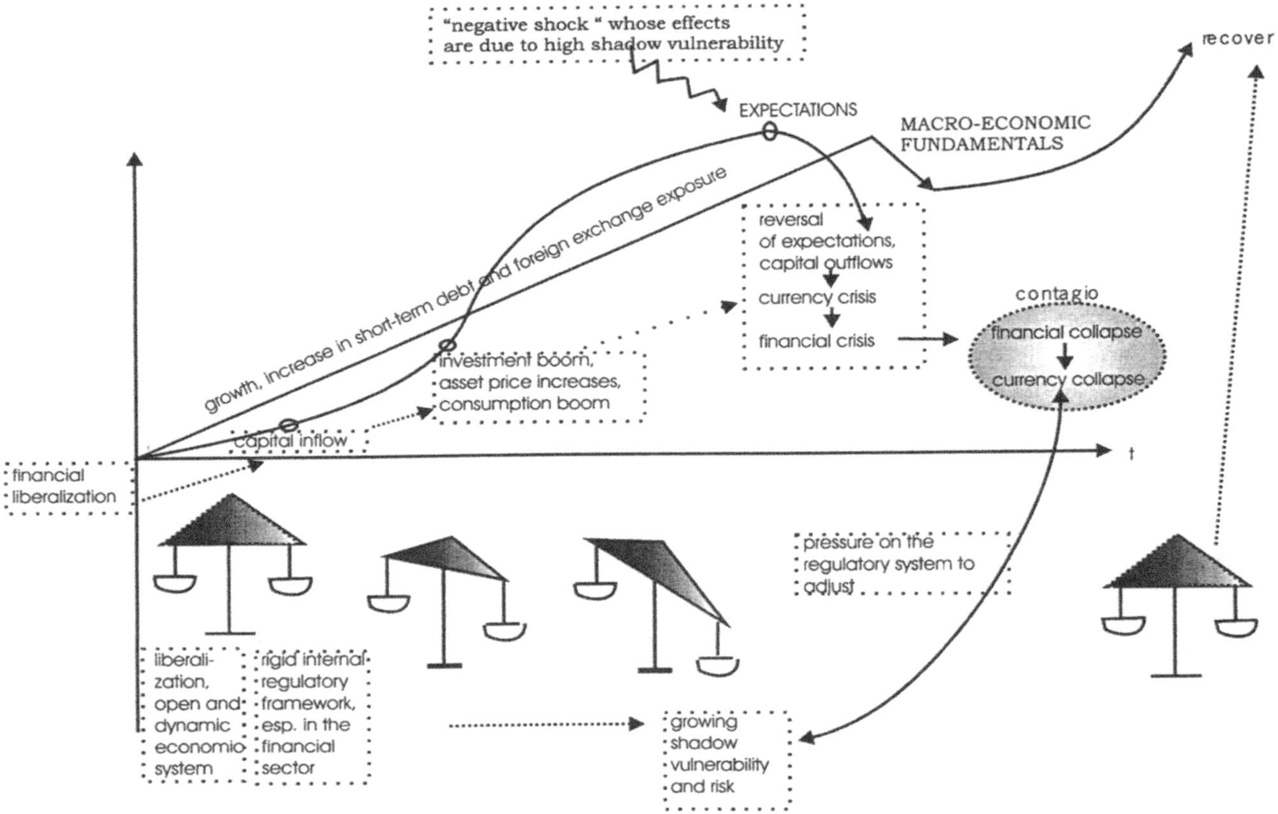

This, however, is a point of view that leads us to conclusions that are hardly related to the discussion as to whether deregulation or regulation are the appropriate strategies for the ASEMECs. It shows that much more attention should be paid to the speed of change in the different sectors of the economy (industrial sector, financial sector and their regulatory frameworks, etc.). In an ideal case we might expect that crisis can be avoided, if we do not permit more rapid growth in the real sector than can be matched by a regulatory framework of the financial sector that allows this sector to grow without an increasing „shadow vulnerability". This seems a simple proposal at first.. At second glance, however, a number of questions arise:

I. Can growth be managed stepwise? Or is industrialization a process of either/or?

II. How can we achieve an optimal fit between change in the regulatory system and growth and change in the real sector?

III. Is the balancing of change – if possible at all – a national task? What can international and supranational institutions contribute to this task?

Even if it is possible to achieve such a balanced growth, we should expect it to be much slower than the experiences of the ASEMECs in the most recent decades. Ideally, however, it would also be a much smoother process.

Table A1: Capital flows to Asian crisis economies: Malaysia, Indonesia, Thailand and Korea (% of GDP)

	1983 - 1988	1989 - 1995	1992	1993	1994	1995	1996	1997
Malaysia								
net private capital flows	3.1	8.8	15.1	17.4	1.5	8.8	9.6	4.7
net direct investment	2.3	6.5	8.9	7.8	5.7	4.8	5.1	5.3
net portfolio investment	n.a.	n.a.	n.a.	n.a.	n.a.	n.a.	n.a.	n.a.
other net investment	0.8	2.3	6.2	9.7	-4.2	4.1	4.5	-0.6
net official flows	0.3	0.0	-0.1	-0.6	0.2	-0.1	-0.1	-0.1
change in reserves	-1.8	-4.7	-11.3	-17.7	4.3	2.0	-2.5	3.6
Indonesia								
net private capital flows	1.5	4.2	2.5	3.1	3.9	6.2	6.3	1.6
net direct investment	0.4	1.3	1.2	1.2	1.4	2.3	2.8	2.0
net portfolio investment	0.1	0.4	0.0	1.1	0.6	0.7	0.8	-0.4
other net investment	1.0	2.6	1.4	0.7	1.9	3.1	2.7	0.1
net official flows	2.4	0.8	1.1	0.9	0.1	-0.2	-0.7	1.0
change in reserves	0.0	-1.4	-3.0	-1.3	0.4	-0.7	-2.3	1.8

Thailand								
net private capital flows	3.1	10.2	8.7	8.4	8.6	12.7	9.3	-10.9
net direct investment	0.8	1.5	1.4	1.1	0.7	0.7	0.9	1.3
net portfolio investment	0.7	1.3	0.5	3.2	0.9	1.9	0.6	0.4
other net investment	1.5	7.4	6.8	4.1	7.0	10.0	7.7	-12.6
net official flows	0.7	0.0	0.1	0.2	0.1	0.7	0.7	4.9
change in reserves	-1.4	-4.1	-2.8	-3.2	-3.0	-4.4	-1.2	9.7
Korea								
net private capital flows	-1.1	2.1	2.4	1.6	3.1	3.9	4.9	2.8
net direct investment	0.2	-0.1	-0.2	-0.2	-0.3	-0.4	-0.4	-0.2
net portfolio investment	0.3	1.4	1.9	3.2	1.8	1.9	2.3	-0.3
other net investment	-1.6	0.8	0.7	-1.5	1.7	2.5	3.0	3.4
net official flows	0.0	-0.3	-0.2	-0.6	-0.1	-0.1	-0.1	-0.1
change in reserves	-0.9	-0.8	-1.1	-0.9	-1.4	-1.5	0.3	-1.1

Source: Singh 1999, p. 22

List of References

Alba, P. et al. (1999): The role of macroeconomic and financial sector linkages in East Asia's financial crisis, in: Agénor, P.-R. et. al. (eds.): *The Asian Financial Crisis*, Cambridge, pp. 9-68.

Bank for International Settlements (2000): 70th Annual Report, Basle.

Corsetti, G./ Pesenti, P./ Roubini, N. (1999): The Asian crisis: an overview of the empirical evidence and policy, in: Agénor, P.-R. et. al. (eds.): *The Asian Financial Crisis*, Cambridge, pp. 127-166.

Dornbusch, R. (1986): Special Exchange Rates for Capital Account Transactions, in: *World Bank Economic Review*, Vol. 1, September, pp. 3-33.

Frenkel, M./ Menkhoff, L. (2000): Neue internationale Finanzarchitektur: Defizite und Handlungsoptionen, in: *Perspektiven der Wirtschaftspolitik*, Vol. 1, 3, pp. 259-281

Gandolfo, G. (1997): Economic Dynamics, Berlin et al.

Grabel, I. (1999): Rejecting exceptionalism: reinterpreting the Asian financial crisis, in: Michie, J./ Smith, J. G. (eds.): *Global Instability*, London, pp. 37-67.

Griffith-Jones, S./ Papageorgiou, V. (1993): Globalisation of Financial Markets and Impact on Flows to LDCs: New Challenges for Regulation, in: Tennissen, J. J. (ed.) *The Pursuit of Reform, Global Finance and the Developing Countries*, The Hague, pp. 65-11.

Krugman, P. R. (1998): Firesale FDI, MIT Paper prepared for the NBER conference „Capital inflows to emerging market economies", mimeo.

Kumar, M. S./ Masson, P./ Miller, M. (2000): Global Financial Crisis: Institutions and Incentives, IMF Working Paper, 00/105, Washington DC.

OECD (1999): Asia and the global crisis, Paris.

Park, K. S./ Tscha, M. J. (2000): Korean Steel Industry after the Economic Crisis: Challenges and Opportunities, paper presented at the 13th Biennial Conference of the Asian Studies Association of Australia „Whose Millenium", 3-5 July 2000, University of Melbourne.

Radlet, S./ Sachs, J. (1998): The East Asian Financial Crisis: Diagnosis, Remedies, Prospects, in: *Brookings Papers on Economic Activity*, Panel, Washington DC, 26-27 March 1998.

Singh, A. (1999): 'Asian capitalism' and the financial crisis, in: Michie, J./ Smith, J.G. (eds.): *Global instability*, London, pp. 9-36

Stiglitz, J. (1998): Restoring the Asian miracle, in: *The Wall Street Journal*, p. 4.

Tobin, J. (1978): A proposal for International Monetary Reforms, in: *Eastern Economic Journal*, Vol. 4, pp. 153-159.

UNCTAD (1997): Trade and Development Report, Geneva.

Winters, J. A. (1999): The Determinant of Financial Crisis in Asia, in: Pempel, T. J. (ed.): *The politics of the Asian economic crisis*, London, pp. 79-100.

Wong, Kar-yiu (1999): Currency crisis and capital control, http://faculty.washington.edu/karyiu/papers/crisis-sur.pdf

World Bank (1993): The East Asian Miracle: Economic Growth and Public Policy, New York.

The Economic Trend of the Last Three Years in Japan

Takafusa Nakamura

The University of Tokyo

1 Introduction

The 1990s have been difficult years for the Japanese economy, especially in the light of the collapse which began in 1997. In this paper, I shall attempt to survey recent economic trends in Japan since 1997. In order to do this, however, it will also be necessary to reflect upon processes ongoing since 1990.[1]

Fig. 1 Business Trend 1990-1999

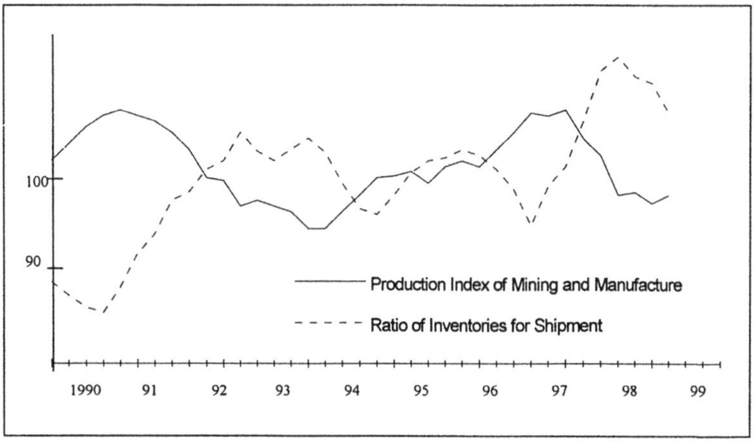

2 Japan's "Ten Lost Years"

"The Ten Lost Years" has become a set phrase referring to Japan's economy in the 1990s. After the bubble boom ended in 1990, the Japanese economy rapidly

1 Source for tables and figures: Kazuo Yoshida: History of 10 Years Slump in Heisei Japan, Tokyo, 2000

slumped and bottomed out in 1993. As we can see in Fig. 1, the industrial production index recorded its peak in the first quarter of 1991, followed by a downward trend lasting until the fourth quarter of 1993. The index declined by around 13 percentage points. This downturn was the worst recorded since 1975.

In spite of this alarming trend, a majority of businessmen and economists remained rather optimistic about future business prospects, because they remembered normal past recessions followed smoothly by revivals once the trough of the slump had been passed. In the 1990s, however, the business cycle acquired an extraordinary momentum. Industrial production increased slowly but steadily until early 1997, to almost the same level as in early 1991. The ratio of inventories for shipment decreased through the end of 1994, and then began to increase. Summing up, the real economic situation was one of very slow but continuous recovery.

In this period, exports were a subtle factor of demand, as shown in Table 1. The exchange rate of the yen against the dollar, which had risen to Y128 in 1988, fell to Y145 in 1990, and then increased to Y94 in 1995. Accordingly, Japanese foreign trade and balance of trade in dollars expanded rapidly, although in terms of yen they remained at about the same level. This was a negative factor in the efforts to stimulate Japan's domestic economy. From an international perspective, Japanese export trade was developing, but in domestic terms the economy was stagnating.

Capital investments showed a swing following the short-term business cycle, but overall their level remained nearly unchanged.

There was no way to embark on the stimulation of the Japanese economy except through government spending and the adoption of a policy of loose money. Spending by the government had to depend upon huge public bond issues because of declining tax revenues, especially in corporate taxes during the recession. The total amount of debts issued expanded radically as seen in Table 2. Japan, well aware that its future burdens would increase, was compelled to issue public bonds. Compared with other major countries, the increase in Japanese bonds is very clear.

Monetary policy was another measure used to stimulate the business situation. The Bank of Japan (BOJ) changed its official discount rate policy and set the rate downward in July 1991 after a tight monetary policy that had lasted two years. Thereafter, a radical trend reduced the official rate all the way down to 0.5% in September 1993. By this process, the BOJ continually lowered rates of interest in order to expand the money supply necessary for economic recovery. In this period, Japan was hit not only by its domestic slump but also by the revaluation of the yen. However, in 1996 the devaluation of the yen brought about a good export situation, and it seemed that a steady recovery had begun.

Table 1: Japan's Foreign Trade

	In Millions of Dollars			In Billions of Yen			Exchange Rate against U.S. Dollar
	Export	Import	Balance	Export	Import	Balance	(yen)
1989	275,175	210,847	64,328	37,823	28,979	8,844	138.12
1990	286,948	234,799	52,149	41,457	33,855	7,602	144.88
1991	314,525	236,737	77,788	42,360	31,900	10,460	134.59
1992	339,650	233,021	106,629	43,012	29,527	13,485	126.62
1993	360,911	240,670	120,241	40,203	26,826	13,377	111.06
1994	395,600	274,742	120,858	40,498	28,104	12,394	102.18
1995	442,937	336,094	106,743	41,531	31,549	9,982	93.97
1996	410,869	349,122	61,747	44,731	37,993	6,738	108.81
1997	420,937	338,739	82,198	50,938	40,956	9,689	120.92
1998	386,544	279,756	106,788	50,645	36,654	13,991	131.02

Table 2: Japan's National Budget and Debt

	Expenditure by the Govt.			Total National Debt (B)	Ratio to GDP (%)	
	National	Local	Net Total (A)		(A)/GDP	(B)/GDP
1989	70,851	72,729	116,307	235,062	28.6	58.4
1990	74,191	78,473	129,393	246,247	28.2	56.1
1991	75,627	83,807	129,559	256,338	28.0	55.3
1992	77,141	89,560	134,804	273,918	28.6	58.0
1993	79,353	93,076	139,856	305,102	29.3	64.0
1994	79,985	93,818	141,441	331,192	29.5	69.2
1995	86,480	98,945	150,761	368,223	30.8	75.6
1996	87,315	99,026	151,405	398,866	30.1	79.3
1997	84,909	32,581	148,749	426,172	29.5	84.4
1998	87,991					
1999	81,860					

3 The Crisis of the Financial Institutions

A notable characteristic of the recession of the 1990s and of the general financial crisis was that Japanese financial institutions, including twenty major banks and four big security companies, had been holding many concealed bad debts in the form of loans to real estate agents and stock speculators ever since the boom period of the second half of the 1980s. In this period, real estate prices, especially for land, and stock prices rose dramatically. During this bubble boom, there was a massive flow of credit to these real estate and stock firms. When the bubble burst, prices of land and stocks fell as shown in Figs. 2 and 3.

Real estate firms suffered fatal losses through falling land prices. The losses grew day by day and year by year. The financial institutions had no way to recover their loans to the firms. They had to hold bad debts as if they had been normal assets. On the stock market, falling prices caused declared or concealed losses to the corporations in almost every sector of the economy. Moreover, the large security companies had made illegal trust contracts guaranteeing fixed rate allotments (of, for example, 5% or 6%). When stock prices fell, they suffered severe losses from these contracts.

Fig.2 Land Prices in City Area

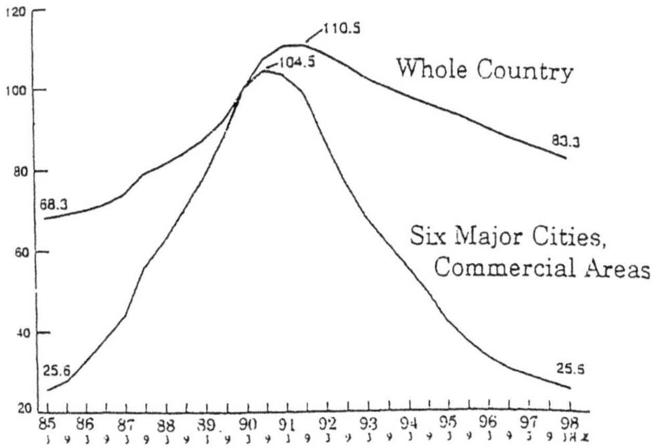

Fig.3 Stock Prices (Nikkei Average, 225 Stocks)

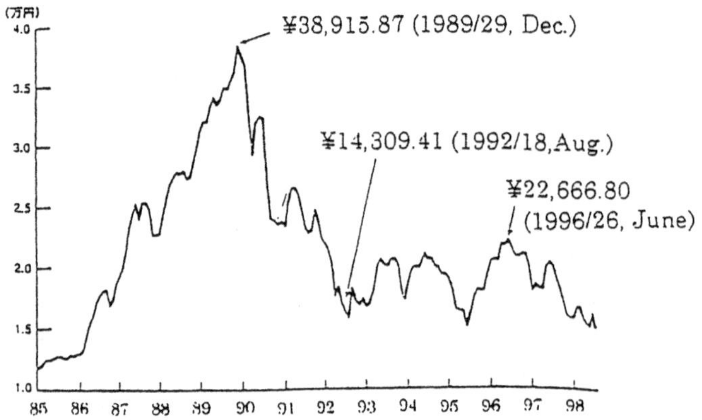

In the early 1990s, these losses cut into the balances of the big companies, especially of financial institutions, even though they were able to cover their running costs. The policy of abnormally low interest rates by the BOJ seemed to be a measure which would relieve these institutions by supplying cheap money and lightening the burden of interest payments on bank deposits.

On the other hand, major Japanese banks carrying on international business were compelled to clear the BIS regulation on capital adequacy, which was required to be over 8%. This ratio is the net equity/(equity+ liabilities). During the recession of the early 1990s, the value of the net worth declined so rapidly that banks tried to increase their net worth by controlling new credit to medium-size and small firms. Consequently, the belief arose on the market that money was not flowing smoothly, because the banks were reluctant to increase these credits. At the same time, big businesses were cautious about starting new projects. Thus, the money supply appeared stagnant.

In 1996, corruption on the part of several non-banking companies specializing in housing and real estate was disclosed. A few credit associations collapsed in 1995. A total of about thirty financial institutions, including a few major ones, went bankrupt between 1995 and 1999.

This slump might be characterized as an asset depression. Since stock and land prices were on a downward trend with no end in sight, banks and companies holding stocks and lands had no way to avoid increasing capital losses. In the early 1990s, banks, security companies and real estate agents did not curtail the assessment of assets on their balance sheets, because they expected an improvement in capital prices. In the mid-1990s, businesses abandoned such selfish expectations and desired to make a fresh start by revealing their capital losses. However, they were unable to declare these huge losses all at once, so that by 1997 they still held many concealed losses.

The Ministry of Finance (MOF) was afflicted by deficits in the annual national budgets and by rapidly increasing public bond issues. The total amount of public bonds expanded so rapidly that it exceeded GDP in 1998. During the depression, direct taxes were supposed to be reduced. In June 1996, the Hashimoto Cabinet decided to raise the consumption tax from 3% to 5%, effective April 1997. This move was due to the strong desire of the MOF and Prime Minister Hashimoto to curtail the national budget deficit. They were, in my opinion, overly optimistic about the negative effect of the tax increase on national consumption and on the true balance of the financial institutions. Perhaps they believed that the worst was now over, and this policy would not have such a grave effect on the Japanese economy. Although consumption did increase under the 3% tax until March 1997, business began to stagnate after April 1997.

The Government still expected that the effect of the tax increase would weaken in the autumn. These expectations were dashed. In November, Sanyo Securities Company collapsed. This was followed by the Hokkaido Takushoku Bank, one of the major twenty banks, closing down its business operations and being absorbed by North Pacific Bank, even though its deposits were paid by the Deposit Insurance Organization supported by the BOJ. At the end of November, the Yamaichi Securities Company, one of the four big security companies, announced that it was going out of business voluntarily on the advice of the MOF. This company had held secret capital loans of over Y200 billion originating from illegal contracts with the Trust Fund to guarantee profit allotments at a fixed rate. The collapse of three major institutions was the gravest shock to the Government and the business community since the financial crisis of 1927. The myth of strong direct control through the "convoy system" by the MOF had now lost its potency.

The Hashimoto Cabinet was on the way to six major reforms, including the epoch-making liberalization of the financial system: the "Monetary Big Bang." Although these plans were implemented on schedule, business went on a downward trend. The Government was unable to take measures to stabilize unrest or to rebuild the banking system. The origin of this turmoil, it seems, can be attributed to the huge amount of worthless loans in major banks, concealed but impossible to collect. The Japanese financial system was suffering from a serious sickness but had no way to cure itself.

Mr. Kiichi Miyazawa, Mr. Seiroku Kajiyama and other experts proposed drastic measures. The MOF announced that the worthless loans held by major banks totalled Y76 trillion (around 13% of GDP). Inputting public funds into the money market was inevitable. The proposal was as follows: (1) The Deposit Insurance Organization (DIO) would receive a national bond for Y10 trillion yen. The Government would guarantee payment of Y20 trillion yen in loans from the BOJ to the DIO. (2) The DIO would allocate Y17 trillion of the Y30 trillion yen in order to restructure the collapsed financial institutions, and Y13 trillion yen to purchase stocks and bonds from banks in order to increase their net capital worth. There were serious debates about inputting public funds into private financial institutions. The problems were matters of principle. Given the magnitude of the crisis, however, such debates were set aside.

In 1998, there was a gradual deterioration of the business trend. Negative growth continued from the last half of 1997. In July 1998, Mr. Hashimoto suffered a severe defeat in the general election for the House of Councillors. He and his Cabinet had to take the consequences and resign. Mr. Keizo Obuchi, the LDP Congressman, succeeded to his post. In order to meet the economic crisis, Mr. Obuchi selected Mr. Kiichi Miyazawa as Minister of Finance and Mr. Taichi Sakaiya as Secretary of the Economic Planning Agency. Mr. Miyazawa is not only a former Prime Minister but also a well-known specialist on economic policy. Mr. Sakaiya is a former official of the MITI and a renowned writer on economic problems. This selection demonstrated Mr. Obuchi's commitment to the priority of economic recovery.

Mr. Obuchi made his Cabinet concentrate on a policy target of stabilization of the financial system and economy. The public fund invested Y7,458 billion in fifteen major banks to bolster their net capital worth. As it turned out, the banks' internal review in March 1998 revealed Y87,527 billion in rotten loans, some of which were highly dubious and had to handled with extreme caution. The total was 2.5 times worse than formerly announced. It was in the light of this situation that the decision was made to input the public funds. The financial institutions reopened and redeemed the hidden losses due to the bad loans on their balance sheets in 1997 and 1998.

In 1998, the Long-Term Credit Bank of Japan, followed by The Nippon Credit Bank were informed by the MOF that their balance sheets showed that their debts exceeded their assets, i.e., their net capital worth was negative. They were required to liquidate and merge with other financial groups.

This marked the end of the enforced reorganization of major financial institutions. Banks and other financial companies, however, began to seek a voluntary way of enlarging their business through merger with other major companies. Dai-ichi Kangyo Bank, Fuji Bank and The Industrial Bank of Japan announced they would form a giant bank in 2002. Sumitomo Bank and Sakura Bank will also form a new bank in 2002. They consider that it will be difficult to survive unless they maintain strong and abundant management resources. They are now preparing themselves for international competition.

4 The Present Economic Trend

As seen in Fig. 1, 1998 was the worst year of the 1990s. Industrial production declined. The money supply shrank to below zero percent of the short run call rate. Loans from financial institutions are still decreasing, as we see in Fig. 4, which shows the rate of increase of loans by financial institutions.

Fig. 4 Rate of Increase of Loans by Financial Institutions (All Types)

(change from one year ago in %)

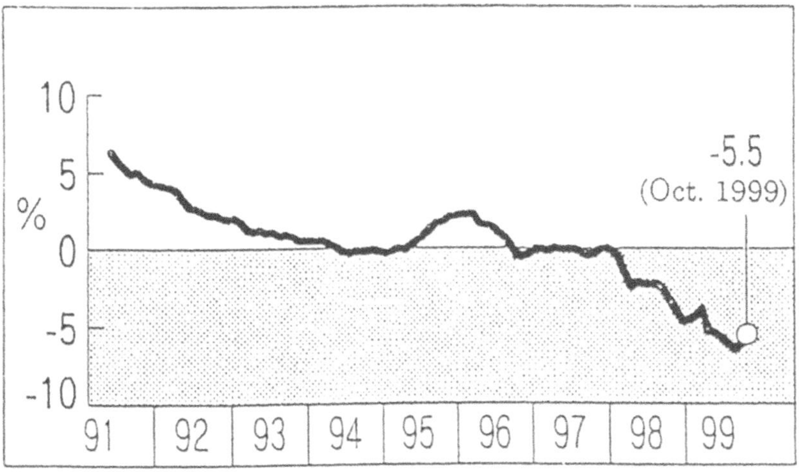

However, there is also some good news. First, the GDP growth rate has been positive since early 1999, and the rate of unemployment has gone down in the past few months. Mr. Sakaiya, the Secretary of the EPA, estimates that a regular recovery of business will be seen after the second half of last year. This is rather optimistic, but perhaps not unrealistic, because of the progress made in clearing away inferior assets and restructuring big businesses over the last two or three years. In addition, the East Asian countries as a whole are recovering from the financial crisis of 1997. It is a good situation for the Japanese economy, which will return to a slow but steady course of growth if economic growth in the U.S. remains favourable.

Effects of Globalization on National Financial Systems

Herbert Hax

Universität zu Köln

1 Introduction

The traditional definition of a national financial system is one subordinated to state regulation, in a state comprising a unified currency zone and with no restrictions upon the movement of capital within its borders. However, such a definition is no longer consistent with current realities. Nowadays the free movement of capital is no longer confined by national borders. Among the nations of the European Union, the movement of capital is completely free. Furthermore, among all the developed industrial nations of the world, and increasingly even among threshold nations and transforming nations, there presently exist hardly any restrictions upon capital movements. Moreover, in Europe the equivalence of currency zone and national territory has also ceased to be a practical reality.

Given this situation, the question as to how the legal framework of financial markets should be structured takes on a completely new form. The legal authority for the regulation of financial systems is still in the hands of the nation states. But the financial markets are no longer national markets, and the players in these markets have many possibilities for avoiding national rules. The question as to whether a supranational regulation of financial systems that cross national borders is necessary presents itself today with special urgency.

2 Prerequisites for the Rise of Global Financial Markets

The decisive prerequisite for globalization, meaning the coalescence of national financial markets into a worldwide market, is the freedom of the movement of capital. This prerequisite has now been met for large parts of the world. Individual nations have voluntarily renounced monitoring and methods of restriction of capital movement because they perceive that a worldwide capital market enables a better allocation of resources, and are moreover aware of the expanded possibilities for diversification created by a more favorable distribution of the risks associated with capital investment. This situation is advantageous for all participants, not least for countries with high potential for development but without the necessary capital to set their development in motion.

Accordingly, inclusion in a worldwide capital market is of especially great importance for developing and threshold countries, although, to be sure, the experiences of recent years show that it also entails high risks. In principle, opening to the worldwide capital market is highly beneficial for economic development, but certain prerequisites must be fulfilled to avoid a simultaneous increase in dangers. A second development, which along with the disappearance of national restrictions upon movement of capital has significantly advanced the worldwide coalescence of financial markets in recent years, has been the introduction of new contracts, which have partly been bought and sold on the stock exchanges in the standard form, but which for the most part have been worked out on a case-by-case basis by the players on the financial markets. With the help of derivative instruments, always as variants of futures and options but with great variety, special risk commitments can be set up according to individual wishes. This expands the possibilities for speculation as well as for switching operations. Since only the derivative contracts are traded and executed, but not the underlying primary financial futures, even elaborate transactions require only a relatively small employment of funds. This enables participants in the market to react quickly and in contrast to trading with the primary financial futures saves considerable transaction costs. A third development, and one that has made its distinctive mark on the worldwide capital market as we know it today, consists of modern communications technology. All the information anywhere in the world can nowadays be made available anywhere else in the world, practically without delays and at trivial cost. The same technology enables contracts to be concluded by widely separated parties without significant transaction costs due to distance. Spatial distance between market participants or between them and their markets no longer has any practical influence.

3 Financial and Currency Crises

Global financial markets open up new possibilities for economic development, but they are at the same time subject to risk. The greatest danger is seen in the fact that the consequences of financial crisis in individual countries very quickly spread throughout the entire world, and not only trigger turbulences in the financial markets but also cause serious non- monetary harm. As a rule, such events begin with a critical but localized development. This leads to a withdrawal of capital from the affected country and, because of the associated downswing in the exchange rate, a currency crisis. Once confidence has been shaken, the crisis spreads to other countries with similar problems. Creditors and other capital investors suffer losses, which lead in turn to slumps in the exchange rates in their own countries. The non-monetary shock hits those countries the hardest which are abruptly cut off from injections of capital. This leads at the same time to a downturn in demand in world trade, which is felt by all the trading partners. The drastic changes in the fabric of exchange rates change the competitive stances and force difficult processes of adaptation even upon the countries which were initially less affected. On top of this, in all the cases in which, due to the spreading worldwide crisis, the financial markets endure asset losses, there is the further consequence of impairment of non-monetary activities, partly due to shortfalls in demand, and partly due to reduction of investment activity.

In the past decade, the world economy has gone through a number of fiscal crises in the form of currency crises with more and less serious non-monetary consequences, most recently the crisis proceeding from Thailand and rapidly embracing all the nations of Southeast Asia in 1997 and 1998 (on the causes and sequence of the Southeast Asian crisis, see Sachverständigenrat 1998/1999, pp. 16-18). The blame for the onset and spread of this crisis was frequently laid on the financial markets, first and foremost those in the threshold countries whose economic development was hard hit. But in Europe as well, there were accusations leveled against "speculators" whose "greed for money" had allegedly plunged the world economy into crisis (Schmidt 1998). This was a major reason for the initiation of a new discussion, under the heading of "Creation of a New Financial Architecture," about the possibilities of international regulation of financial markets.

An initial result of this discussion was the establishment of a new body, the "Forum for Financial Market Stability", by the finance ministers and heads of central banks of the G7 nations in February 1999. At the World Economic Summit Conference in Cologne in June 1999, a report was also submitted on "Reinforcement of the International Financial Architecture" (Sachverständigenrat 1999/2000, p. 20).

The problem about regulating international financial markets is that one wants to avoid the onset and spread of financial crises, without at the same time impairing the capacity of the financial markets to function. Anyone who complains that the withdrawal of capital from a country during a crisis can cause a painful disturbance in its development needs to reflect that without the free movement of capital, the influx of capital that brought about the development in the first place would never have occurred. There is, therefore, little sense in trying to prevent financial crises by limiting the free movement of capital. If we want to create an ordered framework for global financial markets, we need to start with the fundamental causes of the crises, and not with the reactions of the market participants, which are determined by the rationale of the market.

4 Explanatory Models for Financial and Currency Crises

Efforts aimed a finding suitable means for dealing with the onset and spread of financial crises run up against a fundamental difficulty. When one attempts to apply the experience gained from past crises, one discovers that they always had different causes and ran their course in different ways. There can accordingly be no unified rule for countering such crises. Three models used to satisfactorily explain past crises will now be briefly described (on this point see especially Donges 1999, pp. 131-136).

The oldest and most familiar explanatory model takes as its starting point a country that establishes a fixed exchange rate but then undergoes an upward revaluation in real terms because the domestic trend in prices cannot be harmonized with this exchange rate. This leads in turn to increasing deficits in the balance of payments, which cause expectations that a devaluation will occur. The next consequence is capital flight. This reinforces the pressure towards devaluation, and if, nevertheless, attempts are made to maintain the exchange rate, speculation commences, and this ultimately forces the devaluation to take place. As long as the causes continue to exist, this process can go on indefinitely. In this case, the cause of the crisis lies in the discrepancy between an exchange-rate policy aimed at stabilizing the expectations of capital investors, and a macroeconomic policy that does not permit long-term maintenance of a particular exchange rate. Crises of this kind have frequently occurred in Latin American countries, most recently at the beginning of 1999 in Brazil. The only escape route out of a crisis of this type is in a better macroeconomic policy, above all in the reduction of budget deficits, which are fed by monetary policy and thereby promote inflation. A second model proceeds from the same premises, that is, from a fixed exchange rate, but locates the starter of the crisis not in a mistaken policy, but in loss of confidence brought about by external events, which triggers capital flight and thereby creates pressure to devalue, and which cannot be resisted in the long run, so that with benefit of hindsight it appears as if the lack of confidence on the market's part was justified. In other words, in this case we perceive at the outset not real events, but expectations with the character of self-fulfilling prophecies. This explanatory model is often associated with doubts about the rationality of the market participants, who are reproached for behaving as if in accord with a "herd instinct.“ (Schmidt 1998). We should however consider that the actions of the individual market participant are perfectly rational, when he adjusts them to a development which is generally anticipated, even if he himself recognizes that the fears behind the development are really unfounded. To be sure, this explanatory model leaves unanswered the question as to how the expectations that drive the process forward arise in the first place. It is hard to imagine that there are no comprehensible reasons behind them. Be that as it may, there is some basis for the belief that the process just described of how expectations are formed can greatly accelerate and reinforce a critical development determined by other causes.

The forming of expectations likely plays its main role in the contagious effect by which a crisis that has broken out in one country is translated to another in which there is initially no reason for any such thing to be found. Even a change in the competitive position of a country due to the devaluation of its currency can lead to anxieties in other countries engaged in the same markets about a worsening in the balance of payments, and thus influence the formation of expectations to the detriment of these countries. Such contagions played an important role in the spread of the crisis in Southeast Asia in 1997 and 1998. At the same time, however, it was apparent that these countries differed greatly in their susceptibility to contagions of this kind. It is also notable that Taiwan put up a stout resistance to the trend. This, too, indicates that the shaping of disadvantageous expectations normally does not happen without some reason. Behind it are to be found errors in policy and weaknesses, which have possibly been tolerated for a rather long period of time, and then suddenly, due to some trifling cause, produce a change in mood to the detriment of the country.

The third model for explaining financial crises differs from the first two in starting not with actual or anticipated macroeconomic developments, but with microeconomic facts. Central to it is the reliability of the players who are themselves active in the country in question and responsible for the application of imported capital, namely, the governments and firms, primarily banks and other financial-economic intermediaries. If a general misallocation of capital resulting in cancellations of credit and insolvencies among financial intermediaries occurs due to inadequate internal monitoring in the firms and incautious grants of credit, along with, as is not infrequently the case, uninformed political influence, corruption and political instability, then the markets react by withdrawing capital, which triggers a currency crisis with all the subsequent results.

The crisis in Southeast Asia in 1997 and 1998 followed this pattern. It is important to recognize that not all financial and currency crises have the same causes or run their course in same sequence. The main lesson from the crises in Southeast Asia was that not only erroneous developments may be responsible for the outbreak of crisis. Accordingly it was also an error to induce the affected countries to revise their macroeconomic policy, as was done at the beginning. What was really necessary was structural reforms in the microeconomic realm. There will always be new financial and currency crises in the future, and we need to be clear that there is no limit to the different kinds of causes they can have. Therefore, there can be no generally valid rules as to how to meet such crises.

5 Elements of a "New International Financial Architecture"

Behind the current efforts of many governments to construct a "new international financial architecture" there are various motives. One is to divert the non-monetary damage threatened by financial and currency crises. But an important motive is also found in the fact that politicians feel themselves to be limited in their freedom of decision by the reactions of the financial markets. In truth, the financial markets, no longer bound by national borders, are a very quick and effective mechanism for imposing sanctions against misconceived economic policies. A policy that reduces confidence in the security and profitability of capital investments will feel the effects directly in the form of capital outflow and a threat to the value of the currency in terms of its purchasing power abroad. Frequently, politicians who need to distract people from their own mistakes lay the blame for this on the scheming of greedy speculators. Even the demand often heard in connection with reflections about an international regulation of the financial markets, namely, that the primacy of politics over the markets must be preserved, is just another expression of the attempt to escape the constraints stemming from a normal functioning of the markets. But of course politics is in a dilemma here: it would be easy enough to prevent undesirable market reactions, for instance, by restricting movements of capital. But this would have at the same time the effect that the large and important advantages of an efficient allocation of capital would be lost, especially for countries with high potential for development and great need for capital. If one does not wish to lose the advantages of functioning international financial markets, then there is no escaping the constraints imposed by those markets.

Nowadays various instruments for preventing undesirable market reactions are taken into consideration. The creation of a new international currency system for limiting exchange rate fluctuations as well as restrictions upon free movement of capital are under discussion. Furthermore, there are thoughts as to the role that the International Monetary Fund (IMF) can play in future in the prevention and limitation of the harmful consequences of financial and currency crises. Finally, the experiences of recent years have concentrated attention upon the question as to the minimal requirements to be imposed upon the regulatory system for every country's financial system, that is, for its banks and other financial intermediaries.

6 Reference Zones for Exchange Rates

In 1998, instigations for the creation of a new, worldwide currency system with reference zones for exchange rates were felt primarily from German politics (Filc 1999, pp. 19-21; on the reservations about reference zones: Sachverständigenrat

1998/1999, p. 218f.; Siebert 1999, p. 52f.). However, the international response to them was not generally favorable and they have now faded into the background.

An international currency system would have the initial task of regulating the relations among the great currency regions, meaning primarily the Dollar Zone, the Yen Zone, and the Euro Zone. A basic difficulty is that the participating countries would remain essentially unrestricted in the sovereignty of their monetary policies.

A monetary policy required to orient itself to fixed exchange rates would hardly be able to pursue effectively the goal of stabilizing the domestic value of its currency. The possibility that from time to time the exchange rates would have to be adjusted to altered conditions could never be excluded. Experience teaches that with such systems impending change can always be exploited by speculators as a welcome opportunity to make risk-free profits. Apart from this, fixing the exchange rates among the great currency regions as a defense against financial and currency crises which generally proceed from countries in other regions will achieve nothing.

The currency system would, then, have to comprehend not only the great currency zones, but all the countries participating in the free movement of capital. But precisely in such a comprehensive system very serious currency crises could occur. If, for instance, a country were to suffer a loss of confidence on the capital market, whether due to errors in macroeconomic policy, or to serious misapplications of capital, then a fixed exchange rate would immediately feel the pressure. Every attempt to maintain it would merely be an invitation to speculation. In fact, this is the way it was in nearly all the financial and currency crises of the past: the countries involved had, on their own initiative, pegged their own currency to some other currency, usually the Dollar. But since their economic policy was not compatible with such a pegging, they could not maintain the exchange rate they had aimed for. The crisis was in most cases intensified by the attempts to preserve the rate, long after it was a lost cause. Despite these attempts, there was no way of preventing speculation based on the obviously unavoidable devaluation. In such cases, however, the blame is not the speculators‘ but the policy's, which had opened the door to profitable speculation in the first place by clinging to a false exchange rate.

A currency system with fixed exchange rates is utterly unsuitable as a preventive measure against the rise and spread of financial and currency crises. By fixing exchange rates one treats the symptom, not the cause. When capital flows out of a country because of a loss of confidence, a fixed exchange rate is only defensible in the short term; the crisis itself can neither be diverted nor alleviated by this means.

7 Constraints upon the Movement of Capital

Very frequently consideration is given to the idea of preventing the spread of currency crises by restricting the movement of capital (Hoffmann 1999, p. 82f.; on reservations about restricting movement of capital, see: Sachverständigenrat 1998/1999; p. 217, Donges 1999, p. 142f.; Siebert, p. 53f.). If capital cannot easily be withdrawn from a country, then pressure on the currency will also cease. A nation can go down this path unilaterally, and has often done so, like Malaysia, also most recently during the crisis of 1997 and 1998 in Southeast Asia. The consequence is similar to that of a unilateral stoppage of payments. The loss of confidence in the country on the markets will only be more drastic, and the consequences for economic development dependent upon the importation of capital that much more severe. Constraints on movements of capital could be provided for certain cases within the framework of an international regulation of the financial markets. Demands for such are occasionally heard, the reason given being that purely speculative movements of capital are to be hindered. The basic error of these considerations is that there is no way of distinguishing desirable movements of capital for financing investments from undesirable speculative movements of capital. If constraints upon the movement of capital are in fact applied, especially if money invested in a country cannot be withdrawn from it, then the entire movement of capital is necessarily affected. But if capital investors have to reckon that they will be unable to transfer money invested in a country back out of it, then the importation of capital into this country will become extraordinarily difficult, and in any event the interest rate will rise by an appropriate risk premium. There is also little use in differentiating between long-term and short-term movements of capital in the case of constraints on movements of capital. Constraining short-term movements of capital does in fact hinder speculation, but at the same time cuts the country off from access to credit at favorable interest rates on the world market. Moreover, obstacles to long-term movement of capital, as in the case of the transfer of capital gains, can never be avoided. Also, a restriction aimed at the short-term movement of capital requires extensive bureaucratic regulations and monitorings, which are never entirely safe from circumvention, especially if corruption enters the picture. None of this is any way to secure the confidence of capital investors in a country. And so every country has to choose: either it opens itself to the free movement of capital and thereby submits to the rules of the financial markets and also to the sanctions they use to punish errors in economic policy, or it admits, from the outset, importations of capital only with restrictions and under definite conditions, and thereby gives up key possibilities for advancing in its economic development. In every case, certain preconditions need to be fulfilled before a country permits free movement of capital (*Sachverständigenrat* [1998/1999], p. 217, *Siebert* p. 53f.). It has to be ensured that a macroeconomic policy which is both sustainable and guarantees stability can be borne. The same applies to the national financial system, especially banks and other intermediaries, which must ensure an efficient use of the capital taken over into the international markets. This assumes the existence of competition and the monitoring of firms, as well as a state that provides the necessary regulation, but at the same time leaves untouched the investors‘ free, autonomous power of decision. To the degree that these prerequisites are fulfilled, the risk of getting into a serious financial and currency crisis will be lessened. Given these prerequisites, the opening to the international financial markets can bring major impulses for the economic development of a country. On the other hand, a premature opening is dangerous. For it is worse to loosen up the movement of capital initially and then restrict it, than never to free it at all. Confidence, once lost, can only be regained in the markets through years of effort.

8 On the Role of the International Monetary Fund

The International Monetary Fund (IMF) has been the target of sometimes vehement criticism in connection with the crises of recent years, criticism which one must note came from very different directions and was sometimes self-contradictory (Sachverständigenrat 1998/1999, p. 214-216; Hoffmann 1999, p. 75f.).

The criticism accuses the IMF of errors in its developmental policy; the IMF is said to restrict the economic development and contribute to the spread of poverty among the populations of countries affected by currency crises through its imposition of strict requirements. A second charge is that the IMF is too ready to take on the role of a "lender of last resort.“ Because of this, it is said, the IMF gives preferential treatment on the demand side of the capital market to a form of behavior that neglects risks and therefore limits the capacity of the financial markets to function, since risks are valued above market prices. The criticism of the requirements of the IMF from the perspective of developmental policy is based on the demand in many cases for a strict rehabilitation of the budget in order to stabilize the macroeconomic policy, a move that could not be accomplished without a reduction of social services from the state. The consequence was that in countries already suffering from high unemployment rates due to a serious recession brought on by a currency crisis, drastic cuts in the state social services had to be borne by economically weaker segments of the population, on top of the existing problems. The wrath of those affected was directed against the IMF, which was accused of carrying out its rehabilitation to the benefit of foreign dispensers of capital and the detriment of the poor in the population. Such accusations usually overlook the fact that the primary aim is never anything but to downscale state expenditures, which the affected country simply cannot afford at its present level of development. The cause of a financial and currency crisis is almost aways to be found in economic conditions in one or more countries that cannot be sustained in the long run (Pohl 1999, p. 63). The only way of rehabilitating is to change the conditions. Then, the preconditions for capital imports and the advancement of the developmental process can once again be created. Any country affected by a financial and currency crisis can reject the requirements imposed by the IMF and declare itself insolvent. To be sure, if it does this, it will exclude itself for a long period of time from participation in the international capital market. In such cases, most countries find it wiser to follow the path to recovery of the confidence of the markets marked out by the IMF. The criticism of the IMF is more justified when it can be shown that the parameters of macroeconomic policy laid down by it are quite unsuitable for the particular problems of a country. This was partially the case during the crisis in Southeast Asia in 1997 and 1998 (Sachverständigenrat 1998/1999, p. 215; Hoffmann 1999, p. 78). The causes of this crisis were less the errors of macroeconomic policy and more the interdependencies among governments, banks, and firms, which had led to considerable mis-allocations of capital. Despite this, the IMF proceeded with requirements imposed upon macropolicy, which had proven themselves in previous cases, but were an unsuitable therapy for the Southeast Asian nations, especially since their macroeconomic figures were really not all that bad. The criticism from the perspective of developmental policy described here has the aim of placing the IMF under stronger obligations to help the affected countries. Not infrequently, a certain pressure in this direction is exerted from one or another of the member states for political reasons. However, such action forces the IMF into a role which excites criticism from the other side. It becomes the "lender of last resort," which always has to stand ready to help in serious emergencies when all other means have failed. This in its turn has grave consequences for the functioning of the markets. If capital investors can rely upon the IMF to jump to the rescue every time things get really desperate, then they can largely ignore the risks connected with capital investment in any given country. The affected country will always enjoy an influx of capital, and the interest that has to be paid for this need never include the risk premium appropriate to the given situation. When this occurs, then there can hardly be any stimulus to make a special effort towards reducing the risks. The IMF must beware of creating a "moral hazard" in the sense just described through its actions. Financial markets are very well able to create the correct stimuli for dealing with risks. This ability will be lost, however, if people can depend upon a "lender of last resort," on whom they can dump the risks at the end of the day. The critics of the IMF have in some cases gone so far as to declare it a superfluous organisation and call for its dissolution. But the majority opinion is that the IMF, despite all the criticism, still performs important functions. There is little debate over its assignment of preventing crises by providing better information and greater clarity. By the same token, one can hardly make do without the IMF in its role of mediator and leader in negotiations in order to overcome the consequences of a crisis once it has already begun. The assignment of improving the fund of information has at its primary goal the earliest possible recognition of the symptoms of an impending crisis, so that the markets can prepare for it in a suitable way. The experience of recent years shows that it is not enough simply to observe the macroeconomic development.

A financial and currency crisis can arise from microeconomically determined misallocations of capital, even if there is no sign of this in the macroeconomic data. For this reason, the IMF will increasingly need to take microeconomic facts into account in its observations and analyses aimed at early detection of crises. In particular, the financial sector of a country requires scrupulous observation from the point of view that suitable and effective regulations must exist to take account of the risks. The task of mediating and conducting negotiations once a crisis has begun makes especially tough demands on the IMF. In the first place, and for the reasons cited, it must not appear in the role of the "lender of last resort." As a matter of principle, private capital investors must always bear the full burden of risk for their arrangements. In specific cases this can lead to political controversies, and above all to hardships for the country affected. In the second place, there is no avoiding the fulfillment of imposed requirements by the country hit by a crisis, or the enforcement of the requirements by the IMF. Since the hardships are unavoidable, the IMF will have to reckon with severe criticism from the ranks of developmental policymakers. But such criticism is only justified if the requirements are not suited to remove the causes of the crisis and ensure that the country rejoins the international financial markets. As with any institution, there is no guarantee that the IMF will not occasionally make mistakes in the future, but this does not justify the conclusion that an institution for mediation and conducting negotiations in crises can be dispensed with.

9 The Regulation of National Financial Systems

An important and urgent task remains the regulation of national financial systems

(Sachverständigenrat 1998/1999, p. 218; Donges 1999, pp. 138-140). There are minimal standards for this, based on international agreement, adherence to which the IMF is assigned to surveil as part of its informational work. Nowadays it is generally recognized that the practices of banks and other financial institutions that undertake risks cannot simply be left up to their own discretion and to the forces of competition. The negative external effects of the collapse of such institutions are simply too serious to take such an approach. The globalization of the financial markets in connection with the rise of new instruments for trading in risks is currently posing new challenges to such regulation. Politicians have clearly perceived this. Since the financial and currency crisis in Southeast Asia, there have been more energetic efforts to complete the work on unified international standards for regulating banks, which have been in progress for years, and which now have primarily to take account of the conditions arising from new instruments of the financial markets. In the framework of the "Forum for Financial Market Stability," founded in February 1999, working groups were formed to consider both the conditions of legal surveillance of financial market institutions with high-risk portfolios, and the inclusion of offshore centres in the surveillance of financial markets (Sachverständigenrat 1999/2000, p. 20).

A strict surveillance of banks with high standards of risk management can inhibit the rise and spread of financial crises both in nations providing and in those receiving capital flow. The most important requirement is that threshold nations offering excellent opportunities for capital investment limit the contingent risks effectively by constructing a productive financial sector secure from crises. The experience of recent years has shown that bad investments and wrong approaches to crises can plunge a threshold nation into a deep crisis, even if the macroeconomic data give no cause for concern. In judging the susceptibility of nations to crisis, the IMF will in future have to pay close attention to the robustness of the financial sector. Whether the banks are regulated in accord with international standards, and whether the regulation is effectively enforced, will be of great importance.

Regulation in the capital-providing countries will be no less important. Suitable standards of risk management will have to ensure that financial institutions in newly developing markets only take such risks as they can deal with in a crisis with their own resources. It must never be the case that they come to rely on the intervention in a crisis of an international institution like the IMF (Nunnenkamp 1998; Sachverständigenrat 1998/1999, p. 218). In all the participating nations, the financial sector first and foremost must be able to absorb the shocks one knows will repeatedly occur, without their expanding into a major crisis.

10 Conclusion

The globalization of the financial markets opens up great opportunities for efficient capital transfers, primarily for countries with high developmental potential. Risks are an inevitable part of these opportunities. Financial and currency crises, which can spread rapidly on global markets, can always arise from different causes, and they can run their course in different ways. Measures starting from symptoms rather than causes are always mistaken. This is as true of attempts to fix rates of exchange as of restrictions upon the free movement of capital. It is essential for the financial systems in all countries to be robust enough to absorb the shocks on their own, and this must be the goal of regulation of the banking sector. Private capital investors can also not be allowed to depend upon an institution like the International Monetary Fund to intervene with cash assistance when things turn serious and pick up the tab for private losses. A responsible approach to risks on the financial markets can only be achieved if all participants clearly understand that they will have to bear the losses from risky businesses practices.

List of References

Donges, Jürgen B., "Globale Finanzmärkte, Währungskrisen und aufstrebende Volkswirtschaften," *Zeitschrift für Wirtschaftspolitik* 48 Jg. (1999), pp. 129-146.

Filc, Wolfgang, "Leitplanken für Finanzmärkte," in *Globalisierung der Märkte und ihrer Ordnungen*, 8. Volkswirtschaftliches Kolloquium der Bundesvereini-gung der Deutscher Arbeitgeberverbände, Köln 1999, pp. 15-22.

Hoffmann, Lutz, "Währungskrisen—Systemfehler der globalen Marktwirtschaft?" *Zeitschrift für Wirtschaftspolitik* 48 Jg (1999), pp. 72-84.

Nunnenkamp, Peter, "Wie die Gläubiger bei Finanzkrisen in die Pflicht zu nehmen sind," *Handelsblatt*, Oct. 7, 1998.

Pohl, Rüdiger, "Währungskrisen: wie sie entstehen und wie sie (nicht) vorausge-sehen werden können," *Zeitschrift für Wirtschaftspolitik* 48 Jg. (1999), pp. 62-71.

Sachverständigenrat zur Begutachtung der gesamtwirtschaftlichen Entwicklung, "Wirtschaftspolitik unter Reformdruck," Jahresgutachten 1999/2000.

Schmidt, Helmut, "Vorsicht, Finanzhaie," *Die Zeit*, Oct. 8, 1998.

Siebert, Horst, "Ansatzpunkte zur Vermeidung internationaler Währungskrisen," *Zeitschrift für Wirtschaftspolitik*, 48 Jg. (1999), pp. 46-61.

Arisawa Lecture: The Life and Work of Professor Hiromi Arisawa, with Special Reference to his Relationship to Germany

Takafusa Nakamura

The University of Tokyo

Professor Hiromi Arisawa was my father figure in academic life and my mentor on my path through life. I became his student in 1949 and have been his disciple ever since. All my academic work is based on the instruction I received from Professor Arisawa in my student days. It is deeply gratifying for me to speak about the Professor's life and work, with special emphasis on his relationship to Germany, at this meeting before so many of his old friends. Professor Arisawa was born in 1896 in the city of Kochi on Shikoku and passed away in March 1988 at the age of ninety-two. During the first half of his life he experienced many ups and downs, but the second half was an unbroken success. He served as the President of the Japan Academy for six years after 1980. Throughout his long life, he maintained strong ties to Germany. Professor Arisawa completed his studies in the Department of Economics at Tokyo Imperial University and was then appointed as a research assistant in the area of the theory of political economy. The following year, Professor Emil Lederer arrived in Tokyo as a guest professor at the university. Professor Arisawa served as a research assistant to Professor Lederer, who recommended that his young assistant, who had become a friend as well, should come to study at his own university, in Heidelberg. Professor Lederer accompanied his assistant on a trip to Kyoto and Nara, where Professor Arisawa stayed in a western-style hotel for the first time.

In the 1920s, many Marxist and socialist works found their way to Japan, where they greatly appealed to young students, who believed that they contained the key to cracking the secret of capitalist economies. Professor Arisawa was among these students. Some of the most famous of these works, in addition to those of Marx and Engels, were Rudolf Hilferding's *Finanz-Kapital*, Lenin's *Imperialism as the Last Stage of Capitalism*; *State and Revolution* and *Capitalist Development in Russia*, Bukharin's *ABC of Communism*, and Rosa Luxemburg's *Capital Accumulation*, among many others. No fewer than five different translations of *Das Kapital* into Japanese were planned. Moreover, a translation of *The Collected Works of Marx and Engels* was begun in 1928 and completed in 1935. Only *The Communist Manifesto* was not included in the *Collected Works*, due to a ban imposed by the Japanese government. During this period the Communist Party was prohibited from organizing, and even the name "Communist Party" was censored out of all printed matter, XXX appearing in its place.

In 1926, Arisawa was promoted to associate professor and then shifted to the chair in statistics to fill the vacancy in this post. He arrived in Berlin in April 1926 to conduct research. He studied Franz Mehring's *History of Social Democracy in Germany* under the tutelage of Dr. Alexander Conrady. While living in Berlin and travelling in southern Germany, he was greatly impressed by the freedom and democracy of the Weimar Republic. In 1927, he had the opportunity to attend a meeting of the *Sozialdemokratische Akademiker* at the invitation of Professor Lederer in Nuremberg, and he heard Professor Lederer lecture on "Crisis and Imperialism." After the lecture, Professor Lederer introduced Arisawa to Dr. Hilferding. Dr. Hilferding greeted Arisawa most cordially, and then invited the young Japanese to the National Conference held at Kiel that May. Here he developed his famous theory of "Organized Capitalism" in his report on the German economic situation. This well-known theory propounds the idea that cyclical depressions will not appear despite capitalist organizations such as cartels and trusts as long as economic fluctuations can be controlled. Upon his return to Berlin, Professor Arisawa purchased a complete set of the *Neue Rheinische Zeitung*, edited by Karl Marx and published between June 1, 1848 and May 18, 1849, for the Department of Economics at Tokyo University, in whose library it was placed. He also bought such important publications as a first and a second edition of *Das Kapital* at Hugo Streisand's antiquariat: His personal collection of German economics texts was acquired in this establishment.

He became a guest member of the Berlin *Konjunkturinstitut* headed by Ernst Wagemann. This institute published a quarterly devoted to recent world economic trends, and Professor Arisawa was able to absorb their methods of research. At the same time, he organized a reading circle of Japanese students. This group also started up a baseball team and played against a similar American team. As it turned out, he had no time for studies in Heidelberg, even though Professor Lederer's mother had made a room available to him there. His whole time in the Weimar Republic was a personal experience of great freedom and democracy.

On his return to Tokyo, however, Japanese ideological restrictions, particularly upon Marxist groups, became even more severe. In this situation, he formed a new research group for the analysis of the recent currents in the world economy. This group commenced its work in 1928, collecting information from all around the world from newspapers and magazines. With the sudden crash of the New York stock market in October of 1929, a global crisis broke out. Arisawa's group published a paper based on joint research in *Chuo Koron*, a standard review. Thereafter, they actively published the fruits of their research almost every month. They also issued several books: *Cartel, Trust and Concern* (Vol. 1 by Arisawa, Vol. 2 by Ryokichi Minobe), and *World Depression and the Crisis of*

International Politics (by Arisawa and Isamu Abe), among others. The latter work concerned the rise of the Weimar Republic and its final stages during the depression from the Marxist perspective. The group ended their joint research projects in 1932, but they maintained their office and held a weekly meeting until 1937.

Professor Arisawa was active in research and writing until 1937. Then, in July 1937, an undeclared war with China broke out and led to the Pacific War. In February 1938, Professor Arisawa and his university group were arrested on the charge of sympathizing with the *Front Populaire* movement directed by the Comintern. Other members detained included Hyoe Ouchi, Yoshitaro Wakimura (Tokyo University), Ryokichi Minobe and Isamu Abe (Hosei University). This case was called the "Professor Group Incident.“ Professor Arisawa was able to return home from prison after fourteen months. All the members of the group were pronounced innocent in 1944. However, the faculty of the Department of Economics at Tokyo University barred the return of the professors to their posts due to ideological differences.

The Pacific War ended in August 1945 with the acceptance of the Potsdam Declaration. Japan was placed under the control of the Supreme Commander of the Allied Powers. In these changing political circumstances, the University urgently recalled Professor Ouchi, Professor Arisawa and Professor Wakimura, on the condition that many other faculty members were required to leave their posts. At the same time, the Government was faced with the necessity of planning policies for economic recovery. Professor Arisawa was kept very busy, both at the University and with the Government. His most famous contribution to the recovery was his proposal of the Priority Production Plan. His priority was to revive the production of coal and steel by inputting disposable raw materials and funds into these two industries. Their increased outputs were then to be input into each other. As soon as their production reached a suitable level, it could be allocated to other important industries to help overall production recover. This plan was implemented and succeeded in 1947 and 1948. The Japanese industries had now seized the opportunity for selfrestoration.

I was a student at the University during this period and a member of Professor Arisawa's seminar. He taught us that academic work should be based on reality, especially on numerical proofs. He told us that he did not believe any theory if it lacked such proof. This has been the most important principle of my research. The Professor published a book entitled *Inflation and Socialization.* In this book he developed the basic idea of the Priority Production Plan and the method of suppressing runaway inflation in Japan with reference to his experiences in Germany in the early 1920s. His research into the German economy during his young years inspired him to create this policy for the alleviation of Japan's postwar crisis.

In the 1960s, he worked to establish policies for various industries. A majority of the coal companies were inevitably compelled to close their mines, bowing to competition from cheap oil imports from the Middle East. Professor Arisawa assumed the leadership of the team which devised measures to take care of coalminers who had lost their jobs and to revive the coalmining areas. His plan was carried out by the Government and his policies succeeded. Although this is only one example, Professor Arisawa was indispensable to the solution of such difficult problems because of his fairness and his kind, humane personality.

As to Marxist economics, his attitude had gradually changed as he learned about the real conditions in the Soviet Union and the Eastern European countries. He analyzed the Japanese, European and American economies more flexibly through the use of numerical data. He published short works on the Japanese and world economy based on analyses of abundant numerical data for five-year periods carried out in cooperation with his old group, Professor Ouchi, Professor Wakimura and Professor Minobe.

At the age of seventy, he decided to take up once again his study of the history of the Weimar Republic, his ideal state in the 1920s. He set about collecting new materials, reading and annotating them. When I accompanied Professor Arisawa to Bochum for the Conference held in 1969, he visited bookshops to look for works concerning the Republic. In this period, he was still busy with official obligations, so that the only time he had for research was from midnight until two or three a.m. It was our unwritten rule that we should not phone each other before eleven a.m. The Professor's notebook on the Republic eventually comprised about twenty volumes, and these are deposited in the Library of the Department of Economics at the University of Tokyo.

The book resulting from this research, a large volume of over 900 pages, appeared in 1978. He was then eighty-two. Its title was *A Story of the Weimar Republic,* not "A Study." His friend Professor Wakimura advised him to change it to "A Study," but Professor Arisawa would not consent, because, he said, "I am only an amateur historian, not a professional." This book first appeared in a private printing and was not published for a general readership until after his death. My own opinion is that this is the finest of all the Professor's books, and the official political historian, Professor Yoshitaka Oka agrees with me.

In this book, Professor Arisawa showed his sympathy for the Republic. He expressed his esteem for President Friedrich Ebert, Walter Rathenau, Gustav Noske and Gustav Stresemann, because they tried to support the Republic at risk to their lives. On the other hand, he did not conceal his hatred for Hjalmar Schacht and Karl Helfferich, because they betrayed the Republic, even though they were excellent financial technicians. He also expressed his personal sense of attachment to the Republic and its supporters. This is a possible reason for his decision to issue the book privately.

He published a second book on the Republic in 1984, when he was 88. In it, he wrote about the life of Walter Rathenau, whom he described as an ideal businessman. He wanted to write yet another book and solve the riddle of the Republic's collapse, but his death intervened. However, we can guess at his conclusion from the address he gave in January 1987. He said that in the early 1930s, there were many supporters of the Republic, but they did not take action to defend the Republic against its enemies. They were democrats, but not fighting democrats. This statement was the conclusion of his speech. In his last years, Professor Arisawa enjoyed the favourable opinion of China. Japan had invaded and occupied China frequently and for long periods of time, but China had repatriated the Japanese who had lived there peacefully. Professor Arisawa presented his personal collection of twenty thousand volumes, including the first edition of *Das Kapital*, to the Japan Institute of the Social Science Academy of China. This book is displayed in the library of the Japan Institute.

I should like to conclude my address with two personal anecdotes about my beloved Professor. He was constitutionally unable to take any alcoholic beverage. He always enjoyed conversation at the dinner table, but with a glass of Coca-Cola. I am told that when he went to a superb restaurant in Paris, he ordered Coca-Cola, as usual, and the waiter could only stare in astonishment at this curious Japanese man. The Professor smoked, and at age eighty he was still a two-pack-a-day man. In January 1988, I visited him to extend my New Year's greetings. The topic of smoking came up, and I told him that I had been trying to cut down to one pack every three days. The Professor chided me: "Everything comes from smoking. At least one pack every two days!"